Pioneers of Environmental Law

Jan G. Laitos
John A. Carver. Jr. Professor of Law
University of Denver Sturm College of Law

John Copeland Nagle
John N. Mathews Professor of Law
Notre Dame Law School

Twelve Tables Press

ISBN: 978-1-946074-33-1

Twelve Tables Press
P.O. Box 568
Northport, New York 11768
www.twelvetablespress.com

To all the Environmental Pioneers,
past, present, and in our future

Contents

Acknowledgments

By the time this book was sent to the publisher, John Nagle was no longer with us. But Jan Laitos would like to state for the record what a delight it was to work with John as this book was being planned and written.

Jan Laitos also wishes to recognize a number of individuals who helped make this book possible. At the top of the list would be Steve Errick, the legendary uber-publisher of so many law books over the past 30 years, who is now heading up Twelve Tables Press, which is publishing this book. Steve had the foresight and patience to sign up John and I to develop this book, long ago. After some starts and stops, it has finally emerged. Thank you, Steve, for staying the course with us. Jan Laitos wishes also to thank Sharon Ray for her terrific work in copy-editing this entire book. She was both patient and competent in dealing with all of us.

I also must point out the extraordinary depth of talent who agreed to do the actual writing about the Pioneers of Environmental Law. The chapters of this book were written by a pantheon of the best and brightest academic and legal minds. These authors have roamed the halls of leading law schools throughout the United States, and some have led careers as distinguished jurists. As such, they have taught and enlightened generations of law students and lawyers. And now they seek to educate the readers of this book about some prime examples of environmental law pioneers. John and I remain grateful to the authors of the chapters of this book, for delivering such a worthwhile, readable summary of those who first helped to jumpstart and grow environmental law.

Jan Laitos would like to also acknowledge the considerable help of Schyeler Gilman from the University of Denver Sturm College of Law. She helped to proof, copy edit, and organize this book. And she was always there to ensure that the finished product was, indeed, a quality finished product.

Jan Laitos wishes to acknowledge that Prof. Fred Cheever from the University of Denver Sturm College of Law was also to be an author in this book. But he passed away before he was able to begin his chapter. He too will be missed.

And, Jan of course wants to recognize Juliana, for being the ever-loving and always supportive Juliana while this exercise was occurring.

Introduction

This is a book intended to introduce readers to a sampling of those individuals who can be called "Pioneers of Environmental Law." A "pioneer" is among the first to explore a new area. And a pioneer of *environmental law* may be one who (1) first recognized the importance of the natural environment, or (2) helped to invent the relatively new doctrine of environmental law and then ensured that it would survive, or (3) once the new law was accepted, took new and creative approaches to established principles and applied these ideas to environmental law. The pioneers discussed in this book represent these three types, or classes, of pioneers—"True Pioneers," and "Creators and Saviors" and "Innovators."

When John Nagle and Jan Laitos first hatched this idea of launching a book about some representative pioneers of environmental law, they decided that the two of them would not decide who the pioneers would be. Instead, John and Jan turned to some preeminent academics, scholars, and jurists, and asked them to determine who they thought would and should qualify as a featured pioneer in environmental law. And then each expert wrote a short essay on the pioneer they had selected. In some cases, the pioneer chosen was a single person; in other cases, these authors selected a group of people who collectively were deemed to be pioneers. The 10 chapters of this book reflect the choices of the authors. So, this book is really the collective product of some of the most prominent and respected minds in the world of environmental law.

The chapters of this book are not meant to be an exhaustive list of all the various pioneers of environmental law. Rather, the book's chapters are intended to introduce the reader to examples of some of the persons who helped (along with many others not discussed in the book) to invent and develop the field of environmental law. Some of these pioneers are well known; some are more obscure, but still have played critical roles in field of environmental law. The book is meant to be either a companion book to survey courses in law schools on Environmental Law and Natural Resources Law, or a book to be used in college/university Environmental Policy courses.

It is important to recognize that this area of law—environmental law—is relatively new; it really did not exist before the 1960s. Many of the pioneers in this book helped policymakers, long ago, to see the crucial importance of environmentalism. Some of these pioneers also advocated for new laws and doctrines and perspectives to protect and preserve our natural environment. John and Jan thought it might be useful, and interesting, especially to those readers who were new to the field of environmental law, to learn about certain influential figures who were sufficiently creative and far-sighted to help shape this area of law.

John and Jan found a broad minded and innovative publisher—Steve Errick and Twelve Tables Press—who was willing to produce a book that was outside the mainstream of standard environmental casebooks and textbooks. And the result is this book—*Pioneers of Environmental Law.*

Sadly, John Nagle is not here with us to enjoy and appreciate this book. He passed away in 2019, just as the authors were submitting to John and Jan their chapters on their pioneer. John was a kind, intelligent, and dedicated law professor, respected and loved by many. Jan Laitos had the pleasure to work with John in initially brainstorming, organizing, selecting authors, and then putting together this book. We all will miss John, and hopefully what follows in these chapters reflects John's good will, good head, and good heart and spirit.

* * * * *

Here is a too-short summary (excerpted from the Notre Dame Law School website) of John's many professional accomplishments.

John Copeland Nagle was a professor at Notre Dame Law School for more than 20 years. He passed away on May 18, 2019.

Nagle was named the John N. Matthews Professor in 2005. He joined the law faculty as an associate professor of law in 1998 and became a full professor in 2001. He was the law school's inaugural Associate Dean for Faculty Research from 2004 to 2007.

Nagle was the co-author of casebooks on "The Practice and Policy of Environmental Law, "Property Law," and "The Law of Biodiversity and Ecosystem Management. His book "Law's Environment: How the Law Shapes the Places We Live," was published by Yale University Press in 2010. His other writings explored such topics as the relationship between environmental pollution, cultural pollution, and other kinds of "pollution;" the role of religion in environmental law; Chinese environmental law; the scope of congressional power to protect endangered species; alternative approaches to campaign finance reform; and the competing roles of Congress and the courts in correcting statutory mistakes. His articles were published in journals such as the Yale Law Journal, the Columbia Law Review, the Michigan Law Review, the University of Pennsylvania Law Review, and the New York University Law Review.

Prior to joining the Notre Dame faculty, Nagle was an associate professor at the Seton Hall University School of Law from 1994 through 1998. He also worked in the United States Department of Justice, first as an attorney in the Office of Legal Counsel where he advised other executive branch agencies on a variety of constitutional and statutory issues, and later as a trial attorney conducting environmental litigation. Nagle served as a law clerk to Judge Deanell Reece Tacha of the United States Court of Appeals for the Tenth Circuit, and he was a scientific assistant in the Energy and Environmental Systems Division of Argonne National Laboratory. He was a graduate of Indiana University and the University of Michigan Law School.

Nagle participated in numerous activities outside of the law school. He served as a member of the executive committee of the Section on Legislation of the American Association of Law Schools, and as a vice chair on the Endangered Species Committee of the American Bar Association's environmental section. He helped organize the annual meeting of the Law Professors' Christian Fellowship. He served as an elder in the Presbyterian church and was a member of New City Evangelical Presbyterian Church. He was the faculty adviser for the Christian Law Students, the Environmental Law Students, and Young Life.

Jan G. Laitos

Part I

The True Pioneers

We begin with three visionaries who can rightly be considered among the "true pioneers" of environmental law. Before there was "law," there needed to be some recognition of the status, and tenuous sustainability, of the natural "environment." The individuals summarized in Part I were among the first to realize, in the 19th century, that natural resources were not inexhaustible, and not perpetually regenerating. These prescient observers also realized that environmental goods, like air, water, and land, could become polluted, and damaged, and poisoned, and degraded by excessive human exploitation.

There were many true pioneers of environmental law who first pointed out that existing laws served to use and abuse natural resources, leading to their eventual depletion and contamination. Part I focuses on just three of these, who in different ways supplied a necessary condition precedent that had to be in place before environmental law could be invented. And that condition was a realization, and then an articulation, of the fact that human-caused threats to the natural environment could adversely affect, and forever alter, that environment.

These three pioneers discussed in Part I were among those who founded American conservation. Of course, the pantheon of environmental founders includes more than just the three featured in this book. To review all of them would be worthy of a multi-volume treatise, and such a weighty tome would have to include both the well-known (e.g., Aldo Leopold and Rachel Carson) and the lesser-known (e.g., George Bird Grinnell and Mardy Murie). This book instead offers a short "sampling" of three other pioneers of environmental law. These true pioneers were prominent among those who first took up the cause of all that a hyper-expanding 19th Century America was destroying—vast tracts of untrammeled land, wildlife, virgin forests, and endless waterways.

Chapter 1

George Perkins Marsh: Anticipating the Anthropocene

Robin Kundis Craig[1]

In 1864, George Perkins Marsh explored the impacts that human beings were already having on the physical and chemical processes of the world's ecosystems in *Man and Nature; or, Physical Geography as Modified by Human Action*,

[1] Robin Kundis Craig is the James I. Farr Presidential Endowed Professor of Law at the University of Utah S.J. Quinney College of Law in Salt Lake City, Utah. She is also affiliated faculty of the College of Law's Wallace Stegner Center for Land, Resources, and the Environment and the University's Global Change and Sustainability Center, and she serves on the Executive Board of the University of Utah's Water Center. In addition to a J.D. degree with a Certificate in Environmental Law, Craig has a Ph.D. in English from the University of Cali fornia, with a dissertation on 18th- and early 19th-century science and the English Romantic poets, and a Master's in Science Writing from the Johns Hopkins University. Craig specializes in all things water, including the relationships between climate change, fresh water systems, and the ocean; the water-energy-food-climate nexus; the Clean Water Act; the intersection of water issues and land issues; marine biodiversity and marine protected areas; water law; and the relationships between environmental law and public health. She is the author, co-author, or editor of 11 books, including *The End of Sustainability* (Kansas University Press 2017), *Comparative Ocean Governance: Place-Based Protections in an Era of Climate Change* (Edward Elgar 2012), *The Clean Water Act and the Constitution* (ELI 2nd Ed. 2009), and three legal textbooks. She has also written or co-written over 100 law review and science articles and book chapters, including recent publications in the *Proceedings of the National Academy of Science* (*PNAS*) and *Frontiers: Ecology and Evolution*. Craig is an elected member of the American Law Institute and the American College of Environmental Lawyers and a member of the IUCN's World Commission on Environmental Law. She has served on six National Academy of Sciences committees; was selected for the Rockefeller Foundation's Bellagio Center Writing Residency in 2017; was a William Evans Visiting Research Fellow at the University of Otago, New Zealand, in 2018; has consulted on water quality issues with the government of Victoria, Australia, and the Council on Environmental Cooperation in Montreal, Quebec, Canada; and was one of 12 marine educators chosen to participate in a 2010 program in the Papahanamokuakea Marine National Monument, spending a week on Midway Atoll. Craig's comments on contemporary marine, water, and climate change issues have been quoted in *National Geographic*, *The Atlantic*, *The New York Times*, and many other news outlets. At the University of Utah, she teaches Environmental Law, Water Law, Ocean & Coastal Law, Toxic Torts, Property, and Civil Procedure.

republished in 1874 as *The Earth as Modified by Human Action.*[2] Often hailed as "America's first environmentalist," Marsh anticipated—or, perhaps more accurately, recognized the first signs of—the Anthropocene, the era in which human interactions with ecological processes at multiple scales have become *the* major drivers of planetary function and dysfunction. He also helped to inspire new directions in natural resource management, law, and policy, including forest preservation and restoration, fisheries management, and landscape-scale water management.

Context always matters to important thinkers, and it is probably not a coincidence that Marsh was particularly well-positioned temporally and geographically to observe firsthand humans' ability to alter landscapes. Marsh was born in 1801 and grew up in Vermont. His ties to early-19th century New England are crucial to the vision of human influence on nature he later developed: "By 1800, New England was one of the longest settled and most densely populated of the country's regions, and in the first half of the nineteenth century it became the national crucible of a commercial and industrial revolution that was to transform America."[3] The changes occurring in New England were both still fresh in memory—the American Revolution was barely a generation into the past—and still happening, allowing for Marsh to become a personal witness to humanity's increasing ability to engineer landscapes, especially by felling forests. Moreover, the United States still had an active but constantly developing frontier throughout Marsh's life: Thomas Jefferson's Louisiana Purchase occurred in 1803; Lewis and Clark went on their expedition of discovery between 1804 and 1806; the United States annexed Texas in 1845; Mexico and the United States entered the Treaty of Guadalupe Hidalgo in 1848, giving the United States vast new territories in the Southwest; men seeking fortunes flocked to the California Gold Rush between 1848 and 1885, with California becoming a state in 1850; President Abraham Lincoln signed the first Homestead Act into law in 1862, encouraging settlement of the West; and the United States purchased Alaska in 1867. During this time, as well, the national transportation network of railroads was built, connecting the expanding nation; "[n]one had existed as late as the 1820s, but by the 1850s the United States encompassed more miles of track

---

[2] Marsh wrote his most influential work for environmental and natural resources law in the 1850s through 1870s, and his language reflects the usage of his day, where "man" and "humanity" were interchangeable and Nature was almost always personified as female. In addition, as will become clear, he accepts European colonialism without much comment as to the fates of indigenous peoples, although colonization did mean for Marsh the beginning of the degradation of natural systems. While I acknowledge that these usages and attitudes today would subject Marsh to a thorough edit for latent sexism and racism, I have chosen, other than in this footnote, to let his language stand without comment, viewing it as an historical artifact in its own right.

[3] Robert L. Dorman, A Word for Nature: Four Pioneering Environmental Advocates, 1845-1913, at 5 (University of North Carolina Press: 1998).

than the rest of the world combined."[4] Americans were building other things, as well, including "scores of dams, [] hundreds of miles of canals, and [] thousands of miles of roads...."[5] The young nation's population grew from 5 million at the Revolution to 31 million in 1860, but it was also shifting west and was centered west of the Appalachian Mountains for the first time right before the Civil War. The United States before the Civil War also experienced the highest rate of urbanization in its history. A changing national map, the progressive acquisition of new landscapes, and the European-American settlement and transformation of new territories were thus the constant and unavoidable realities of Marsh's life.

By the age of seven, Marsh suffered from strained and damaged eyesight from intensive reading. The treatment was to send him outdoors,[6] and he became an avid walker and fisherman. As a boy in Woodstock, Vermont, he observed firsthand what deforestation was doing to the landscape, particularly in terms of water supply. Thirty years of settlement had rapidly deforested the area surrounding Woodstock, as residents converted the once-abundant forests into farms, firewood, and potash.[7] A frequent user of the Quechee River, Marsh noticed "that the spring freshets grew increasingly violent as more trees were cut into the hills" but also that in the summer streams and rivers increasingly dried up, making summer fishing less and less productive over time.[8] Aided by his lawyer-father's instruction as they toured the New England landscape, Marsh recalled beginning to understand how the various physical facets of nature worked together:

> "My father pointed out the most striking trees as we passed them, and told me how to distinguish their varieties. I do not think I ever afterward failed to know one forest tree from another. He called my attention to the general configuration of the landscape, pointed out the direction of the different ranges of the hills, told me how the water gathered on them and ran down their sides, and where the mountain streams would likely be found. But what struck me, perhaps most of all, he stopped his horse on top of a steep hill, bade me notice how the water there flowed in different directions, and told me such a point was called a *water-shed*.... I never forgot that word, or any art of my father's talk that day."[9]

---

[4] *Id.* at 6.

[5] *Id.*

[6] Jane Curtis, Will Curtis, & Frank Lieberman, The World of George Perkins Marsh 13 (1982).

[7] David Lowenthal, George Perkins Marsh: Prophet of Conservation 4 (2000).

[8] Curtis, Curtis, & Lieberman, *supra* note 6, at 15.

[9] *Id.* at 15, 18.

In addition, at school in Royalton, Vermont, starting in 1811, the 10-year-old fisherman also observed the striking differences between the forested streams of his home and the thoroughly deforested White River.

Despite his eyesight, Marsh remained a voracious lifetime scholar—but he was also a 19th-century Renaissance man. Over the course of his varied and often unsuccessful careers, he taught Greek and Latin at the Norwich American Literary Scientific and Military Academy, advocated training in sign language for deaf-mutes, practiced law in Burlington, Vermont (reflecting much later, in 1875, that "[o]nly odd or perverse people go into law"[10]), "amassed one of the largest collections of Scandinavian literature" in the United States,[11] lectured on "The Goths in New England" (1843) and produced dictionaries of American English, raised sheep and ran a woolen mill, worked as a quarryman, contributed as an amateur architect to the designs for the Washington Monument and the Vermont State House, collected art, invested in railroads, and convinced the U.S. military to adopt camels for use in the American West. Marsh was also a politician, serving first in Vermont's General Assembly and then in Congress, as an anti-slavery and pro-protective tariff Whig, for two terms beginning in 1843. As a member of the Joint Library of Congress Committee and then the seven-man Smithsonian Select Committee, Marsh exhorted his fellow congressmen to use the founding $500,000 bequest from James Smithson to create national museums and research institutions rather than to support practical training in agriculture and experimental science. His efforts, together with those similarly-minded individuals like John Quincy Adams, eventually bore fruit, as the Smithsonian Institution became a place of knowledge and research as well as a home to various natural history collections. Marsh himself became a Smithsonian trustee.

Marsh's post-Congress public service fed the observations that would help shape *Man and Nature*. Proficient in languages from an early age, Marsh eventually spoke about 20 of them, contributing to his qualifications for the diplomatic service. Beginning in 1849, under appointment by newly-elected President Zachary Taylor, Marsh served as the United States Minister in Residence to the Ottoman Empire (Turkey), a post that allowed him to travel to Paris, Rome, Nubia, Egypt, and the Holy Land and that included an assignment to unravel a complex land dispute in Athens. Exploring the transformed landscapes of Greece and Turkey, he could see even more profoundly and over a longer temporal scale than he had in New England the long-term results of human interactions with their environments. "It was here Marsh first saw that men had everywhere left their mark; soon he realized how far that touch had transformed nature. The mangled forests and disrupted rivers of New England had already shown him the

---

[10] LOWENTHAL, *supra* note 7, at 34.

[11] *Id.* at 19 (quoting CAROLINE CRANE MARSH, LIFE AND LETTERS OF GEORGE PERKINS MARSH 7 (1888)); *see also* CURTIS, CURTIS, & LIEBERMAN, *supra* note 6, at 25 (quoting the same language).

immediate impact of human improvidence; the deserts of the Levant revealed the ultimate effects of similar processes when long continued."[12] Marsh also collected specimens and set up museum swaps for the Smithsonian.

After President Pierce appointed Marsh's successor to Turkey in late 1953, Marsh spent a year traveling in Europe. Significant financial difficulties kept Marsh in a battle with Congress to get paid for his diplomatic expenses, and after returning home he gave a series of lectures that tried to educate Americans that they needed to start conservation efforts if they were to avoid the European environmental fate. Americans, he argued, "were 'already beginning to suffer from the washing away of vegetable soil from our steeper fields, and from the drying up of the abundant springs which one watered our hill pastures, and from the increased violence of our spring and autumnal freshets.'"[13] Europe revealed where these processes were going, because "'only in countries that have been laid bare ... for generations [could] the extent of the devastation thus produced be comprehended.'"[14] Marsh recommended a number of land management reforms to avoid the geographical transformations he had seen in Europe and the Near East, including logging prohibitions on steep slopes, grazing restrictions, mandated reforestation, and stream conservation.[15]

Eventually, in 1957, Vermont's governor, Ryland Fletcher, appointed Marsh to the positions of Vermont Railroad Commission, Fish Commissioner, State House Commissioner, and head of the Ethan Allen Monument Committee. From his position as Fish Commissioner, in particular, Marsh once again observed the deep and long-term human impacts on natural systems. "Fishing in Vermont was now even worse than it had been in his boyhood. The Legislature had passed act after act to protect what was left, but the plump salmon, the silvery trout had all but vanished from the waters"[16]; the former had been extirpated as a result of dam building, while the latter had been eaten to extinction by the pickerel that early settlers had introduced to Vermont's streams and rivers.[17] Marsh recognized that the causes of the loss were complex, encompassing not only over-fishing and dam building. Indeed,

> "other and more obscure causes have had a very important influence on producing the same result ... much must doubtless be ascribed to the general physical changes produced by the clearing and cultivating of the soil.... It is certain that while the spring and autumnal freshets are more violent, the volume of water in the dry season is less in all our water courses than it formerly

[12] LOWENTHAL, *supra* note 7, at 134.

[13] *Id.* at 160 (quoting Marsh's public lectures).

[14] *Id.* (quoting Marsh's public lectures).

[15] *Id.*

[16] CURTIS, CURTIS, & LIEBERMAN, *supra* note 6, at 94.

[17] LOWENTHAL, *supra* note 7, at 183.

> was, and there is no doubt that the summer temperature of the brooks has been elevated.... The clearing of the woods has been attended with the removal of many obstructions to the flow of water.... The general character of our water courses has become in fact more torrential.... In inundations, not only does the mechanical violence of the current destroy or sweep down fish and their eggs, and fill the water with mud and other impurities, but it continually changes the bed and banks of the streams, and thus renders it difficult and often impossible for the fish ... to return to their breeding places and deposit their spawn."[18]

Humans, Marsh concluded, had been the architects of the physical, chemical, and ultimately biological changes that they now lamented, and "it is enough to say that human *improvements* have produced an almost total change in all the external conditions of piscatorial life ... and we must of course expect that the number of fish will be greatly affected by those revolutions."[19] In his fisheries report, Marsh recommended careful use of fish breeding and restocking, with controls to prevent the harmful side effects that he had seen in Europe. As a start, "he proposed restocking Lake Champlain with the shad, salmon, and trout 'which formerly furnished so acceptable a luxury to the rich, and so cheap a nutrient to the poor of Western Vermont, but which now are become almost as ... extinct as the game that once enlivened our forests.'"[20] In addition, Marsh exhibited a thorough understanding of the complex interrelationships among species and even a nascent version of what has now been dubbed "ecosystem services," chastising Vermonters for their "mistaken prejudices" against "birds, quadrupeds, and reptiles" because of the supposed damage they inflict upon crops. Instead, Marsh argued, "they 'much more than compensate the little injury they inflict upon the crops' by consuming 'vast numbers of noxious insects.'"[21]

The Vermont Legislature praised Marsh's report but declined to act on it. However, fifteen years later, Spencer Baird, U.S. Commissioner of Fish and Fisheries and a Marsh protégé, relied heavily on Marsh's fish report in his own 1872-1873 federal fisheries report. Baird credited Marsh with initiating salmon restoration efforts in the United States and adopted Marsh's conservation

[18] Curtis, Curtis, & Lieberman, *supra* note 6, at 94 (quoting George Perkins Marsh, *Report, on the Artificial Propagation of Fish* 19-21 (1857)).

[19] *Id.* (quoting George Perkins Marsh, *Report, on the Artificial Propagation of Fish* 19-21 (1857)).

[20] Lowenthal, *supra* note 7, at 183 (quoting George Perkins Marsh, *Report, on the Artificial Propagation of Fish* 19-21 (1857)).

[21] *Id.* at 185 (quoting George Perkins Marsh, *Report, on the Artificial Propagation of Fish* 10-11 (1857)).

approach for federal fisheries management.[22] As such, "Marsh had played a truly pioneering role" in U.S. fisheries management and policy.[23]

Marsh ended his career, and life, as the U.S. Minister to the newly-formed country of Italy, in which position he died in 1882. Appointed by President Lincoln, Marsh left the United States eleven days before the American Civil War broke out in 1861. After Lincoln's assassination, first President Johnson and then President Grant kept him on as Minister. Marsh wrote *Man and Nature* from Italy, and the book was published in 1864, with a second revised edition appearing in 1874 and a third, posthumous, edition in 1885.

In *Man and Nature*, Marsh posited that humans were geological agents, transforming geographic, physical, and chemical processes through the changes—both modest and extravagant—that they bring to natural systems. He was the first person to offer such a theory, and he "was considered by many as a radical crank," because "[t]he conventional idea held by his contemporaries ... was that the physical aspect of the earth was entirely the result of natural phenomena, mountains, rivers, oceans."[24] He focused on the great transformational activity of his day: deforestation. Specifically, he sought "'to show the evils resulting from too much clearing and cultivation, and often so-called improvements in new countries like the United States.'"[25] However, his observations remain highly relevant and generalizable beyond the cutting of trees and even anticipate in many ways the premise of Jared Diamond's *Collapse*.

Man and Nature is a historic and geographic *tour de force*. All of human history, all of natural history, and all geographies are with Marsh's scope. As one commenter notes, "The immediate sources of *Man and Nature* are wildly heterogeneous. Interspersed with excerpts from French engineers on stream abrasion and German foresters on tree physiology are piquant anecdotes from Marsh's boyhood and travels."[26] *Man and Nature* begins, for instance, with the natural advantages that the Roman Empire enjoyed, only to have Marsh graphically describe the degradation that has since occurred:

> If we compare the present physical condition of the countries of which I am speaking, with the descriptions that ancient historians and geographers have given of their fertility and general capability of ministering to human uses, we shall find that more than one-half of their whole extent—and not excluding the provinces most celebrated for the profusion and variety of their spontaneous and their cultivated products, and for the wealth and social

---

[22] *Id.* at 184.

[23] *Id.*

[24] Curtis, Curtis, & Lieberman, *supra* note 6, at 102.

[25] Lowenthal, *supra* note 7, at 268 (quoting letter from George Perkins Marsh to Secretary of State William H. Seward, July 7, 1863).

[26] *Id.* at 296.

> advancement of their inhabitants—is either deserted by civilized man and surrendered to hopeless desolation, or at least greatly reduced in productiveness and population. Vast forests have disappeared from mountain spurs and ridges; the vegetable earth accumulated beneath the trees by the decay of leaves and fallen trunks, the soil of the alpine pastures which skirted and indented the woods, and the mould of the upland fields, are washed away; meadows, once fertilized by irrigation, are waste and unproductive because the cisterns and reservoirs that supplied the ancient canals are broken, or the springs that fed them dried up; rivers famous in history and song have shrunk to humble brooklets; the willows that ornamented and protected the banks of the lesser watercourses are gone, and the rivulets have ceased to exist as perennial currents, because the little water that finds its way into their channels is evaporated by the droughts of summer, or absorbed by the parched earth before it reaches the lowlands; the beds of the brooks have widened into broad expanses of pebbles and gravel, over which, though in the hot season passed dryshod, in winter sealike torrents thunder; the entrances of navigable streams are obstructed by sandbars; and harbors, once marts of an extensive commerce, are shoaled by the deposits of the rivers at whose mouth they lie; the elevation of the beds of estuaries, and the consequently diminished velocity and increased lateral spread of the streams which flow into them, have converted thousands of leagues of shallow sea and fertile lowland into unproductive and miasmatic morasses.[27]

While some of this change, Marsh admitted, resulted from natural forces and human violence, "a far greater proportion" is "either the result of man's ignorant disregard for the laws of nature, or an incidental consequence of war and of civil and ecclesiastical tyranny and misrule."[28] Moreover, while humanity seems puny compared to the forces of geography and climate, "it is certain that man has reacted upon organized and inorganic nature, and thereby modified, if not determined, the material structure of his earthly home."[29]

Marsh acknowledged that he could not provide quantitative proof of humanity's influence on geography and climate,[30] only qualitative observations—his own; instead, his aim "was to stimulate, not to satisfy, curiosity...."[31] He nevertheless started with some basic observations. First, climate and geography matter to what can grow and thrive in specific locations.[32] Second, life can adjust over time to new conditions, as evidenced by the fact that introduced species such as maize and the tomato have adjusted over time to their new

---

[27] GEORGE PERKINS MARSH, THE EARTH AS MODIFIED BY HUMAN ACTION 20 (1878).

[28] *Id.* at 21.

[29] *Id.* at 24.

[30] *Id.* at 28.

[31] *Id.* at 26.

[32] *Id.* at 30-31.

locations.[33] Third, we know from a variety of examples that both human farming and human engineering can change the character of a place's water resources: clearing of forests, whether in central Africa, Arabia, or California, tends to dry out that locality, while as a result of "injudicious husbandry, or the diversion or choking up of natural water-courses, [an area] may become more highly charged with humidity."[34]

Part of the importance of *Man and Nature* lies in Marsh's keen recognition that the environment is a system—that "the organic and inorganic world are ... bound together by such mutual relations and adaptations as secure, if not the absolute permanence and equilibrium of both, a long continuance of the established conditions of each at any given time and place, or at least, a very slow and gradual succession of changes in these conditions."[35] Thus, he argues at great length that plant and animal life are relevant to modern geography,[36] and he recognizes that ecosystems affect climate and the weather as much as climate and weather affect ecosystems. Forests, for example, influence meteorology, the mixture of gases in the atmosphere, and the distribution of heat.[37] Marsh also postulated that forests reduce malaria by breaking up "miasmatic vapors"[38]; Sir Ronald Ross did not discover the role of mosquitoes in malaria transmission until 1897. Forests also shape the landscape itself: trees shelter ground leeward of the prevailing winds.[39] It total, "in countries in the temperate zone still chiefly covered with wood, the summers would be cooler, moister, shorter, the winters milder, drier, longer, than in the same regions after the removal of the forest, and that the condensation and precipitation of atmospheric moisture would be, if not greater in total quantity, more frequent and less violent in discharge."[40]

Equally important to the enduring importance of *Man and Nature* to environmental and natural resources law is Marsh's early recognition that humans are *not* too insignificant to seriously affect physical and chemical geographical realities, not just biological. Indeed, human enterprises regularly upset ecosystems' deep relationships and alter those systems' balances, causing long-term "unforeseen and undesirable results."[41] (Notably, the title Marsh first proposed for his book was "Man the Disturber of Nature's Harmonies."[42]) For example,

---

[33] *Id.* at 31.

[34] *Id.* at 32.

[35] *Id.* at 41-42.

[36] *Id.* at 57-120.

[37] *Id.* at 125-26, 140-41.

[38] *Id.* at 126.

[39] *Id.* at 128.

[40] *Id.* at 155.

[41] *Id.* at 47.

[42] LOWENTHAL, *supra* note 7, at 291.

"[w]ith the extirpation of forests, all is changed"—"the climate becomes excessive, and the soil is alternately parched by the fervors of summer, and seared by the rigors of winter."[43] Precipitation events become more violent, soil is carried away, and rivers and lakes become choked on sediment.[44] Similarly, humans have significantly changed the character of inhabited coasts by reclaiming solid land from tidelands and wetlands, by "resist[ing] new encroachments of the sea upon the land,"[45] by draining and redirecting freshwaters, and by using groundwater. Marsh also noted some of the newer forms of significant changes humans might bring to natural geography. For example, cutting across more isthmuses—like the Isthmus of Panama—with canals like the Suez Canal could aid navigation in other parts of the world, but "[a] new channel may deflect strong currents from safe courses, and thus occasion destructive erosion of shores otherwise secure, or promote transportation of sand or slime to block up important harbors, or it may furnish a powerful enemy with dangerous facilities for hostile operations along the coast."[46] Another new development, hydraulic mining, "is producing important geographical effects in California," where "the process is resorted to o a vastly greater scale than in any other modern engineering operations, and with results proportional to the means"—"[n]aked hills and fertile soils are alike washed away by the artificial torrent, and the material removed—vegetable mould, sand, gravel, pebbles—is carried down by the current and often spread over ground lying quite out of the reach of natural inundations, and burying it to the depth sometimes of twenty-five feet."[47] Marsh thus found an enormous array of observations relevant to his thesis in *Man and Nature*, and "[n]o book before it had ever treated of subject of environmental abuse in such a comprehensive, systematic, and compelling fashion."[48]

Finally, *Man and Nature* also continues to be important because of Marsh's full-throated commitment to conservation, including restoration. The New World, he emphasized, was in trouble:

> Comparatively short as is the period through which the colonization of foreign lands by European emigrants extends, great and, it is to be feared, sometimes irreparable injury has already been done in the various processes by which man seeks to subjugate the virgin earth; and many provinces, first trodden by homo sapiens Europae within the last two centuries, begin to show

[43] Marsh, *supra* note 27, at 224.

[44] *Id.*

[45] *Id.* at 297.

[46] *Id.* at 437-38.

[47] *Id.* at 450.

[48] Dorman, *supra* note 3, at 41.

> signs of that melancholy dilapidation which is now driving the peasantry of Europe from their native hearths.[49]

This decay, Marsh asserted, "should be arrested"[50]; humans had to act again, because their changes meant that nature could no longer heal itself.[51] Specifically, "man's utmost ingenuity and energy must be tasked to renovate a nature drained, by his improvidence, of fountains which in a wise economy would have made plenteous and perennial sources of beauty, health, and wealth."[52] Moreover, Marsh acknowledged that law is an important component of the conservation approach, emerging directly from government's duty to supply public goods, which includes the environment as much as roads, canals, railroads, and a postal service.[53]

As one might expect for a work from the 1870s, Marsh's science wasn't perfect. For example, he generally fails in *Man and Nature* to identify overuse of natural resources as an important human driver of ecological change,[54] despite his work as Vermont's Fish Commissioner and his recognition there that greedy fishermen were part of the reason native fish stocks were declining. He considered forests to be the earth's most natural condition, positing that "the surface of the habitable earth, in all the climates and regions which have been the abodes of dense and civilized populations, was, with few exceptions, already covered with a forest growth when it first became the home of man."[55] His preference for forests also leads him to view even natural forces that change forests—for example, beavers and the creation of bogs—as "destructive in character."[56] Marsh's "Calvinist, Enlightenment, utilitarian progressivism predisposed him to segregate and exalt humanity as above and at war with the cosmos,"[57] and he clearly identifies humanity as a species apart from nature,[58] whose "self-conscious will"

---

[49] MARSH, *supra* note 27, at 52.

[50] *Id.*

[51] LOWENTHAL, *supra* note 7, at 294.

[52] MARSH, *supra* note 27, at 53.

[53] *Id.* at 56.

[54] Even here, however, Marsh does note problems of over-consumption: "Man has too long forgotten that the earth was given to him for usufruct alone, not for consumption, still less for profligate waste." *Id.* at 41.

[55] *Id.* at 121.

[56] *Id.* at 37.

[57] LOWENTHAL, *supra* note 7, at 290-91.

[58] "The fact that, of all organic beings, man alone is to be regarded as essentially a destructive power, and that he wields energies to resist which Nature—that nature whom all material like ad all inorganic substance obey—is wholly impotent, tends to prove that, though living in physical nature, he is not part of her, that he is of more exalted parentage, and belongs to a higher order of existences, than those which are born of her womb and live in blind submission to her dictates." MARSH, *supra* note 27, at 42.

in acting upon nature pursues both primary and secondary, and short-term and long-term goals, operates as a different category of force than is exercised by animals like beavers.[59] He accepts without question the embedded stationarity and Balance of Nature model of a personified Nature left to her own devices, reflecting the dominant view of both contemporary catastrophists and uniformitarians:

> Nature, left undisturbed, so fashions her territory as to give it almost unchanging permanence of form, outline, and proportion, except when shattered by geologic convulsions; and in these comparatively rare cases of derangement, she sets herself at once to repair the superficial damage, and to restore, as nearly as practicable, the former aspect of her dominion. In new countries, the natural inclination of the ground, the self-formed slopes and levels, are generally such as best secure the stability of the soil. They have been graded and lowered or elevated by frost and chemical forces and gravitation and the flow of water and vegetable deposit and the action of the winds, until, by a general compensation of conflicting forces, a condition of equilibrium has been readied which, without the action of man, would remain, with little fluctuation, for countless of ages.[60]

Finally, as his recurring references to the United States as a "new country" attest, Marsh wholly ignores (or, more charitably, may have been legitimately ignorant of) the pervasive influences of Native Americans on the geography and ecology of what became the United States and Canada. Indeed, Marsh downplays or ignores the influences of "uncivilized" cultures more generally. For example, on the subject of peat bogs, Marsh notes that "[i]n countries somewhat further advanced in civilization that those occupied by the North American Indians, as in mediaeval Ireland, the formation of bogs may be commenced by the neglect of man to remove, from the natural channels of superficial drainage, the tops and branches of trees felled for the various purposes to which wood is applicable in his rude industry...."[61] More generally, "[p]urely untutored humanity ... interferes comparatively little with the arrangements of nature," and while the "earliest dawn of civilization" was accompanied by "domestication of the organic

---

[59] *Id.* at 47.

[60] *Id.* at 36. "In fine, in countries untrodden by man, the proportions and relative positions of land and water, the atmospheric precipitation and evaporation, the thermometric mean, and the distribution of vegetable and animal life, are maintained by natural compensations, in a state of approximate equilibrium, and are subject to appreciable change only from geological influences so slow in their operation that the geographical conditions may be regarded as substantially constant and immutable." *Id.* at 40. *See also id.* at 44 ("without man, lower animal and spontaneous vegetable life would have been practically constant in type, distribution, and proportion, and the physical geography of the earth would have remained undisturbed for indefinite periods").

[61] *Id.* at 39.

world," "the conquest of inorganic nature [belongs] almost [] exclusively to the most advanced stages of artificial culture."[62]

Nor was *Man and Nature* wholly without intellectual precedent. As the numerous and fascinating footnotes in *Man and Nature* reveal, Marsh, like Newton, "stood on the shoulders of giants." In particular, his immediate predecessors Alexander von Humboldt and Charles Darwin both influenced him tremendously, the former through his systemic view of nature and the latter through his various exegeses of change in living organisms. When Humboldt died in 1859, he was considered the greatest scientist of his day. Like Marsh, Humboldt's interests were broad, his publications many (Marsh devoted an entire section of his library to Humboldt's works), and his views of the universe shaped by many travels. However, Humboldt's *Cosmos*, the best-selling first volume of which appeared in 1845, perhaps most succinctly illustrates the connections between the two thinkers. Humboldt sought to know everything, and *Cosmos* journeys from outer space to the inner earth, reflecting Humboldt's views that "[e]verything was part of this 'never-ending activity of the animated forces,'" and that nature was "a 'living whole' where organisms were bond together in a 'net-like intricate fabric'."[63] Like Marsh, Humboldt brought together a wide range of subjects, but his interest was in showing connections. For example, "Humboldt was the first to understand climate as a system of complex correlations between the atmosphere, oceans, and landmasses."[64] Humboldt also occasioned some of Marsh's "aha!" moments. For example, as he traveled in Turkey, Egypt, Greece, and the Levant, "[e]verything that Marsh had read in Humboldt's books suddenly made sense," including Humboldt's observation that humanity "left trails of destruction ... 'wherever he stepped'."[65] Darwin, in turn, published *On the Origin of Species* in 1859, and Marsh was quite familiar with Darwin's work more broadly, as the various references to Darwin in *Man and Nature* attest. Notably, Marsh took pains to distinguish *Man and Nature* from Darwin's work, noting that while "[t]he modification of organic species by domestication is a branch of philosophic inquiry which we may almost say has been created by Darwin," "the geographical results of these modifications do not appear to have yet been made a subject of scientific investigation."[66] In addition, both *On the Origin of Species*

---

[62] *Id.* at 45. Notably, however, Marsh's conception of "civilized" culture was broader that many of his contemporaries and included more than white, European- or Greco-Roman-derived "western civilization." His experiences in Turkey and the Holy Land had given him great respect for Islamic civilization, for example. LOWENTHAL, *supra* note 7, at 109-135.

[63] ANDREA WULF, THE INVENTION OF NATURE: ALEXANDER VON HUMBOLDT'S NEW WORLD 290 (Viking Books first ed. paperback 2016).

[64] *Id.* at 291.

[65] *Id.* at 339-40.

[66] MARSH, *supra* note 27, at 25.

and *Man and Nature* focus on change in nature, often slow and gradual, and both books upended traditional views about humanity's place in the universe.

Nevertheless, *Man and Nature* was a pioneering work in its own right. "Next to Darwin's *On the Origin of Species*, Marsh's *Man and Nature* of 1864 was the most influential text of its time to link culture with nature, science with society, landscape with history."[67] Cultural historians also rank *Man and Nature* with Aldo Leopold's *A Sand County Almanac* (1949) and Rachel Carson's *Silent Spring* (1962) in terms of its role in reconceptualizing humans' relationship to their surroundings in a politically salient way:[68]

> No one had ever pointed out the total effect of all the works of man. No one had ever before turned to the study of the earth as the home of mankind. Others had voiced concern about the silted rivers, deforested hills, but only Marsh saw the *total* interdependency of the environmental and social relationships. The 18th Century naturalists had considered man's action as beneficial, order and cultivation being wrested from chaos. Marsh knew better.[69]

Man and Nature "made a growing public aware of how massively humans transform their milieus," directly contradicting the popular perception at the time that human impacts "were largely benign, [and] that malign effects were trivial or ephemeral."[70] Indeed, "[m]ost inquirers before Marsh had trusted earth's plentitude, assumed resources inexhaustible, and never doubted that they could and should master nature; the conquest was God's command and national destiny."[71] Environmentalist and writer Wallace Stegner called *Man and Nature* "the 'rudest kick in the face' to America's optimism," exhorting Americans to be more cautious in their race to develop their country.[72]

Marsh's work both influenced and anticipated natural resources and environmental law and policy in the United States: "*Man and Nature* was the first work of natural history fundamentally to influence American politics."[73] For example, *Man and Nature* helped to crystallize land conservation efforts in the United States, underscored by the creation of Yellowstone as the first National Park in 1872. Marsh himself took significant interest in preserving landscapes through protective legal designation, becoming for example "an early and active advocate

---

[67] LOWENTHAL, *supra* note 7, at xv.

[68] William Cronon, *Forward: Look Back to Look Forward*, *in* LOWENTHAL, *supra* note 7, at ix, xiii.

[69] CURTIS, CURTIS, & LIEBERMAN, *supra* note 6, at 104.

[70] LOWENTHAL, *supra* note 7, at 268.

[71] *Id.* at 273.

[72] WULF, *supra* note 63, at 350.

[73] *Id.*

of setting aside part of the Adirondack wilderness as parkland."[74] John Muir would read and be influenced by *Man and Nature*. *Man and Nature* remained the "only general work in the field" for decades, and "[t]he third (1884) edition was last reprinted in 1907, on the eve of the White House Conference that led Theodore Roosevelt to create a national conservation commission under Gifford Pinchot,"[75] the predecessor agency to the U.S. Forest Service. Marsh's insights regained popularity again during the 1930s Dust Bowl, and "Marsh's prescient ecological warning were hailed at a 1955 Princeton symposium, 'Man's Role in Changing the Face of the Earth.'"[76] *Man and Nature* was finally reissued in print in 1965, just as the United States' nascent environmental movement was gaining steam, and President Lyndon B. Johnson's Secretary of the Interior Stewart Udall credited the book with helping to create the United States' conservation movement,[77] calling it "'the beginning of land wisdom in this country.'"[78]

As might be expected from Marsh's emphasis on forests, *Man and Nature* was particularly instrumental in launching forest conservation efforts. For example, "Marsh's warnings led Franklin B. Hough at the American Association for the Advancement of Science in 1873 to petition Congress for a national forestry commission," relying heavily on *Man and Nature*, and "[e]very leading forestry figure was inspired by the book and sought Marsh's advice."[79] *Man and Nature* both "encouraged the passage of the 1873 Timber Culture Act to encourage settlers on the Great Plains to plant trees as a way of increasing rainfall" and laid the groundwork for protecting U.S. forests at both the state and federal levels.[80] "Several state forestry commissions founded in the 1870s were also attributable in part to Marsh's consciousness-raising efforts," leading within a decade of his death to state forest reserves.[81] At the federal level, Hough's petition to Congress bore fruit, and in 1876 Congress created the Office of the Special Agent for forest research within the Department of Agriculture. Hough served as the head of this office, which Congress expanded in 1881 to the Division of Forestry. The Forest Reserve Act of 1891 authorized the withdrawal of federal lands for forest reserves, which fell under the U.S. Department of the Interior's jurisdiction. The first such withdrawal occurred on March 30, 1891, establishing the Yellowstone Park Timber and Land Reserve, which eventually evolved into

---

[74] LOWENTHAL, *supra* note 7, at 430.

[75] *Id.* at 300.

[76] *Id.* at 414.

[77] CURTIS, CURTIS, & LIEBERMAN, *supra* note 6, at 122.

[78] LOWENTHAL, *supra* note 7, at 431-32 (quoting Stewart Udall).

[79] *Id.* at 298.

[80] Cronon, *supra* note 68.

[81] DORMAN, *supra* note 3, at 42-43.

the Targhee, Teton, Wyoming, Bonneville, Absaroka, Shoshone, and Beartooth National Forests that surround Yellowstone and Grand Teton National Parks.

In 1901, the Division of Forestry became the Bureau of Forestry, and in 1905, Congress used the Transfer Act of 1905 to move the federal forest reserves from Interior's jurisdiction to the Bureau's, which became known as the United States Forest Service. Gifford Pinchot, the first Chief Forester of the U.S. Forest Service, knew *Man and Nature* well, and "[t]he U.S. Forest Service, the Sierra Club, and finally even the timber companies acted within an ecological mindset whose broad premises Marsh had set."[82] By 1907, President Roosevelt had doubled the acreage of the National Forest reserves. In 1911, Congress passed the Weeks Act, allowing the federal government to purchase private land to protect streamflow and to manage the purchased lands as national forests. In effect, the Weeks Act allowed the growing national forest system to extend into the eastern states—including back to Marsh's state of birth, through the establishment of what is now the Green Mountain National Forest. Today there are 154 National Forests throughout the United States, covering more than 192 million acres.

Man and Nature also greatly influenced forestry practices in Europe, including France and Italy, and in India, Australia, New Zealand, South Africa, and Japan. Notably, when Marsh died in Europe in 1882 at the age of 81, "his coffin was borne down the mountain by an honor guard of foresters,"[83] a tribute to how quickly he had influenced forestry policy and management.

Importantly, Marsh's conservation ethic included careful human use of the earth, and that balanced approach also can be traced forward into 21st-century U.S. environmental and natural resources law. Unlike both the caricature of his near contemporary Henry David Thoreau and the actual aims of 1960s ecological reformers who sought to limit all human impact on the environment (for example, by preserving wilderness), Marsh did not oppose all human action that changed the environment. He admitted, for example, that "[t]he physical revolutions thus wrought by man have not indeed all been destructive to human interests, and the heaviest blows he has inflicted upon nature have not been wholly without their compensations."[84] Instead, and again anticipating contemporary issues in environmental and natural resources law, he examined such changes through a cost-benefit approach, concluding in many circumstances that the benefits to humans outweighed the adverse ecological effects. His point in *Man and Nature* was more subtle: that humans should not act in ignorance,

---

[82] LOWENTHAL, *supra* note 7, at 298-99.

[83] DORMAN, *supra* note 3, at 43.

[84] MARSH, *supra* note 27, at 25.

unaware of their potential to wreak long-term and damaging change that they themselves would come to regret.[85]

In this sense, therefore, there is a direct line of self-awareness connecting *Man and Nature* to the United States' 1969 National Environmental Policy Act (NEPA) and to environmental impact analysis requirements more generally. Indeed, Marsh both emphasized the importance of cumulative impacts over time and was unwilling to accept uncertainty as an excuse for acting greedily and rashly. Marsh distinguished law and nature in this regard:

> It is a legal maxim that "the law concerneth not itself with trifles," de minimis non curat lex; but in the vocabulary of nature, little and great are terms of comparison only; she knows no trifles, and her laws are as inflexible in dealing with an atom as with a continent or planet.
>
> The human operations mentioned…, therefore, do act in the ways ascribed to them, though our limited faculties are at present, perhaps forever, incapable of weighing their immediate, still more their ultimate consequences. But our inability to assign definite values to these causes of the disturbance of natural arrangements is not a reason for ignoring the existence of such causes in any general view of the relations between man and nature, and we are never justified in assuming a force to be insignificant because its measure is unknown, or even because no physical effect can now be traced to its origin.[86]

In addition, Marsh recognized profoundly that human well-being is intimately intertwined with natural functions, anticipating the contemporary focus on this interrelationship that is generally captured, albeit imperfectly, in the concept of *social-ecological systems.*

Finally, Marsh also recognized that geographical and ecological systems do not always respond as humans intend, emphasizing the importance of "the contingent and unsought results which have flowed" from human interactions with the environment.[87] He of course lacked the 20th- and 21st-century terminology to describe *complexity theory*, *systems theory*, *complex adaptive systems*, and *panarchy*, but his recognition of unintended consequences and realization that nature does not always behave as humans expect encapsulate the core insight for natural resources managers of these later developments in ecological and social-ecological theory. This core insight has, if anything, become even more critical in the Anthropocene, in which we are living out the truly global and long-term consequences of industrialization and the increasing dependence, already

---

[85] *Id.* at 44 (for humanity to thrive, "a certain measure of transformation of terrestrial surface, of suppression of natural, and stimulation of artificially modified productivity becomes necessary," but "[t]his measure man has unfortunately exceeded.").

[86] *Id.* at 457-58.

[87] *Id.* at 36.

accelerating in Marsh's time, on fossil fuels—namely, global climate change and ocean acidification. Management surprise and a continually changing set of natural and coupled social-ecological systems have become our new reality, and yet, as in Marsh's time, there remain those who will not see or who still hew to the worldview of balance and divine providence that dominated Marsh's America. As Marsh biographer David Lowenthal has summarized, "Unlike most modern environmentalists, Marsh had come to terms with nature's 'baffling complexity, its inherent unpredictability, its daily turbulence,'"[88] anticipating by a century and a half a mindset that now has become universally necessary for effective environmental management.

It is perhaps the American West, however, that provides one of the most enduring monuments both to Marsh's general influence and to the continuing relevance of his observations in *Man and Nature* about the unintended consequences of humanity's often overexuberant and unreflective manipulation of the physical world. A bit ironically, Marsh became one of the architects of what is arguably the greatest geographical transformation in the United States: the human-engineered irrigation of the West. Toward the end of his life, at the request of the U.S. Commissioner of Agriculture, Marsh wrote an influential report on irrigation, recommending a thorough survey of the American West to see whether and how to invest in irrigation projects there. His report eventually helped prompt Congress to create the Bureau of Land Reclamation and to enact the Reclamation Act of 1902.

That agency and that law have made absolutely clear humanity's capacity to transform an entire region. Pursuant to the Reclamation Act, the Bureau of Reclamation operates in 17 western states, from the west coast to the line of states from North Dakota south to Texas. Since 1905, when it built its first project, the Klamath Basin project straddling southern Oregon and northern California, the Bureau has built more than 600 dams and reservoirs in the West, including Hoover Dam on the Colorado River and Grand Coulee Dam on the Columbia River. Its 338 reservoirs have a total storage capacity of 140 million acre-feet (an acre-foot contains 325,851 gallons of water), and the Bureau remains the United States' largest water wholesaler, delivering 10 trillion gallons of water each year to 31 million customers. One out of five farmers in the West still rely of Bureau projects for irrigation, watering 10 million acres of cropland. The Bureau also operates 53 hydroelectric facilities that produce, on average, 40 billion kilowatt-hours of electricity each year.

While the many large-scale dam-and-reservoir Reclamation projects allowed farming, ranching, and settlement of the arid West, they came at an environmental cost. No rivers of any size in the West flow free, dozens of fish and other river-dependent species have declined so much that they are listed for protection

[88] Lowenthal, *supra* note 7, at 432 (quoting Marsh, *supra* note 27, at 91-92).

under the federal Endangered Species Act, few coastal estuaries receive the freshwater they need for productive ecosystems, and the huge reservoirs have drowned habitats and affected climate. Contradicting Marsh's cautions to tread slowly and carefully, engineers built effectively every dam that *could* be built, regardless of how marginal the human benefit or how high the ecological cost.

The result is what Marc Reisner famously dubbed "the Cadillac Desert."[89] Reisner, like Marsh, recognized that the engineered changes to the physical world that make human settlement and comfort possible also have a habit of coming back to bite us, complete with unintended consequences:

> Like so many great and extravagant achievements, from the fountains of Rome to the federal deficit, the immense national dam-construction program that allowed civilization to flourish in the deserts of the West contains seeds of disintegration; it is the old saw about an empire's rising higher and higher and having farther and farther to fall.[90]
>
> None of this is to say that we shouldn't have gone out and tried to civilize the arid West by building water projects and dams. It is merely to suggest that we overreached ourselves. What we achieved may be spectacular; in another sense, though, we achieved the obverse of our goals. The Bureau of Reclamation set out to help the small farmers of the West but ended up making a lot of rich farmers even wealthier at the small farmers' expense.... We set out to tame the rivers and ended up killing them. We set out to make the American West secure; what we really did was make ourselves rich and our descendants insecure. Few of them are apt to regret that we built Hoover Dam; on balance, however, they may find themselves wishing that we had left things pretty much as they were.[91]

George Perkins Marsh first published *Man and Nature* over 150 years ago, but his basic lessons remain relevant to U.S. environmental and natural resources law and policy far beyond forest protection and reforestation. Indeed, given the widespread agreement that we have entered the Anthropocene, his lessons are perhaps even more relevant now than they were at the beginning of the conservation era.

Humanity has set climate change in motion, the impacts of which—from the behavior of glaciers in Greenland and Antarctica to the worsening of tropical storms to the burning of Norwegian sub-Arctic forests and the Amazon rainforest—continually surprise us. Humanity has set ocean acidification in motion, perhaps signing the death warrant for coral reefs worldwide. We have covered the planet in plastic and seasoned it with an increasing variety of toxics and are

---

[89] Marc Reisner, Cadillac Desert: The American West and Its Disappearing Water (1993 Viking Penguin paperback ed.).

[90] *Id.* at 480.

[91] *Id.* at 486.

still figuring out the extent of *that* damage. Cumulatively, we appear to have set in motion the planet's sixth mass extinction event, to who knows what end.

Marsh, in other words, hadn't seen *anything* yet—and he nevertheless still got the core message right. Humans are agents of massive geographical and ecological change. However, we never have a complete idea of what we're doing because we are acting on complex adaptive systems in which causation is inherently problematic and results inherently uncertain. Changes accumulate and feed each other over time, and those synergies often lead to results that we neither wanted nor like. The damage, once done, is often hard to undo, warranting caution.

Unfortunately, humanity has not yet fully absorbed Marsh's warning. The American West—and the rest of the world, for that matter—continues to cope with the consequences of human modifications to planetary systems, from Marsh's deforestation and dammed rivers to urbanized landscapes to climate change. If Marsh could observe these "new" challenges shaping contemporary environmental and natural resources law and policy, he might just shake his head in frustration and mutter, "I told you so!"

However, Marsh also saw ways out of the transformation trap—exit routes from prior behavior that we must hope can still work to thwart at least the worst of the futures that we have probably already set in motion. Human agency can work to better the environment as well as to destroy it. We can conserve what remains and try to restore some of the systems that have changed—or at least, using modern parlance and acknowledging climate change realities, we can act to preserve and restore ecosystem function and the production of ecosystem services, building system resilience, even if the system in question is partially or wholly transformed from what it used to be. Above all, we can be less greedy, curbing our desires to consume and control the natural systems within which we are embedded in favor of a far more modest footprint on the planet.

Chapter 2[1]

The Remarkable Legacy of John Wesley Powell[2]

Mark Squillace,[3] Travis Miller,[4] and Cody Phillips[5]

Introduction

John Wesley Powell may seem like an odd choice to cast as a pioneer of environmental law. He was not a lawyer. He never even graduated from college. Yet he was a visionary leader, admired by his peers as a first-rate intellect, who understood the American West better than any of his contemporaries. And alongside his familiarity with the West came an abiding appreciation of the limits that water resources would foist on western development.

Powell is perhaps best known for his audacious trip down the Colorado River through the heart of the American West—a feat recounted in a thrilling journal published in 1875 by the U.S. Geological Survey as *The Exploration of the Colorado River and its Tributaries.* Powell's vivid descriptions of a landscape

[1] This chapter draws on the works of the many scholars who have written extensively about the life and work of John Wesley Powell. While these works are cited throughout the article, citations are generally limited to direct quotes from other manuscripts.

[2] The principal author of this chapter is Prof. Mark Squillace.

[3] Mark Squillace is the Raphael J. Moses Professor of Natural Resources Law at the University of Colorado Law School. Professor Squillace joined the Colorado Law faculty in 2005. He served as the Director of Colorado Law's Natural Resources Law Center from 2005-2013. Before joining the Colorado law faculty, Professor Squillace taught at the University of Toledo College of Law, where he was named the Charles Fornoff Professor of Law and Values, and at the University of Wyoming College of Law, where he served a three-year term as the Winston S. Howard Professor of Law. He is a former Fulbright scholar and the author or co-author of numerous articles and books on water resources law, public lands, natural resources, and environmental law and policy.

[4] Travis Miller has a degree in Environmental Studies from the University of California, Santa Barbara and is a second-year law student at the University of Colorado Law School.

[5] Cody Phillips has a dual degree in Biology and Geology from Whitman College and is a second-year law student at the University of Colorado Law School.

bursting with natural beauty, of the privations suffered by his men during their epic journey, and of the remarkable feats of bravery required to complete their expedition into the unknown assured his place among the great explorers of the American West. But his remarkable accomplishments as an explorer and field scientist aside, it was his subsequent career as a public servant that secured his legacy as a pioneer of environmental law, or perhaps more accurately, as a pioneer of natural resources law and policy. Donald Worster, author of the definitive biography of Powell, *A River Runs West*, compares his subject to John Muir and Gifford Pinchot, "two figures [who] stand like gods"—and suggests that "[w]e might call him our prophet of the inhabited environment—the prophet of the watershed and of watershed democracy."[6]

Powell wore many hats during his long and productive career, but he was especially committed to restructuring the system of public land management, especially in the arid expanses of the American West. And while he would not see his most ambitious ideas enacted into law, his achievements were legendary. He was instrumental in founding two federal agencies devoted to two important branches of science. Most prominent was his work to establish the U.S. Geological Survey in the U.S. Department of the Interior. Powell served as the second director of the USGS and the Survey's mapping tradition can be traced directly to his work. But Powell also had a deep and enduring passion for the Bureau of Ethnology, an agency now situated under the Smithsonian Institution as the Department of Anthropology. Powell served as the Bureau's founding director and continued to oversee the agency until his death in 1902.

Young John Powell

John Wesley Powell was born on March 24, 1834, in Mount Morris, New York. He was the fourth child of British emigrants Mary Dean and Reverend Joseph Powell, a Wesleyan Methodist preacher.[7] His deeply religious parents named him after John Wesley, the founder of the Wesleyan Methodist movement, perhaps in the hope that he would follow his father in the path of a preacher.

After migrating to the United States and a difficult first eight years in New York, Reverend Joseph Powell, like many emigrants, saw an opportunity to build a better life for his family in the American West. In 1838, he moved his family to Jackson, Ohio where they remained for much of John Powell's childhood. However, the Powell family was quickly met with new troubles due to the Reverend's

---

[6] Donald Worster, *Watershed Democracy: Recovering the Lost Vision of John Wesley Powell*, 23 JLRENVL 57, 58 (2003).

[7] M. D. Lincoln (Bessie Beach), Grove Karl Gilbert, Marcus Baker, and Paul Carcus, John Wesley Powell A Memorial To An American Explorer And Scholar xi, 1 (Grove Karl Gilbert ed. 1903).

outspoken position in the locally unpopular abolitionist movement. When copies of *Wesley's Thoughts on Slavery*, an abolitionist pamphlet written by John Wesley Powell's namesake, were anonymously spread throughout the town, pro-slavery advocates mobbed and beat many of the abolitionists in the region. Although Reverend Powell escaped this mob, tensions ran high in Jackson.

Fearful for her son's safety, Mary Dean removed young John Powell from the local school. Luckily, George Crookham, another member of the anti-slavery movement and friend of the Powell family, offered to tutor John privately. It was Crookham, an amateur naturalist who had built a library, museum, and schoolhouse on his property, who first exposed Powell to the natural sciences and often took Powell into the woods in lieu of assigned readings. And Crookham's tutelage undeniably played a large role in shaping the young mind of John Wesley Powell.

In 1846, Reverend Powell left Ohio and moved his family westward again, this time purchasing a farm in Walworth County, Wisconsin Territory, just two years before Wisconsin achieved statehood. However, Reverend Powell was more interested in preaching than working the land and laid the responsibilities for the farm on his twelve-year-old son, John. Four years later, John Powell marked his occupation in the 1850 federal census as "Farmer." Interestingly, less than a hundred miles away from the Powell farm, a young John Muir tilled his own land, as the Muir family had also moved to Wisconsin in the late 1840s.

In 1851, the Powell family moved again, this time to Boone County, Illinois. Once there, John Powell turned the farming over to his younger brother, W.B. Powell, and began to self-educate, teaching himself grammar, math, and geography. One year later, eighteen-year-old John Powell passed the teachers' proficiency test and was certified to teach in Jefferson Prairie, Wisconsin. Although he was self-taught and younger than many of his students, Powell continued to teach for the next three years in the winters and spent his time farming in the summers, saving money for a college education.

Powell enrolled at Wheaton College in 1855, but quickly ran out of funds during his first year and left to make money by teaching public school in the town of Clinton, Wisconsin. Powell was not deterred from his effort to gain a formal education, however, and the following year he enrolled at another institution of higher learning—this time at Illinois College in Jacksonville, Illinois—where he remained for less than a year. In 1857, at Reverend Powell's urging, John Powell enrolled in a third institution, Oberlin College where he spent five months before leaving to re-enroll at Illinois College. True to form, he dropped out again after just one year. Despite having attended three different colleges, Powell never received a degree.

Powell's lackluster performance in the academic world likely resulted from his time with Crookham, where he had learned that there was more to education than brick and mortar classrooms. Bessie Beech described John Powell's unorthodox style of learning in her biography of his life:

> To a large extent his school-room was in the forest and the field, on the prairie and the mountain, and along the river bank and the lake shore; for he early became a student of nature, and studied in the solitudes of nature.[8]

Between his formal academic semesters at official institutions of higher learning, Powell took many excursions into the great outdoors, his preferred classroom. In the summer of 1855, Powell went up the Mississippi by boat to Wisconsin, and then by foot to the Straits of Mackinac in Michigan where he collected mollusk samples for his personal collection. It was on this trip that he met his wife-to-be, Emma Dean, the daughter of his mother Mary Dean's half-brother. The next summer, Powell took a skiff down the Mississippi River from St. Anthony Falls south to its mouth in New Orleans, and in 1857, he rafted the Ohio River to the Mississippi River. After reaching the town of St. Louis on the Mississippi, he proceeded on foot further south towards the Iron Mountains, collecting mineral samples along the way. Powell kept many of the specimens he collected on these trips and gifted many others to various institutions of learning in Illinois for use in the classroom.

Despite having never earned a degree, these trips lent an academic weight to Powell's work and many considered Powell to be a genuine naturalist. In 1859, the same year that Darwin's *On the Origin of Species* was published, John Wesley Powell was elected to the position of Secretary of the newly-founded Illinois Natural History Society. When the next census came around in 1860, Powell was able to update his profession from "Farmer" to "Naturalist."

By then, America was on the brink of civil war. In 1861, at the age of 27, John Wesley Powell enlisted in the Union Army. Like his father, Powell was a staunch abolitionist who "felt thoroughly convinced that American slavery was doomed."[9] Powell was an extremely capable soldier and quickly rose up the Army's ranks, earning the title of second lieutenant within a month. Before seeing combat, Powell requested brief leave from General Ulysses S. Grant to go to Detroit to marry Emma Dean. When he returned he was again promoted, this time to captain.

On April 6, 1862, Powell led Battery F of the Second Light Artillery in the Battle of Shiloh in Tennessee. The battle began when 44,000 Confederate soldiers ambushed the Union forces near the Tennessee River and resulted in an estimated 23,700 casualties, which, at the time, was the bloodiest battle in

---

8 Lincoln et al., *supra* note 7, at 11.

9 P.C. Warman, *John Wesley Powell. Proceedings Of A Meeting Commemorative Of His Distinguished Services: Held In Columbian University Under The Auspices Of The Washington Academy Of Sciences*, 5 Proceedings of the Wash. Acad. of Sci., 99, 101 (1905).

American history. Unfortunately, Powell did not escape unscathed. While signaling his troops to fire, Powell was struck by a confederate musket-ball in his right arm, just above the wrist. Two days later, his right arm was partially amputated.[10]

Despite his injury, Powell continued to command artillery batteries under General William Tecumseh Sherman and General George Henry Thomas, and in 1864 he was promoted to the rank of Major. Powell's time in the army ended less than three months before the end of the Civil War when he received an honorable discharge from military service on January 14, 1865.

With the war behind him, Major Powell returned to teaching. He became a professor of geology at Illinois Wesleyan University and taught there for three years. Drawing from his own educational experience with Crookham, Powell often used the natural world as his classroom and frequently took students on field excursions to study the geology of the surrounding region. "Although he probably did not realize it, Powell was revolutionizing the teaching of science. And when he took a group of students on an extended field trip to the Rocky Mountains, it was one of the first such trips of its kind in American higher education."[11]

Powell also gave lectures at the Normal University near the Illinois Natural History Society where he continued to serve as secretary, a position he had maintained throughout his tenure in the army. In the winter of 1866-67, due to his many accomplishments as a naturalist and soldier, the Illinois Natural History Society elected Powell to travel to Springfield, the capitol of Illinois, to secure funding for a natural history museum at Normal. On his successful return to Normal from the capitol, Powell was elected curator of the museum.

By the beginning of 1867, at the age of 33, John Wesley Powell was a decorated war veteran, an accomplished professor of natural resources, the curator of a museum of natural history, and the secretary of the Natural History Society of Illinois. However, one of the most impactful experiences of Powell's career came in the summer of 1867 when he organized a federally-funded expedition to study the geology of North and South Park—two large valleys on the west slope of the Rocky Mountains in the Colorado Territory.[12] It was on that expedition

---

[10] "In the same battle of Shiloh, a Southern officer, Col. Charles E. Hooker, afterwards Member of Congress from Mississippi, lost his left arm, and after the war the warriors met and became friends. It happened that their hands were of the same size, and henceforward whenever either purchased a pair of gloves he sent the unnecessary one to his enemy; the two veterans ever after remained friends."

See Lincoln et al., *supra* note 7, at 16.

[11] James M. Aton, John Wesley Powell: His Life and Legacy 4 (2010).

[12] In a letter from Powell to Ulysses S. Grant:

A party of Naturalists, under the auspices of the State Normal University of Illinois, will visit the Mauvaises Terres of Southwestern Dakotah for the purpose of making a

that Powell climbed Pikes Peak, explored the Front Range of the Rocky Mountains, and was first exposed to the mighty rivers of the West.

Powell, The Explorer

John Wesley Powell first became captivated with the Colorado River and its tributaries during his summer expedition of 1867.[13] The expedition explored many of the small side canyons of the Colorado River; a region which kindled in Powell an overwhelming desire to fill in the last significant hole in the map of the United States—the canyons of the Colorado Plateau.

Powell returned to Colorado in the winter of 1868-69 to survey the geography, geology, ethnography, and natural history of the area. During this trip he camped along the White River and made excursions to the Grand, Green, and Yampa Rivers. With each excursion into the river canyons, Powell's interest in the area, and his ambitions for exploration grew. By the spring of 1869, Powell had organized what would become one of the most famous and audacious river journeys in history. It began on the Green River in Wyoming, moved south to where the Green River joins the Colorado River (at the time, the Colorado above the confluence was known as the Grand River), through Glen Canyon and the Grand Canyon, and onward toward the Gulf of California in Mexico.

The Powell Survey, or Colorado River Exploring Expedition, was made up of ten men, including hunters, trappers, and seven of Powell's fellow Civil War veterans. All were capable outdoorsmen, though most had little if any experience gathering scientific data. The Expedition piloted four boats of Powell's design, each with two sealed air-compartments which kept them buoyant even when swamped with water. Powell captained the *Emma Dean*, a smaller and lighter pilot boat named for his wife that was used to scope the rapids ahead. Powell designed the other three boats—the *Maiden of the Cañon*, *Kitty Clyde's Sister*, and the cleverly-named *No Name*—to be much heavier vessels as each needed to carry one-third of the supplies. The Illinois Natural History Society, where Powell continued to serve as secretary, and the Illinois Industrial University funded the Expedition. The Smithsonian Institution and the Chicago Academy of Sciences provided Powell with the scientific instruments he would need. For food, the Expedition relied on an 1868 congressional resolution that allowed Powell to withdraw rations from any western federal outpost. Rather

---

> more thorough geological survey of that region. From thence the party will proceed to explore the 'Parks' in the Rocky Mountains.

The Papers of Ulysses S. Grant: Volume 17 January 1–September 30, 1867, 406-407 (John Y. Simon, David L. Wilson, J. Thomas Murphy, eds., 1991).

[13] John Wesley Powell, *The Exploration of the Colorado River and Its Canyons* 117 (2003).

than withdraw the full amount of food to which he was entitled, Powell instead withdrew part of his allotted bacon rations as cash. Powell then used that money to pay the hunters who came along on the expedition, using them to supplement the bacon rations with fresh meat. These hunters, however, seem not to have been very accomplished at their sport. In his journal, George Bradley, one of the Expedition members, complained that the hired men were the worst hunters in the group, comparing them more to "school-boys on a holiday than like men accustomed to live by the chase."[14]

Although Powell documented the Expedition in his journal, his tale of the journey was not published until 1875, six years after the initial Expedition had ended. Powell was finally persuaded to publish his journal by future-president James Garfield, who was then head of the House Appropriations Committee.[15] Powell relied heavily on this Committee to fund his surveys of the Colorado Plateau.

The story of Powell's first expedition was published by the Government Printing Office in 1875, as *The Exploration of the Colorado River of the West and its Tributaries in 1869, 1870, 1871, and 1872.* Powell's account of the Expedition varies somewhat from the accounts of the other members of the party but these variations were explained by Powell as the use of "those embellishments which help to make a story complete."[16] Historians, however, widely believe that Powell did more than merely embellish the adventurous aspects of the expedition. He apparently also swapped data from the initial expedition with more accurate survey data obtained in subsequent trips down the River in order to give the first trip a stronger scientific pedigree.[17]

The Expedition set off from Green River City, Wyoming on May 24, 1869. The boats were heavy with equipment and the crew inexperienced, but the Green River was forgiving in these first weeks. Around May 29, the Expedition encountered their first true canyon rapid in Flaming Gorge, and the explorers "took off boots and coats and prepared for a swim."[18] Nonetheless, all four boats survived these early rapids intact. Despite this early success, Powell was extremely cautious, forcing the group to portage their heavy boats and supplies around many other rapids rather than risk running the narrow, rock-filled channels, much to the ire of the men who bore the brunt of the portage duties.

---

[14] George Y. Bradley, *George Y. Bradley's Journal*, 15 Utah Historical Q. 51, 56 (1947).

[15] Garfield was the chair of the House Appropriations committee during the 42nd and 43rd Congress and was elected the 20th President of the United States in 1880. *See* U.S. *House of Representatives*, History, Art, and Archives: Garfield, James Abram. https://history.house.gov/People/Listing/G/GARFIELD,-James-Abram-(G000063)/ (last visited Sept. 28, 2019).

[16] Powell, *supra* note 13, at 123.

[17] Donald Worster, A River Running West: The Life of John Wesley Powell 256 (2001).

[18] Bradley, *supra* note 14, at 55.

Even as the Expedition was taking extra care, the waters were becoming increasingly turbulent. After passing through the relatively calm waters of Brown's Park, Utah on June 8, they entered into a new canyon full of powerful rapids in present day Dinosaur National Monument. The boats capsized several times in the strong waters, inspiring Powell to name this area the Canyon of Lodore, after the Robert Southey poem, *The Cataract of Lodore*, about a raging river.

On June 9, just two weeks after setting off, disaster struck the Expedition. Powell's pilot boat, the *Emma Dean*, signaled for the others to make for shore above a series of two falls. Two of the larger boats safely made shore, but the current carried the *No Name* down the rapids, slamming it broadside against a rock in the lower falls. Powell had split the rations up evenly among the three heavy ships to avoid total ruin in case of such an incident. Even so, the *No Name* went down loaded with three months of rations and all of the team's barometers, necessary tools for accurately measuring the height of the cliffs and the descent of the river. Luckily, the next morning the men were able to salvage all of the lost barometers, along with a three-gallon keg of whiskey, which, unbeknownst to Powell, the men had snuck onto the boat. Fittingly, the Expedition dubbed these rapids Upper and Lower Disaster Falls.

Though none of the members of the Expedition were harmed during the ordeal, the three men piloting the *No Name*—Seneca Howland, O.G. Howland, and Frank Goodman—were three of the four men who would later choose to leave the Expedition. Goodman was the first to go, departing the party the first chance he got on July 5, when the Expedition reached the mouth of the Uinta River near Ouray, Utah. Powell described the parting matter-of-factly, noting that "[Goodman] was one of the crew on the 'No Name' when she was wrecked. As our boats are rather heavily loaded, I am content that he should leave, although he has been a faithful man."[19]

Between the Green and the Colorado, the Expedition was constantly tested. Day by day the party faced "rocks, rapids, and portages,"[20] even as their food was constantly "wet and spoiling."[21] Still, the Expedition carried on in relatively good spirits, gathering fossils, measuring the canyon walls, and collecting geological information.[22]

As part of their research, Powell and his companions climbed up the canyon walls, while carrying scientific instruments, to document the river canyons from both above and below. The route from the river to the rim of the canyon

---

[19] POWELL, *supra* note 13, at 187.

[20] *Id.* at 158, 280; Bradley, *supra* note 14, at 96.

[21] POWELL, *supra* note 13, at 158.

[22] *Id.* at 176.

was often steep and perilous. During one such excursion he took with George Bradley, Powell, the one-armed war veteran, described how the team climbed:

> We determine to attempt a passage by crevice ... so we climb as men would out of a well. Bradley climbs first; I hand him the barometer. So we pass each other alternately until we emerge from the fissure, out on the summit of the rock.[23]

From atop the canyon near the confluence of the Colorado and Green Rivers, Powell described in his journal some of the stunning sandstone shapes familiar to anyone who has traveled to the canyons of southern Utah:

> When thinking of these rocks one must not conceive of piles of boulders or heaps of fragments, but a whole land of naked rock, with giant forms carved on it: cathedral-shaped buttes, towering hundreds or thousands of feet, cliffs that cannot be scaled, and canyon walls that shrink the river into insignificance, with vast, hollow domes and tall pinnacles and shafts set on the verge overhead; and all highly colored—buff, gray, red, brown, and chocolate—never lichened, never moss covered, but bare, and often polished.[24]

In early August, the party floated through one of the more serene canyons of the Expedition. The men spent two days camped in a large cavern, "doubtless made for an academy of music by its storm-born architect."[25] Powell later dubbed this cavern the Music Temple, after his brother, a man known for his sour attitude but beautiful singing voice, filled the cavern with song.[26] This section of the canyon gripped Powell, but a lack of rations forced Powell to depart after two days.[27] Powell described the process of naming this canyon in his journal on August 2:

> So we have a curious *ensemble* of wonderful features—carved walls, royal arches, glens, alcove gulches, mounds, and monuments. From which of these features shall we select a name? We decide to call it Glen Canyon.[28]

The Music Temple, along with the rest of Glen Canyon, is now submerged under Lake Powell, the result of the Glen Canyon Dam which was completed in 1964. The dam and reservoir are a significant source of hydroelectric power, but they do little to enhance the water supply for the millions of people who rely on

---

[23] *Id.* at 212.

[24] *Id.* at 206.

[25] *Id.* at 231.

[26] *Id.*

[27] Bradley, *supra* note 14, at 82.

[28] Powell, *supra* note 13, at 232-33.

Colorado River water. This fact is especially true today as the Basin confronts the realities of persistent drought and climate change.[29] One wonders what Powell would think, were he alive today, about the inundation of that "ensemble of wonderful features" that were once found in Glen Canyon. Not only are the wonders of the canyon lost, probably forever, the dam causes serious negative impacts to the ecology of the Grand Canyon situated just downstream.

After leaving Glen Canyon on August 5th, the Powell Expedition entered the Grand Canyon. Powell waxed poetic at the stunning scenery and the massive walls that form Marble Canyon:

> And now the scenery is on a grand scale. The wall of the cañon, 2,500 feet high, are of marble, of many beautiful colors, often polished below by the waves, and sometimes far up the sides, where showers have washed the sands over the cliffs.... As this great bed forms a distinctive feature of the cañon, we call it Marble Cañon.[30]

Powell named many other features of the Grand Canyon during the voyage, including Silver Creek, which he later renamed Bright Angel Creek as a counterpart to the Dirty Devil River.

During the 24 days the men spent in the Grand Canyon, the party endured several more mishaps. Anyone who has floated through the Grand Canyon knows of the frequent encounters with steep granite walls and massive rapids. The men carried out several difficult portages, but in many cases they were unable to forge a path between the canyon walls and the River, and were forced to run these rapids, often swamping or capsizing their boats. Barely a week after entering the Grand Canyon, the expedition had lost all of their hats, blankets, and spare clothes, and nearly sank the pilot boat, the *Emma Dean*.

---

[29] The waters of the Colorado River were divided between the upper and lower river basin states in the 1922 Law of the River Compact. However, the writers of the Compact over-estimated the average amount of water in the Colorado River by approximately 1 million acre-feet per year, effectively allocating out more water than the River carries. Both Lake Powell, and the lower reservoir created by the Hoover Dam, Lake Mead, have been below capacity for a decade. Lake Powell is so low that it is approaching the point where it would no longer be able to produce hydropower. Neither reservoir is likely to meet capacity again, as research by the U.S. Bureau of Reclamation indicates that both population and drought intensity will only increase in the region. Further, not only does Lake Mead have the capacity to additionally hold the water of Lake Powell, but the lower basin states can claim the water of Lake Powell if the upper states fail to supply the mandatory minimum amount of water as dictated by the 1922 Compact, making Lake Powell largely redundant. *See* Brittany Patterson, Scientific American, Climate Wire: *Should Iconic Lake Powell Be Drained?* (Oct. 27, 2017), https://www.scientificamerican.com/article/should-iconic-lake-powell-be-drained/; Scott K. Miller, *Undamming Glen Canyon: Lunacy, Rationality, or Prophecy?* 19 Stan. Envtl. L.J. 121, 173-174 (Jan. 2000); Colo. Rev. Stat. §37-61-101 (2017); U.S. Bureau of Reclamation, *Glen Canyon Unit* (last updated May 13 2019), https://www.usbr.gov/uc/rm/crsp/gc/.

[30] POWELL, *supra* note 13, at 237, 241.

By August 17, less than three months after setting out from Green River, Wyoming, Powell observed that the initial ten-month's worth of rations had become "only musty flour sufficient for ten days and a few dried apples, but plenty of coffee."[31] Morale in the men had become dangerously low, most of the scientific equipment had been lost or destroyed, and the River seemed to be only growing in intensity and danger. This discontent came to a head at what is now known as Separation Rapids.[32]

The party had spent half a day attempting to portage around the rapid, but were unable to forge a path. With only a few days left of food and what seemed like numerous other large rapids ahead, Powell had two options—run the rapids or abandon the expedition. Powell spent a sleepless night weighing his choices. Using a sextant, he meticulously measured his exact location and determined it was 75-80 miles to the mouth of the Virgin River where Mormon missionaries had settled. It was possible to walk away. However, at the end of the night, Powell came to the steadfast determination that he could not pull himself away so close to the end of the Expedition:

> To leave the exploration unfinished, to say that there is a part of the canyon which I cannot explore, having already nearly accomplished it, is more than I am willing to acknowledge, and I determine to go on.[33]

George Bradley's journal entry for August 28 simply states they "came to the determination to run the rapid or perish in the attempt."[34]

For three of the men, the two Howland brothers and William Dunn, the risk seemed too great. Both the Howland brothers were on the *No Name* when the River splintered the boat, while Dunn, an experienced hunter and trapper in the Colorado Rockies, likely trusted his own survival skills in the desert over the dangers of the last stretch of the river.

On August 28th, the three men climbed out of the canyon and made their way overland 75 miles to the nearest American settlement. They carried only weapons, no food or water, opting to rely on their hunting skills and pools of rainwater rather than deplete the already meager remaining rations of the Expedition. Powell attempted to persuade the men to stay, but both sides equally felt that the other was facing certain ruin. The remainder of the expedition party regretted the splitting, as the three who left were skilled outdoorsmen and had proven their worth time and again throughout the Expedition.

---

[31] *Id.* at 260.

[32] Separation Rapids was lost to Lake Mead with the construction of Hoover Dam; Worster, *supra* note 17, at Ch. 5 fn.59.

[33] Powell, *supra* note 13, at 279.

[34] Bradley, *supra* note 14, at 96.

Tragically, the three men died before they ever reached the settlement, most likely killed by members of the Shivwits band of the Paiute people who apparently believed they were encroaching on Shivwits territory. The story of their demise remains the subject of much debate and is now part of the lore of the Grand Canyon.[35]

As the two groups separated, the remainder of the Expedition lightened their boats to better navigate the life-threatening rapids by leaving behind, along with any extra gear, all the geologic samples and fossils they had collected. Powell was also forced to abandon the badly damaged *Emma Dean*.

Ironically, the rapids proved less daunting than had been anticipated and the remaining members of the party made it through without incident. Just one day later, around noon on August 29, 1869, the Expedition safely floated out of the Grand Canyon, and on August 30, 1869, Powell called an end to The Colorado River Exploring Expedition at the confluence of the Virgin and Colorado Rivers, a site now inundated by present-day Lake Mead in Nevada.

Powell's research conducted during this expedition down the Colorado River placed the first broad brush strokes on the otherwise blank region of the map where the waters of the West flowed, opening the door to further studies of the region. Powell himself returned to the Colorado River for a second, more scientific expedition after two summers of scouting the area and gathering more data.

The Powell Survey

Powell's second expedition down the Colorado River was focused on thoroughly cataloguing the river canyons of the West through a scientific survey, which Powell had not been able to do on the first trip. More detail meant more time on the River and within its side canyons. This meant that Powell needed to bring more supplies for his new ten-man crew, most of whom were selected primarily for their scientific acumen. Additionally, Powell employed two artists to document the trip, including E.O. Beaman, a photographer skilled in the intricacies of field photography.

The knowledge of the River that Powell had gained from the first trip allowed him to cache food and supplies at the few points accessible by horseback. The goal was to ensure that the survey team had sufficient time to take accurate

---

[35] Two years after the expedition, Powell came across a band of Shivwits who admitted to the murder of Dunn and the Howland bothers. However, conspiracy theories range from murder by Mormons to fear of cannibalism by the Howland brothers, who were cousins of Franklin and Elizabeth Graves, members of the infamous Donner party twenty years prior.

DON LAGO, *THE POWELL EXPEDITION: NEW DISCOVERIES ABOUT JOHN WESLEY POWELL'S 1869 RIVER JOURNEY, 320* (2018); WORSTER, *supra* note 17, at 213.

measurements of the canyons without having to leave the region to resupply. Even so, it took two years for the Powell Survey to complete this second trip down the Colorado River.

The party left from Green River City, Wyoming in May 1871 and reached Lees Ferry[36] at the mouth of the Grand Canyon five months later in October. In comparison, the original expedition covered this same distance in only three months. With the entirety of the Grand Canyon still before them, Powell arranged to spend the winter in the Mormon township of Kanab, Utah where the survey crew established baselines for their topographical mapping. Powell, a dedicated anthropologist who had spent a great deal of time over the previous summers meeting with the native people of the surrounding region, continued his ethnological research during his winter in the Kanab area. Powell was well-known for treating native people with humanity and he found their cultures and mythologies fascinating. Powell's many interactions with the native tribes of the region led the tribes to confer on Powell the nickname *Kapurats*, which in the Kaibab Paiute language means "he is who is missing an arm."[37] In studying the native people, Powell documented their different styles of agriculture and sophisticated use of irrigation.[38] Here is one description from *The Exploration of the Colorado River and Its Tributaries*:

> Wherever there is water, near by an ancient ruin may be found; and these ruins are gathered about centers, the centers being larger pueblos and the scattered ruins representing single houses. The ancient people lived in villages, or pueblos, but during the growing season they scattered about by the springs and streams to cultivate the soil by irrigation, and wherever there was a little farm or garden patch, there was built a summer house of stone.[39]

In that same work, Powell also documented the similarities between the Mormon pioneers around Kanab and the ancient Puebloans of the region, highlighting how both societies chose to settle in the same water-rich areas and how the Mormons even used the stones of the old pueblos in their buildings.

During his winter in Kanab, Powell likely saw the Mormon settlements as models for the large-scale water planning that would bring settlers out West. The Mormons of Utah built their communities around a spirit of cooperation, which stood in stark contrast to other western settlements where new pioneers often

---

[36] Lees Ferry was named for the Mormon settler John D. Lee, best known for leading the Mountain Meadows massacre in 1857, which killed 120 'gentile' emigrants attempting to travel west to Los Angeles. *See* PBS, *John Doyle Lee*, New Perspectives on The West, https://www.pbs.org/weta/thewest/people/i_r/lee.htm (last visited Sept. 15, 2019).

[37] Worster, *supra* note 17, at 261.

[38] Talking about the Pimas, Maricopas, and Papagos: "They are skilled agriculturalists, cultivating lands by irrigation." Powell, *supra* note 13, at 24.

[39] *Id.* at 53.

competed with each other at the expense of community. The collective enterprise that characterized the Mormon settlements promoted, and later codified,[40] the creation of irrigation districts in the state of Utah. Landholders within those districts were equally entitled to use the water and regulate its use without regard to priorities.

Powell's experience with the Mormon and native communities and their communal irrigation practices undoubtedly influenced his appreciation of water allocation systems and their suitability to the American West.

Powell, The Visionary

Before winter's end, 1872, Powell left his survey for Washington D.C. to ask Congress for additional funding for the following summer, wisely bringing along the first photos of the Colorado River Canyons taken by E.O Beaman. As the years progressed and the Powell survey continued its work, Powell would occasionally return to the West, but he spent increasingly more time in the nation's capital. In June 1872, while the men of the Powell survey were approaching the confluence of the Dirty Devil River, Powell and his wife moved from Chicago to Washington, D.C. Powell had gained fame and influence by bravely running the Colorado River, unlocking its mysteries and opening it to the larger world. By moving to Washington, D.C., Powell forged for himself an opportunity to influence the federal government's western lands policy so as to better reflect the scientific work that he and others had carried out. While he ultimately fell short of his most ambitious dreams, the ideas he introduced and the influence he exerted as a public servant remain a powerful and enduring force, even today. The Powell Survey did not stand alone in its scientific study of the American western territories. It was one of four surveys, each important in their own way, that provided baseline data and information that was critical to setting government policy for the western United States. Powell's Survey, which was funded by the Smithsonian Institution, was one of four surveys that came to be known as the Great Surveys of the West, and, together they formed the backbone for our early understanding of the arid west. The King Survey (1867-1869; 1872) focused on mapping out coal and iron deposits, and surveyed the transcontinental railroad from California's Sierra Nevada Mountains to Colorado's Front Range. The Wheeler Survey (1871-1879), which was funded by the U.S. Army, created topographical maps for the military and surveyed "the number, positions, and character of the Indian tribes." The Hayden Survey (1867-1879),

[40] "The county court having jurisdiction may proceed to organize the county or part thereof into an irrigation district; and thereafter the landholders of such district shall be equally entitled to the use of the water in or to be brought into such district, according to their several needs." Law of Jan. 20, 1865, Title 11, ch. 3, §505, 1876 Compiled Laws of the Terr. of Utah 1, 219, https://babel.hathitrust.org/cgi/pt?id=hvd.hl3co6&view=1up&seq=237c.

which was funded by the Department of the Interior, was the first to map the Yellowstone region.

Despite the many remarkable achievements of the Great Surveys, only the Powell Survey concerned itself directly with the human settlement of the West. Ferdinand Hayden's survey was perhaps closest to Powell's, in that it focused not just on the discovery of mineral wealth, but also on cataloguing the possible uses of land. However, the Hayden Survey seemed more interested in pleasing members of Congress than providing an accurate description of the land, and as such released grand exaggerated claims on the wealth of resources in the region.[41] For example, in 1873, the Hayden Survey published a report erroneously claiming that the increase in rainfall in the early 1870s was undeniably "connected with the settlement of the country; and that, as the population increases, the amount of moisture will increase."[42] The report was so popular that over 8,000 copies were ordered and printed. Thus, just as Powell was busy making a new home in Washington D.C., a cadre of notable scientists, funded by Congressional appropriations, were influencing policy and promoting the theory that "rain follows the plow."

Powell, meanwhile, continued to manage his own survey and, from his seat in Washington, worked to debunk claims such as "rain follows the plow." In 1873, the same year Hayden's report was published, Powell convinced his long-time friend and director of the Smithsonian, Joseph Henry, to release all of the Smithsonian's rainfall data collected since 1846 to more accurately map out the water patterns of the American West. What they discovered was a tale of two countries: one humid, flat, and well-disposed to agriculture; the other dry, rugged, and in need of irrigation. The line separating them was more or less at the 100th meridian—a north-south line coincident with the eastern border of the Texas panhandle. It was roughly around that line where annual rainfall dropped below 20 inches a year, the amount needed to sustain agriculture without irrigation.

Although Powell had made his name exploring the desert canyons of the southwestern United States, he proved himself equally adept at the very different enterprise of Washington politics. The four Great Surveys all served a similar function of exploring the American territories of the West, and all but the King Survey lacked a defined border. So, it was perhaps inevitable that the surveys would overlap. In 1873, the Hayden and Wheeler surveys duplicated efforts in

[41] *See, e.g.*, F.V. Hayden, *Notes on the Lignite Deposits of the West*, 198, 204 (Mar. 1, 1868), where Hayden claimed that iron ore found in Boulder county will have the same influence on the progress of the West as the coal of Pennsylvania has on the country as a whole.

[42] F.V. Hayden, *Preliminary Field Report of the United States Geological Survey of Colorado and New Mexico, Conducted Under the Authority of John. J.D. Cox, Secretary of the Interior* at 141 (1869).

South Park, Colorado Territory, catalyzing a Congressional hearing on the purpose behind the four surveys.

Powell used this hearing as an opportunity to accomplish two goals. First, he outlined the uniqueness of his survey by highlighting the work that was being done to determine which areas of the West could be farmed through irrigation. This convinced Congress to take his survey out from under the Smithsonian Institution and place it under the direction of the Department of the Interior as the Second Division of the United States Geological and Geographical Survey, a veritable promotion. Second, and more importantly, Powell used the Congressional hearing as a platform to warn of the social and economic consequences of ignoring the Smithsonian rainfall data.

Powell determined that even if pioneers diverted all of the free flowing bodies of water in the west for irrigation, "not more than three per cent, can eventually be cultivated."[43] There was simply not enough water to irrigate the entire western estate.

Powell implored Congress to create a general survey for the purpose of determining which areas of the West could be redeemed by irrigation. Yet, despite his convincing scientific evidence, Congress refused Powell's plea, primarily because it clashed with the government's effort to promote western settlements.

Since the 1840s and over the next several decades, Congress passed a series of legislation encouraging the movement of people out West. The 1841 Preemption Act allowed squatters on federal land to purchase up to 160 acres for a minimum of $1.25/acre, thus encouraging squatting on public lands. The 1862 Homestead Act allowed homesteaders to acquire 160 acres of land for an $18 filing fee and five years of farming their new homestead. The 1873 Timber Culture Act gave homesteaders an additional 160 acres in return for planting trees on a quarter of their land. Finally, the 1877 Desert Lands Act allowed individuals to claim arid and semi-arid lands for the purpose of irrigating and cultivating the land.

Settlers made land claims using the Public Lands Survey system, a system devised by Thomas Jefferson that divides land into six-square mile Townships and one-mile square sections. The system simplified legal descriptions and it helped define and catalogue new states after the revolutionary war. But the straight lines and square corners that characterize the system[44] do not conform

---

[43] COMMITTEE ON THE PUBLIC LANDS, GEOGRAPHICAL AND GEOLOGICAL SURVEYS WEST OF THE MISSISSIPPI, H.R. REP. NO. 43-612, at 3 (1st Sess. 1874) (hereinafter "1874 Committee").

[44] The system took new territory and divided it "by lines to be run and marked due North and South, and others crossing these at right angles," Because of its right angles, the Public Lands Survey System gained the nickname the "Rectangular System." National Archives, Report of a Committee to Establish a Land Office, 30 April 1784, https://founders.archives.gov/documents/Jefferson/01-07-02-0148

well to the rugged western landscape and its natural watershed. Moreover, land allocations of 160 acres, which may have been appropriate in the more humid east, proved largely inadequate to sustain agriculture in the arid west. Thomas Donaldson colorfully describes the problem in an 1881 essay:

> An acre of land in the Middle States means almost a sustenance for one person; in the Mississippi valley it means fifty bushels of corn; but on the plains among the railway lands it generally means a crop of sage-brush, with a colony of prairie-dogs.[45]

Notwithstanding their many short-comings, pioneers took advantage of the homestead and preemption laws and their offer of cheap land, trusting that rain would indeed follow the plow. Powell, of course, knew that this was fantasy but he also knew that someone would need to marshal the science and sell it to the Congress and the American people. What followed was a document that today stands as his greatest contribution to the debate over the settlement of the West—the *Arid Lands Report.*

The Arid Lands Report

The *Arid Lands Report* is both a comprehensive scientific study of the western United States region, as well as a provocative blueprint for societal change. Powell presented the report—his vision of "inhabiting the land, of knowing its limits as well as its promise, and of working cooperatively within the context of nature"[46]—to the House Public Lands Committee in 1878. The Report begins with science. Powell methodically laid out the physical and hydrological characteristics that define the arid region, and used facts and figures to lay the groundwork for his theories and to debunk popular myths, such as "rain follows the plow." At its core, however, Powell's plan could not co-exist with the established system of distributing public lands and he called for replacing the old methods with a new model grounded in science and steeped in communitarian ideals. Only by working cooperatively and within the limits of available resources, Powell argued, could humans expect to live sustainably in such a harsh, arid climate.

The heart of the Report is found in the second chapter, *The Land Systems Needed for the Arid Region*, where Powell proposed his revolutionary theory on

---

[45] Thomas Donaldson, *The Public Lands of the United States*, 133 The North Amer. L. Rev. 204, 205 (Aug. 1881).

[46] Donald Worster, *Watershed Democracy: Recovering the Lost Vision of John Wesley Powell*, 23 JLRENVL 57, 58 (2003).

land allotment for the arid west.[47] Here, Powell pulls no punches, beginning the chapter with a simple prediction: "The growth and prosperity of the Arid Region will depend largely upon a land system which will comply with the requirements of the conditions and facts [that applied to western lands.]"[48] Powell argued that while the existing land laws were adequate for irrigable lands fed by minor streams, as was true throughout the eastern half of the United States, "these methods are insufficient for the settlement of the irrigable lands that depend on the larger streams, and also for the pasturage lands and timber lands, and in this are included nearly all the lands of the Arid Region."[49]

Accordingly, the Report proposed a piece of legislation composed of two radical ideas, each aimed at remaking the way public land was distributed throughout the arid west. Drawing on the lessons he had learned from the Mormon settlers and ancient Puebloans, Powell proposed that:

> A general law should be enacted under which a number of persons would be able to organize and settle in irrigable districts, and establish their own rules and regulations for the use of the water and subdivision of the lands, but in obedience to the general provisions of the law.[50]

Powell believed that bending the dry harsh climate to the needs of man, and thereby "redeeming the land" with irrigation, was too daunting a task for any one farmer to accomplish alone. Therefore, his proposed law would require settlers to form groups of nine or more persons before being granted title to any land.[51] Each individual within the group would receive 80 acres—half of the 160 acres promised under the Homestead Act—in which to build their homestead and plant their crops, distributed not in an unworkable square plot, as was mandated under the existing laws, but in plots that conformed to the realities of nature and consisted only of land certified by surveyors as irrigable. Together, the individual plots would comprise an "irrigation district" wherein every individual property would have a guaranteed share of the water that flowed through the district.[52] Thus, "[a]n essential principle underlying Powell's irrigation and

---

[47] John Wesley Powell, *Report on the Lands of the Arid Region of the United States with a More Detailed Account of the Lands of Utah*, 45 Cong., 2d Sess., Ex. Doc. 73 Serial 1805, at 25 (1878).

[48] *Id.* at 25.

[49] *Id.* at 27

[50] *Id.*

51 *See id.* at 30-33.

[52] The second piece of proposed legislation called for the creation of "ranch districts," which concerned the distribution of pasturage land as opposed irrigable land. Like with the irrigation districts, the ranch districts would be comprised of at least nine persons. But unlike the irrigation districts, which called for smaller plots of 80 acres, the ranch districts would be comprised of plots of no less than 2,560 acres per family. *Id.* at 33-37.

grazing districts was this: the lay of the land should dictate land use and land distribution.... In other words, Powell was saying that a thousand years or so of European, wetlands agricultural ideas and parceling systems could not work in the arid region."[53]

But Powell went even further with his recommendations. In addition to changing the size and shape of land parcels, "[h]e wanted to change the centuries-old system of water appropriation."[54] Powell understood the value of water in the arid west, and predicted that if individual greed were left unchecked, "[a]ll the waters of all the arid lands will eventually be taken from their natural channels" and be depleted.[55] Even the mighty Colorado, running through its awe-inspiring canyons, would one day become little more than a trickle as irrigators diverted its entire flow to their fields. To combat this tragedy of the commons, Powell argued that by establishing water rights in common and allowing each irrigation district to set their own rules for how it was shared, farmers would be forced to work together to conserve their water, lest the entire enterprise fail.

Not surprisingly, the Report generated significant controversy. In *John Wesley Powell: His Life and Legacy*, James M. Aton aptly sums up the reasons why Powell's report was so controversial:

> It questioned the Homestead Act, a well-meaning land law that proved mostly useless in the West. It questioned the capitalistic practices of land and water speculation and urged a more socialistic system of apportionment. It questioned the applicability of Anglo-Saxon riparian water law in an arid region. It questioned various pseudoscientific ideas like the rain-follows-the-plow theory. It questioned the myth of the West as a garden, a myth that had been propounded by railroads, speculators, and western congressmen. And finally, it questioned our national myths of rugged individualism and self-reliance, as well as the belief that it is an American birthright to acquire enormous wealth. In short, Powell wanted to remake America in the West.[56]

Powell received plenty of resistance from congressmen who refused to confront the scientific reality that the arid west was an altogether different beast than the east, one that would not be easily tamed and that was ill-suited to the old public lands distribution system. But settlers and speculators were also predisposed to ignore Powell's message. "Those who suspected their pocketbooks might suffer or their fundamental beliefs be overturned by reason and facts rose up, thumped their chests in self-righteous indignation, and said 'no.'"[57] As Wallace

---

[53] Aton, *supra* note 11, at 37.

[54] *Id.*

[55] Worster, *supra* note 17, at 357.

[56] Aton, *supra* note 11, at 35.

[57] *Id.* at 36.

Stegner wrote, the West had "not so much been settled as raided—first for its furs, then for its minerals, then for its grass, then in some places for its scenery."[58] Up until Powell's report, the West was widely believed to host bountiful, verdant land, ripe for the taking. The *Arid Lands Report* warned about the danger looming behind this mistaken belief. It reads like a clarion call to government decision makers, warning that land policies that failed to account for the arid conditions and rugged nature of the landscape were doomed to fail and would lead to severe ecological damage and political upheaval. Nonetheless, "the raiders and boosters fought [Powell] as they fought reality," and, ultimately, the Report, and the radical blueprint for western development, died in committee.[59]

Despite the negative reception given the *Arid Lands Report*, Powell continued to develop and tinker with the recommendations in the Report until his death in 1902. And time has proved them to be remarkably prescient. James Aton sums up the Report's importance well:

> Whatever one might say about Powell's vision or blindness in the *Arid Lands Report*, it remains a singularly important contribution to American land policy. Many of its ideas ultimately found form in the various laws and government agencies established to protect grazing (the Bureau of Land Management), water (the Bureau of Reclamation), and timber (the U.S. Forest Service). It also laid the foundation for Theodore Roosevelt's and Gifford Pinchot's sweeping Progressive conservation reforms in the early 1900s, and it simpered the New Deal's Soil and Water Conservation Districts. For better or worse, it has been called the first environmental impact statement. It certainly speaks to our own age, even if it could not make itself heard above the roar of its own times.[60]

The USGS and the Irrigation Survey

In March 1888, ten years after the *Arid Lands Report* was left for dead in committee, western congressmen, led by Senator William Stewart of Nevada, went to the Director of the newly-formed United State Geological Survey to determine the cost of conducting an irrigation survey to "investigate the practicability of constructing reservoirs for the storage of irrigation water in the arid region."[61] Powell was then serving as the second Director of the USGS, having been appointed in 1881. He quickly replied that it would cost $250,000 to start, and subsequently explained that the first step of an irrigation survey would be to create a topographical map of the arid region. The entire project, however,

---

[58] WORSTER, *supra* note 17, at 360.

[59] *Id.*

[60] ATON, *supra* note 11, at 19.

[61] WORSTER, *supra* note 17, at 473.

would require more than $5 million, most of that for completing the topographical mapping. "The map would provide a systematic overview of the region's drainage system, indicate all the potential reservoir sites, and show which lands could make the most efficient use of the limited water supply."[62] Yet, while "Congress could see the Major's far-sighted organizing mind at work,"[63] the body was nevertheless divided in opinion, with eastern senators skeptical about the wisdom in funding western development.

Ultimately, in October 1888, Congress passed legislation funding an irrigation survey—with a budget of $100,000 rather than the $250,000 Powell had initially requested. Notably, Congressman Symmes of Colorado included a clause reserving all irrigable lands, reservoir sites, and ditch sites from entry, at the president's request. In other words, settlers would be unable to claim any federal land in the arid region until the project was complete. Much as Powell had predicted in his *Arid Lands Report*, Symmes had watched as greedy speculators in his state deprived small farmers of inexpensive farm land with legal access to water, and he was concerned that speculators would follow in the wake of Powell's survey and buy up the best irrigable land for moneyed interests. It was a controversial decision that, however well intentioned, ultimately contributed to the survey's eventual demise two years later.

The limited budget notwithstanding, Powell undertook the task with great enthusiasm. By the end of that fiscal year, the survey had mapped over 22,000 square miles of the West, and had selected 127 reservoir sites, thirty-four of which had been surveyed.[64] The work covered the Snake, Bear, Missouri, Yellowstone, Owens and Rio Grande River Basins. Congress, impressed with the work, increased the survey's budget to $250,000.[65] Under Powell's direction—

> [o]vernight the USGS had swelled like a bubble.... Even the lively Major could not keep up with all the inquiries afoot or speak the languages of all the specialists he had on the payroll. He concentrated on what excited him most—scientifically guiding the economic development of the West.[66]

In support of this pursuit, "Powell and his agency created language as well as techniques"[67] that are still used today in discussion of water law. He coined the

---

[62] *Id.*

[63] *Id.*

[64] Worster, *supra* note 17, at 479.

[65] Interestingly, Congress was willing to give Powell even more money for his budget, but he requested that they only appropriate the $250,000 he had originally requested, explaining that he was not yet ready to spend more without more men. *Id.*

[66] *Id.*

[67] Worster, *supra* note 17, at 477.

terms "runoff" and "flyoff"—referring to the rainfall that was not absorbed by soil—as well as a new measure of water volume, the "acre-foot."[68]

The most important innovation, however, was the idea that the West was made up of a series of "hydrographic basins," or watersheds.[69] Donald Worster explains the concept in *A River Running West*:

> Every stream, regardless of its size, had a natural terrain that produced it, a set of slopes that collected falling water and concentrated it. The landscape had never been systemically analyzed in that way except by the old Powell Survey. The purpose now was to see the entire region as a mosaic of interconnected watersheds, as integrated units of water and land, not to deepen geological understanding so much as to guide settlement. Each of those carefully mapped and measured watersheds furnished the natural boundaries for a series of "irrigation districts" into which settlers could come and work out their problems together.[70]

Powell understood that each watershed or basin is utterly unique, "unduplicated even in the next valley."[71] "Everything within its borders, from one divide to the other, is bound together by the forces of geology, rainfall, evaporation, soil absorption, runoff, and drainage."[72] Within each watershed, Powell argued, was "a set of interrelated ecological zones, each with its own appropriate economic use."[73] There were forests on the upper slopes, pastures below them, and finally irrigable lands in bottomlands, where the creeks and rivers make agriculture possible. Because each zone was its own unique system, each should have, according to Powell's plan, its own community rules to prevent over usage of the land, as first suggested in his *Arid Lands Report*.

In keeping with this community approach to western development, Powell instructed his surveyors "that the ends in view are not actual construction [of irrigation projects] by the Government but plans and estimates for the use of the people and Reports should be prepared in the simplest manner possible."[74] "By those criteria," Worster argues, "Powell was not projecting massive dams on major rivers such as the Colorado or Colombia. Only rarely did any of the dams he imagined rise higher than one hundred feet."[75]

---

[68] *Id.*

[69] *Id.*

[70] *Id.*

[71] Worster, *supra* note 6, at 60.

[72] *Id.*

[73] Worster, *supra* note 6, at 61.

[74] Letter from John Wesley Powell to Clarence Dutton, May 28, 1889, USGS Letters Received, Roll 25, No. 2705.

[75] WORSTER, *supra* note 17, at 479.

Meanwhile, Senator Stewart of Nevada convinced six of his colleagues to create a Select Committee on Irrigation and Reclamation of Arid Lands, with himself as chairman. In the summer of 1889, the Select Committee set out on a fact-finding tour of the West to inquire about local needs for irrigation, and they invited Powell to accompany them. Powell caught up with the senators late in the season, and on August 5, the group reached Bismarck, where a North Dakota constitutional convention had been convened. Powell addressed the assembled crowd briefly but urgently:

> 'I was a farmer boy,' he told the agriculturists and lawyers before him. He knew first-hand the problems of settling and cultivating a new land, for he had been a participant in the 'march of progress' through the wilderness. He knew a little history too, and what it taught him was that they need not be reluctant to look the problem of aridity squarely in the face, for civilization was born in arid lands. Four thousand years of experience provided that it was possible to turn a deficiency of water into a promise of prosperity. Then he turned blunt and exhortative. 'You hug to yourself the delusion that the climate is changing,' but you must accept the facts of nature and adapt. Above all, you must realize that whoever controls water in an arid country controls society. 'Fix it in your Constitution,' he urged, 'that no corporation—no body of men—no capital can get possession and right to your waters. Hold the waters in the hands of the people.'[76]

Powell, however, stood facing the same barriers he faced ten years earlier with the *Arid Lands Report* and ultimately, was unable to convince these frontiersmen to adopt such a seemingly radical idea. America was founded on the principles of free enterprise and rugged individualism; Powell's plan for the West verged on socialism. As such, it quickly became apparent to Stewart, a red-blooded capitalist, that he and Powell had very different goals for the Irrigation Survey. "Stewart saw the survey locating dam sites and irrigable lands, then turning them over to private enterprise. He wanted laissez-faire capitalism to continue as it had in the West—with a little boost from the government."[77] Powell, meanwhile, called for cooperative control of water resources within a particular watershed, and government supervision over land and water monopolies. "The two ideologies clashed, and by the fall of 1889 these two men had become political enemies."[78]

Powell's political problems only compounded from there. That same summer, President Grover Cleveland adopted Symmes' clause from the 1888 appropriations bill that established the Irrigation Survey, thereby effectively suspending the public land laws in all of the arid west, and making it impossible

[76] Worster, *supra* note 17, at 480-81.

[77] Aton, *supra* note 11, at 20.

[78] *Id.*

for anyone to acquire title to a piece of the public domain until the Survey was completed. Opposition to this decision was swift and furious. At the same time, Powell's old enemy Edward Cope, a close associate of Hayden (of the Hayden Survey), rose up again and leveled several damaging allegations against Powell, including cronyism, plagiarism, and misuse of public funds. Regardless of the veracity of these claims, the timing proved disastrous.

Just days after Cope's story hit the press in June 1890, Powell was summoned to testify before Stewart's Select Committee on Irrigation and Reclamation of Arid Lands to answer questions regarding the allegations leveled against him. However, the purpose of the hearing was not to discover the truth as "Stewart and others were waiting in ambush."[79] True to form, Powell came bearing facts and figures, as well as several maps that the USGS had drawn for the occasion, and he presented his vision of development in the West. One of these maps in particular—a General Map of the Western Drainage Districts—was especially evocative. The map, a "patchwork quilt of colors in which faded shades of red, green, brown, and yellow were supposed to tell legislators and settlers how the West looked from the perspective of a drop of water[,]" was the visual embodiment of Powell's revolutionary thinking—"the icon of his vision."[80]

The map's resemblance to a colorful jigsaw puzzle, however, belies the simplicity of its message. Powell insisted that nature follows its own logic, and therefore "the very shape of a human community, the shape of its rights and rules, should be tailored to some extent to that logic."[81] He argued that communities needed to adapt to their place; they needed to mimic and respect the watershed that supported them. Instead of drawing political lines over mountains and across rivers with no regard for topography, as was customary, Powell used the lay of the land and drew a map that logically fit the region's natural geography.

In a trilogy of articles for *Century* Magazine, published a few months earlier in the spring of 1890, Powell laid out his proposals in detail, almost as an updated version of his original *Arid Lands Report.* After acknowledging his indebtedness to Mexican and Mormon models of communitarian development, he wrote that "[t]he plan is to establish local self-government by hydrographic basins," wherein each would be "a common-wealth within itself."[82] Under Powell's plan, each irrigation district would own all the water within its boundaries and have no rights to any other water. Each landowner would have rights in common to that water, and each district would make its own laws and build its own irrigation system. All existing landowners—which Powell estimated had

---

[79] ATON, *supra* note 11, at 21.

[80] William deBuys, *Visions of Western Governance: Powell and his Successors*, 23 JLRENVL 15, 15 (2003).

[81] Worster, *supra* note 6, at 60.

[82] John Wesley Powell, *Institutions for the Arid Lands.* THE CENTURY MAGAZINE, May 1890, at 115.

already privatized half of the irrigable lands in the West—would be absorbed into their respective irrigation districts. The federal government, meanwhile, would hold in perpetuity the remaining public domain—those lands not suited for homesteads, mines, or towns—and turn it over to local residents to manage. "I say to the Government: Hands off!" Powell wrote. "Furnish the people with institutions of justice, and let them do the work for themselves."[83]

The politics, however, eventually drowned out everything else. A few weeks after the hearings ended, Stewart commenced "a campaign against Powell of personal slander and defamation that would last through the ensuing summer."[84] This included re-airing the grievances provided by Cope, as well as tying Powell to the Symmes reservation clause that had proved unpopular. In response, Powell gave an interview to the *Washington Star*, where he explained that "[t]he struggle that I am at present engaged in ... is a fight against the speculators pure and simple. I am doing what I can to prevent moneyed sharks from gobbling up the irrigable lands of the arid belt, together with the waters upon which they will depend for fruitfulness, and so establishing a sort of hydraulic feudal system, to which American farmers would be helplessly subject."[85] But his words fell largely on deaf ears. Powell's facts and figures—his fidelity to scientific knowledge and agrarian ideals—proved completely ineffective in the face of Stewart's bombast and hyperbole.

In July of 1890, debate on the irrigation survey opened before the entire House and Senate and lasted for several days, overshadowing even the Sherman Anti-trust bill that was being considered that same month. Powell was pilloried as a corrupt and un-American bureaucrat who was attempting to steal the West for his own purposes. Eastern congressmen, who had opposed irrigation spending from the beginning, saw their opening, and eight days later the Irrigation Survey was dead, as were Powell's dreams of reforming western agriculture through scientific planning. "It was the worst defeat Powell had ever suffered at the hand of Congress.... Stewart had thoroughly beaten him, without scruple or regard for the truth."[86] Nevertheless, the Appropriations Committees continued to support Powell and, despite the death of the Irrigation Survey, increased his budget for the USGS.

As a result of Stewart's crusade, Powell's second shot at irrigation legislation in the West died at the federal level, and remained dead for a dozen more years. In the void, private companies struggled to develop water projects, and all large-scale development of the West came to a grinding halt. Much of the blame

[83] *Id.* at 113-14.

[84] Worster, *supra* note 17, at 500.

[85] *Washington Star* interview reprinted in *CR*, May 29, 1890, 5419.

[86] Worster, *supra* note 17, at 506.

belonged with Stewart, but as Worster argues, Powell himself played a major role in the failure:

> If Stewart spit in his own face, Powell hurt himself by unresolved conflicts in his thinking. He never seemed to realize how much his blueprint for the arid region contradicted his repudiation of nature as a guide to human affairs. When he came down from the heights of cosmic progress, when he looked closely at the land and its rivers, he found, if not a guide to ethics at least a guide to adaptive settlement. While he echoed the idea of conquest, he tried to preach adaptation to place. He called for the liberation of humanity from the constraints imposed by nature but then turned around to advocate a sense of natural limits, a skepticism toward industrial progress, and a populist program of agrarian democracy. It was confusing and ambiguous. For all his brilliance, his message contained fatal flaws.[87]

Powell's Legacy as a Public Servant

Few would question Powell's stature as pioneer of western natural resources policy and ultimately, of environmental law. His foreword thinking on western public lands and water law and policy remains as relevant today as when he wrote about these issues in the 19th century. But Powell's influence and importance extended well beyond these issues.

One of the most enduring contributions was his seminal role in establishing the United States Geological Survey. In October 1878, just months after submitting his *Arid Lands Report* to Congress, Powell received a letter from the National Academy of Sciences, soliciting his advice on what plan should be adopted for surveying and mapping the territories. Powell, who was in the field with his survey crew when he received the letter, hastened back to Washington and, on November 1, delivered his statement to the committee—"a long, brilliant, combative treatise that threw into the shadows much briefer communications from the Corps of Engineers, the Land Office, and Dr. Hayden."[88] And in so doing, "he instantly assumed the generalship of a battle to reorganize science in the federal government—a battle he would decisively win, though it would cost him a war."[89]

The National Academy of Sciences was chartered by Congress during the Civil War for the purposes of providing expert scientific advice on demand, and its ranks included the self-selected elite of American science.[90] In the spring of 1876, the Academy was directed by Congress to look into the "survey jumble"

[87] WORSTER, *supra* note 17, at 507.

[88] *Id.* at 360.

[89] *Id.* at 361.

[90] Powell, himself, would become a member two years later, in 1890. *Id.* at 361.

in the West and recommend changes. The idea for the committee came from Abram Hewitt, Representative of New York's 10th District, though the proposal likely originated with Clarence King, head of the King Survey, who had been elected to the Academy earlier that same year. It had become increasingly clear that the present system of competing private surveys was inefficient and expensive—and Congress wanted a change. With Powell, the former Army Major, leading the charge, that is exactly what they got.

Powell's blunt and forceful statement before the committee "was a blast that reduced the entire jerry-built system of western surveying to a pile of kindling."[91] Despite his position atop one of those western surveys, Powell's comments laid siege to the private contract framework of land-office surveys. "The present multiplication of organizations," Powell said, "is unscientific, excessively expensive, and altogether vicious, preventing comprehensive, thorough, and honest research, stimulating unhealthy rivalry, and leading to the production of sensational and briefly popular rather than solid and enduring results."[92] Given the constraints exacted by the arid landscape, Powell argued that laying out six-mile square townships across wide swaths of uninhabitable desert was a waste. Yet contractors driven by their bottom line, were paid handsomely to do just that. Thus, while the government had spent $23 million on contracted work, Powell argued that "it was absolutely valueless for scientific purposes."[93] Besides being able to point out the tract of land on a map, Americans could get little useful information out of such work.[94]

Powell's solution to this problem was to place all surveying work into the hands of scientific experts employed on a fixed federal salary. In other words, he was proposing the formation of a new federal agency—a single comprehensive "geographical and geological survey" tasked with producing a better understanding of the country's vast natural resources, something he had been an outspoken advocate for since the early 1870s. Science, Powell argued, was critical to the continued prosperity of American life and deserved government support. Accordingly, he expected extensive social benefits to flow from the government's embrace of science, especially in the West, "a region of vast and inexhaustible wealth" just waiting for scientific discovery to locate that wealth and show how to develop it.[95]

This approach, however, represented a subtle but important evolution in Powell's thinking. Whereas just a few months prior, Powell had extolled the virtues of self-organizing common folk, a theme he would return to later in his life,

---

[91] *Id.*

[92] *Surveys of the Territories*, 45 Cong., 3 Sess. House Misc. Doc. 5, 16, cultivating lands by irrigation overnight?

[93] *Id.*

[94] Worster, *supra* note 17, at 361.

[95] *Id.* at 362-63.

his recommendations to the Academy were more akin to "a Faustian dream of scientific experts managing the earth and all its resources."[96] "Nature put limits on humankind, but they could be eased by the power of organized science."[97]

Five days after Powell delivered his statement, the Academy adopted the committee's recommendations, which, in turn, primarily followed the framework provided by Powell. In short, the recommendation called for the consolidation of the major surveys into a new federal agency within the Department of the Interior: the United States Geological Survey. The Academy also recommended that the Powell Survey, specifically, be renamed the Bureau of Ethnology and be moved to the Smithsonian Institution. On March 3, 1879, following a winter full of political maneuvering, the legislation was passed by both houses of Congress, and both the USGS and Bureau of Ethnology were born. "Although he worked behind the scenes, Powell was the man who made the consolidation come into being."[98]

Some of Powell's behind the scenes work involved the co-founding of the Cosmos Club, which first met in Powell's home in 1878. Both King and Powell, the first two directors of the USGS, were founding members of the Club. The Cosmos Club was established as a place where scientific minds could gather and work towards solving the problems of the time. Moreover, it was meant to create a unified scientific front in the seat of the federal government in Washington D.C. Since its inception, the Cosmos Club has attracted prominent members of Washington D.C. society, including Presidents Taft, Wilson, and Hoover, as well as other notable men including Henry Kissinger, Alexander Graham Bell, Oliver Wendell Holmes, and Carl Sagan. Notably, the Club is credited with inspiring the creation of several other remarkable scientific organizations, including the National Geographic Society, the National Parks Association and the Wilderness Society. Today, these societies stand at the forefront of the American environmental movement, pioneers in their own rights.

To this day, the Cosmos Club remains an important meeting place for intellectuals in the nation's capital. It hosts visitors and elected members of the Club for a wide range of lectures, music concerts, and literary conversations at its elegant facility on Massachusetts Avenue in Washington, D.C.

In addition to orchestrating the consolidation of the western surveys, Powell's unwavering dedication to the study of ethnology made him the obvious candidate to be the first director of the newly established Bureau of Ethnology, a title he would hold until his death in 1902. Powell's fascination with and dedication to studying native populations began long before Congress created the Bureau. His formal research began when Joseph Henry, head of

---

[96] *Id.* at 363.

[97] *Id.*

[98] Aton, *supra* note 11, at 17.

the Smithsonian, urged Powell to use his first expedition down the Colorado River in 1869 to study the native people of the region. Up until the late 1800s, American settlers had largely left the original inhabitants of the region alone, the Mormon pioneers notwithstanding. This presented Powell with a unique opportunity to greatly expand the country's knowledge of the Native American people of the region.

Powell took Henry's advice and used his time in the American West to build relationships with these tribes and study their cultures. Powell recognized that the government's inconsistent policies of either assimilating native people into American culture or resettling them on smaller reservations of land[99] would likely compromise and might even destroy native languages, native governments, and native arts and cultures. This gave an urgency to Powell's work.

Powell was a firm believer that one could not understand a native culture without understanding the native language. In 1877 he published *Introduction to the Study of Indian Languages, with Words, Phrases, and Sentences to Be Collected*, one of the first dictionaries of this variety, as a way to catalogue the native people who lived in the American Territories. This important work opened the door to understanding the cultures of the native tribes.

With the creation of the Bureau of Ethnology, Congress found a way to put Powell's wealth of knowledge to good use. Immediately following its creation, Congress ordered the Bureau of Ethnology to categorize the numerous complex treaties the Federal Government had signed with the various American tribes. Over the next thirty years, Powell poured himself into that task, even after being named the second Director of the USGS in 1881. Through his time at the Bureau, he continued the work he had started on the linguistics of native peoples, and completed the first comprehensive survey of North America's indigenous tongues, *Indian Linguistic Families of America, North of Mexico*, in 1891. Eventually, the Bureau of American Ethnology was combined with the Department of Anthropology of the Museum of Natural History in the Smithsonian Office for Anthropological Research in 1970. James Aton, in his work on the life and legacy of Powell, summed up the Bureau's importance in this way:

> The founding of the Bureau of [ ] Ethnology in 1879, and Powell's subsequent direction of that bureau until his death in 1902, was, as Wallace Stegner puts it, "one of the two great works of his life." Powell's genius for organization and delegation expressed itself most clearly in anthropology. When Powell began practicing anthropology it was a nascent science, full of amateurs and wild theories. When he left it, his bureau had stamped the seal of "serious science" on the discipline. While many of Powell's own

[99] The Trail of Tears took place in the early 1830s; The Indian Appropriations Act creating the reservation system was passed in 1851. *See* Patrick W. Wanders, *Indian Land Claims: Sherrill and the Impending Legacy of the Doctrine of Laches*, 31 Am. Indian L. Rev., 131 (2006).

> anthropological theories have been discarded, the bureau he founded, like the USGS, became on the foremost scientific organizations in the world. It remains so today.[100]

While ethnology was arguably Powell's greatest passion, it was his role in creating and shaping the United States Geological Survey that likely left the biggest mark on the history of the United States. Despite his prominent role in its formation and unimpeachable qualifications for the job, Powell was a reluctant USGS Director. His most important contributions, he believed, lay not in the natural sciences but rather in ethnological research. Nonetheless, many wanted Powell to take on USGS Director role. As one geologist at the University of Cincinnati put it in 1878:

> '[N]o other man in the continent is so well qualified to take charge of this work.... What is wanted is a man who has the proper appreciation of the *comprehensive character of such* [ ] *work*.'... But as his protégé [Clarence] Dutton explained, '[Powell] renounces all claim or desire or effort to be the head of a united survey and would merely ask for a subordinate position under it secured to him by executive appointment. The administrative duties of such a position would render it impossible for him to acquire the only thing he really covets and that is a standing among men of science resting upon his own personal contribution to it.'[101]

Despite this pressure, Powell successfully recommended his friend Clarence King as the first USGS Director. King was a co-founder with Powell of the Cosmos Club, and King's own survey had just recently been completed. Due to failing health, however, King's tenure atop the USGS was brief, and when he eventually left the Survey in March 1881, President James Garfield immediately named Powell to succeed him. "The self-taught farm youth who had learned about rocks and Indians from another self-taught scholar now headed two government bureaus specifically established to support two growing branches of science. In reality Powell had founded them both."[102]

Between 1881 and 1894, when he eventually stepped down as Director, "Powell built the USGS into the pride of American science."[103] It was, at the time, the largest scientific organization of its kind in the world. Universities across the western world bestowed on Powell honorary degrees and other awards, while Congress continued to support his efforts, raising his budget from a $100,000 annual appropriation to as much as $719,000 per year. "Most important, however, were the number and quality of the survey's publications during Powell's

[100] Aton, *supra* note 11, at 39.

[101] Worster, *supra* note 17, at 364.

[102] Aton, *supra* note 11, at 18.

[103] *Id.*

tenure there. One need only turn to any American geology bibliography today to find a number of works from Powell's men written between 1881 and 1894."[104]

Powell's primary goal as director of the USGS was to produce a complete set of topographical maps of the United States, finishing a task that began in 1869 when he first led his men down the Colorado and into the last major blank space on the map of the American Territories. Among Powell's many contributions was developing a standardized system of mapping conventions—symbols, colors for different rock ages, nomenclature, and the like. And in 1881 Powell pushed through a new uniform system that became the American standard and greatly influenced the European standard as well.

Despite Powell's success at running the USGS, his fight with Stewart over the Irrigation Survey ultimately proved too damaging and too draining for Powell. Following his defeat to Stewart in 1890, with irrigation reform effectively dead for several more decades, Powell decided it was time to leave the USGS and set about getting his affairs in order and grooming a successor. Four years later, in 1894, Powell tapped Charles D. Walcott, a long-time associate from the early days of the USGS, to succeed him. Powell's career as Director of the USGS was over. And while Powell still had the Bureau of Ethnology to run, as the years passed his enthusiasm even for that started to wane. By the turn of the century, Powell had largely turned the bureau over to W. J. McGee, leaving the dedicated public servant with little to do.

In November 1901, Powell suffered a stroke. While he recovered after a few months, he suffered a second stroke the following summer while living in Maine. He died there on September 23, 1902, at the age of sixty-eight.

Conclusion

Looking back at Powell's *Arid Land Report*, and his support for a science-based approach to public lands policy one might think that Powell's ideas were borne from an environmental ethos. To be sure, Powell's vision was to promote western settlement that was harmonious with the land and nature. In that sense one might fairly place Powell at the vanguard of the environmental movement. But Powell was working on these issues well before the American environmental movement had obtained a strong foothold. The writings of American authors George Perkins Marsh, Henry David Thoreau, and Ralph Waldo Emerson were beginning to influence a new generation of Americans while John Muir was developing a love of nature that would later lead to his founding of the Sierra Club and his advocacy for nature. But Powell's drive seemed to come not so much from a desire to conserve nature as from his desire to keep the land and water in the hands of the small farmers who lived and worked there. Powell's

[104] *Id.*

1890 admonition to the North Dakota State Constitutional Convention that they should ensure that "no corporation—no body of men—no capital can get possession and right to your waters" and further that the water should be held "in the hands of the people" was quintessential Powell and reflected a strong populist sensibility.

But without diminishing his enormous scientific accomplishments, Powell is perhaps best remembered because of his genius for organizing. "Both his supporters and critics commented on his remarkable powers of classification and synthesis."[105] Drawing on the lessons learned during his extensive studies of canyon country geology, Powell quickly grasped the larger picture and relied on outstanding assistants to paint in the details. Powell shared his wealth of knowledge with them, but then let them work independently. Meanwhile, he took on the task of presenting his findings to an often-incredulous Congress, organizing his facts and presenting them so clearly that even the most unlearned congressman could understand them. According to William Davis, a contemporary of Powell's in the National Academy of Sciences, when Powell appeared before legislators with his charts and maps, "he had so full command of all pertinent facts that his opponents in Congressional committees were often left with nothing but their opposition to stand on."[106]

John Wesley Powell's legacy has to be appreciated on many levels. He was an audacious explorer with a remarkable talent for scientific field work. Despite lacking much formal education, he was perhaps the most profound intellectual of his time, particularly on issues involving western settlement and water resources management. He was a remarkable leader, respected by his peers, and renowned for his skill at carrying out complex scientific work and explaining that work to lay audiences. Given his extraordinary intellect and his myriad accomplishments, one would be hard-pressed to deny his rightful place among the most important pioneers of natural resources and environmental law.

---

[105] *Id.*

[106] William Morris Davis, *Biographical Memoir of John Wesley Powell, 1834-1902*, NAT'L ACADEMY OF SCIENCES 8 (February 1915): 29.

Chapter 3

Theodore Roosevelt: Of Mice and Men, Birds and Bison

Sandra B. Zellmer[1]

Introduction

In one sense, it is easy to write a chapter about a pioneering president like Theodore Roosevelt. After all, he was widely known during his lifetime and is still renown today for environmental conservation. But the task is less straightforward than one might imagine for at least two reasons. Roosevelt was a complicated person with a complicated legacy. When he won the Nobel Peace Prize in 1906, it was not for his impact in the environmental realm, but for his role in negotiating a conclusion to the Russo-Japanese War, which in turn propelled the United States into the limelight of global diplomacy. Possessing characteristics more of the hawk than the dove, Roosevelt and his brand of "Big Stick Diplomacy"—walk softly and carry a big stick in case negotiations fail—relied on thinly veiled threats and on a willingness to deploy the military as an international police force. Roosevelt's complex nature was expressed in his environmental policies as well, for he was both a naturalist who relished the beauty and

[1] Sandra Zellmer is a Professor and Director of Natural Resources Clinics at the University of Montana School of Law, where she teaches public lands, wildlife law, water, torts, and related courses. Zellmer has published dozens of law review articles and several books, including Water Law & Policy (2018) (with Thompson, Abrams, and Leshy), Natural Resources Hornbook (2015) (with Laitos), and A Century of Unnatural Disasters: Mississippi River Stories (2014) (with Klein). Zellmer served as a trustee of the Rocky Mountain Mineral Law Foundation for many years, and she is a member scholar of the Center for Progressive Reform. She is active with the American Bar Association's Section on Environment, Energy, and Resources (Committees on Public Lands and on Water Resources). Previously, Zellmer held the Robert B. Daugherty Chair at the University of Nebraska College of Law. Before teaching, she was an attorney for the U.S. Department of Justice Environment and Natural Resources Division, litigating public lands issues for the National Park Service, Forest Service, and other federal agencies. She also practiced law at Faegre & Benson in Minneapolis, Minnesota and clerked for the Honorable William W. Justice, U.S. District Court, Eastern District of Texas.

serenity of wild places and an avid hunter who delighted in bagging big game species to add to his long list of trophies. The more ferocious, the better.

Doing justice to Teddy Roosevelt as a pioneer of environmental law is challenging for another reason. What hasn't already been said about Roosevelt's creation of millions of acres of forest reserves? About the dozens of national monuments that he protected? About his role in the conservation of wildlife and birds?

Roosevelt took center stage during a pivotal moment in conservation history, and he charted a course for subsequent presidents, both with respect to conservation-related measures and with respect to the exercise of sweeping presidential powers. Drawing parallels between the early twentieth century executive office and the early twenty-first century executive office reveals some compelling themes relevant to conservation and democracy.

Just over a century after Roosevelt left the West Wing in 1909, another Republican moved into the Oval Office, President Donald Trump, in 2017. The contrasts between Roosevelt and Trump are many. At first blush, one might note that, while Roosevelt was the youngest president to take the oath of office in 1901, Trump is the oldest. Also, Roosevelt worked tirelessly to bust up powerful corporate monopolies like Standard Oil, while Trump embodies corporate economic—and political—power.[2] More to the point, Roosevelt is viewed as one of the greatest conservation Presidents in the nation's history with a deep respect for science, while Trump has been billed as the worst, with a palpable disdain for science.[3]

However, several parallels can be drawn. Both Roosevelt and Trump qualify as flamboyant, loud, media-centric, wealthy, and markedly different than any other president that came before them. More importantly for purposes of this chapter, both exhibit a penchant for asserting strong executive powers to accomplish his goals, with little concern for the checks and balances of the legislative and judicial branches of government. In both cases, the environmental stakes couldn't be higher. For Roosevelt, the destruction and outright disposal of public lands loomed large; for Trump, a rapidly warming climate is bringing the planet to a tipping point.

This chapter celebrates the conservation victories of Teddy Roosevelt, and examines the lasting implications of sweeping, often unilateral, executive power over federal public lands and wildlife. It assesses Roosevelt's ability to deploy his expertise as a naturalist in the campaign for wildlife protection and hunting

---

[2] Joe Romm, *Donald Trump is the Anti-Teddy Roosevelt,* Think Progress, Dec. 13, 2016, at https://thinkprogress.org/trump-the-anti-teddy-roosevelt-753c595c1459/.

[3] Chris Peak, *Which Presidents are the Greenest in U.S. History?*, Sept. 16, 2016, http://nationswell.com/greenest-u-s-presidents/; Bill Press, *The Worst Environmental President Ever,* July 10, 2019, https://tribunecontentagency.com/article/the-worst-environmental-president-ever/.

ethics. It also highlights the creation of wildlife refuges, in particular Pelican Island and the National Bison Range, and national monuments, including the Grand Canyon. Along the way, Roosevelt's impacts on the nascent National Park System are illuminated. Although much ink has been spilled on all of these subjects, this chapter strives to present Roosevelt's legacy in a new and different light by placing it in the context of modern environmentalism and executive power. The chapter concludes with a comparative assessment of Roosevelt and President Trump, and draws insights about the role of the presidency in national conservation initiatives and counter-initiatives.

The Conservation Context of the Late Nineteenth Century

Born near Madison Square Park in New York City on October 27, 1858, Theodore (Teddy) Roosevelt, Jr. entered the world at a propitious time for conservation. In 1858, the first trans-Atlantic telegraph cable was delivered, making international communication much quicker and easier than ever before. Abraham Lincoln made his anti-slavery "House Divided" speech at the Illinois Republican Convention to launch his senatorial run against Stephen Douglas, who believed that slavery should be allowed in new states as a matter of popular sovereignty. Forty-Niners streamed into the Rocky Mountains of the western United States during the Pike's Peak Gold Rush, and the City of Denver was founded not long afterwards.[4]

Teddy came of age during the years between the Civil War and the turn of the twentieth century. As children, he and his brother Elliot watched Abraham Lincoln's funeral procession passing by their grandfather's mansion in Union Square in 1865, and Teddy later identified Lincoln as his "great hero," who meant "more to me than any other of our public men," not only for emancipation but also because Lincoln was plain-spoken and stood for "plain people."[5]

As a young man, Teddy studied natural history and government at Harvard College from 1876-1880, and then enrolled at Columbia Law School, but found the law "irrational." Instead of studying law, he spent the bulk of his time writing a book on the War of 1812 and preparing to launch his political career by building allies in the local Republican party. He dropped out of law school and was elected to the New York Assembly in 1882, and immediately set out to make his mark by fighting corporate and political corruption.[6]

---

[4] Wikipedia, 1858 in the United States, https://en.wikipedia.org/wiki/1858_in_the_United_States#Events (updated July 12, 2019).

[5] Richard Striner, Lincoln's Way: How Six Great Presidents Created American Power 48 (2010).

[6] H.W. Brands, T.R.: The Last Romantic 126 (1997).

Roosevelt had his work cut out for him. Corruption ran rampant during the Gilded Age. Although Victorian values and high moral principles predominated social life, Robber Baron-industrialists amassed vast amounts of wealth and dominated every major commercial sector, from railroads to oil fields and steel, and from timber, tobacco, and liquor to meatpacking and banking. While urban middle-class families enjoyed electric lighting, millions of struggling immigrants and dirt-poor farmers poured into New York, Chicago, and other major cities looking for work and outpacing social and sanitation systems. In far greater numbers than ever before, people subscribed to newspapers and magazines, while investigative journalists dug through "the muck" of the Gilded Age to expose scandal, corruption, and injustice.[7]

Meanwhile, railroad companies and their executives received generous amounts of land—as much as 200 million acres in the West—from the U.S. government. The Transcontinental Railroad was finished in 1869, which cut the 3,000-mile journey across the United States from a matter of months to less than a week. Railroads facilitated the rapid settlement of the western United States, and settlers, tourists, and market hunters began to stream West. The Homestead Act, which Abraham Lincoln signed into law in 1862, granted 270 millions acres of the public domain to private citizens in the Midwest and the western territories and states.[8] Westward expansion escalated conflicts between settlers and Native American tribes, with tribes suffering horrific losses of life and land. The non-Indian population skyrocketed from five million in 1800 to 63 million in 1900. By comparison, in 1800, there were about 600,000 Native Americans living in the United States, but the 1890 census reported only 248,253.[9]

The 1890 U.S. census was notable for another reason. It revealed that there was no longer a western frontier line beyond which the population density was less than two persons per square mile. In his 1893 address to the World Congress of Historians in Chicago, Frederick Jackson Turner announced his frontier theory of American democracy. For Turner, free land and the westward movement of settlement epitomized the American experience. He argued that frontier life gave rise to distinctive American cultural traits—"that coarseness and strength combined with acuteness and acquisitiveness; that practical inventive turn of mind, quick to find expedients; ... that restless, nervous energy; that dominant individualism."[10] These individual traits, in turn, meant that "American

---

[7] Matthew E. Stanley, *The Gilded Age*, 105 J. of American History 772-74 (2018).

[8] Act of May 20, 1862 (Homestead Act), Pub. L. 37-64, 12 Stat. 392.

[9] *See* Robert N. Clinton, *Redressing the Legacy of Conquest: A Vision Quest for A Decolonized Federal Indian Law*, 46 Ark. L. Rev. 77, 79 (1993); C. Blue Clark, *How Bad It Really Was Before World War II: Sovereignty*, 23 Okla. City U. L. Rev. 175, 177 (1998).

[10] David Hamilton Murdoch, The American West: The Invention of a Myth 79 (2001).

democracy ... gained new strength each time it touched a new frontier."[11] Once the frontier line was gone, Turner feared that U.S. innovation and democratic ideals would disappear along with it.

Turner's frontier theory became so widespread that some scholars view it as "most influential piece of writing in the history of American history."[12] Roosevelt was not only familiar with Turner's argument, he viewed it as a supplement to his own theories published in his 1896 multi-volume tome *The Winning of the West*. To Roosevelt, the frontier settlers' frequent encounters with "hostile races and cultures" in the struggle for mastery of the land was essential to the formation of a uniquely American character.[13]

Whether the geographic frontier is truly "closed" or not, the concept of the frontier continues to have profound consequences for the environment and culture of the West. Historian Patricia Limerick explains, "The conquest of Western America shapes the present as dramatically—and sometimes as perilously—as the old mines shape the mountainsides."[14] As for Roosevelt, his environmental agenda was shaped by his experiences with, and passion for, the Wild West, and his conservation policies and initiatives still shape our landscape and national psyche today.

In the waning years of the nineteenth century, Roosevelt was gaining political power just as the American public was experiencing an environmental awakening.[15] The kick-off meeting of John Muir's Sierra Club—generally acknowledged as the first environmental group in the United States—occurred in 1892.[16] Audubon Societies were launched that same decade. In 1896, Muir hiked along the Crown of the Continent in present-day Glacier National Park and camped out in the Grand Canyon with Gifford Pinchot, who became Roosevelt's Chief Forester, during a National Forest Commission research trip through the West. Pinchot was enchanted by Muir's stories, but puzzled by Muir's seemingly extreme "hands off" stance on preservation.[17]

---

[11] Frederick Jackson Turner, The Significance of the Frontier in American History 293 (1920).

[12] PBS, New Perspectives on The West: Frederick Jackson Turner, https://www.pbs.org/weta/thewest/people/s_z/turner.htm (2001).

[13] Richard Slotkin, *Nostalgia and Progress: Theodore Roosevelt's Myth of the Frontier*, 33 American Quarterly 608–637 (1981).

[14] Patricia Nelson Limerick, The Legacy of Conquest 18 (1987).

[15] Darrin Lunde, The Naturalist: Theodore Roosevelt, A Lifetime of Exploration, and the Triumph of American Natural History 173 (2016).

[16] Samuel P. Hays, Conservation and the Gospel of Efficiency: The Progressive Conservation Movement, 1890-1920 192 (1959).

[17] John Clayton, Natural Rivals 165-66, 183-84 (2019). The Commission later produced a report recommending the establishment of 13 new forest reserves (21 million acres) to be retained in federal ownership. This led to President Grover Cleveland's Washington's Birthday Reserves on Feb. 22, 1897.

While Roosevelt respected Muir, as President, he ultimately aligned with Pinchot on the side of sustained use of resources and land, which Pinchot characterized as "the greatest good for the greatest amount of people in the long run."[18] In any event, as Douglas Brinkley notes, "The educated class was coming to believe that the federal government needed to intervene before the rivers ran dry and the forests disappeared like the buffalo herds."[19] The time was ripe for Theodore Roosevelt to take center stage in the conservation theater.

President Roosevelt's Conservation Legacy

Among all of his accomplishments, Theodore Roosevelt believed that conservation was the most important contribution of his domestic agenda as President.[20] His conservation agenda synthesized four major themes: American heritage; nationalism; science, especially evolutionary biology; and utilitarian progressivism.[21] For Roosevelt, a deep romanticism for the West and a sense of moral responsibility to future generations provided a subtext for these themes.

These facets of President Roosevelt's conservation legacy are addressed here in three parts: empire-building; wildlife protection; and national monuments.

Resource Conservation and Empire-Building

When President William McKinley was assassinated in 1901, Teddy Roosevelt, age 42, became the youngest man to assume the U.S. presidency. The assassin's bullet that propelled Roosevelt into the White House galvanized the conservation movement that was beginning to gain traction at the turn of the century.[22]

Resource conservation was a key aspect of the deeply Progressive streak that marked the early twentieth century, and conservation went hand in hand with related reform movements that sought to counterbalance the challenges faced by a newly industrialized society. Popular books and magazines such as *McClure's* and *Forest and Stream* created a growing sense of alarm at the excesses of the "wasteful" nation between 1900 and 1910. Much more than just the rhetoric of learned scholars or the political elite, this was a genuine grass roots

---

[18] Charles Wilkinson, "*The Greatest Good of the Greatest Number in the Long Run*": *TR, Pinchot, and the Origins of Sustainability in America,* 26 Colo. Nat. Resources, Energy & Envtl. L. Rev. 69, 71-72 (2015).

[19] Douglas Brinkley, The Wilderness Warrior: Theodore Roosevelt and the Crusade for America 295 (2009).

[20] *Id.* at 20.

[21] *Id.* at 19.

[22] Ian Tyrell, Crisis of the Wasteful Nation 16 (2015).

environmental movement, championed by major social institutions of the era, such as churches, schools, Chautauqua assemblies, women's clubs, and debating groups.[23]

Roosevelt personified the ideal of Progressive Era conservation. His policies reflected his belief that the national government could and should do everything in its power to prevent the waste of forests, watersheds, soil, and wildlife; only if it did would national prosperity be secured.

During his time in the White House, Roosevelt quadrupled the amount of protected land, from 42 million acres to 172 million acres. Although Roosevelt's predecessors in office, Presidents McKinley, Benjamin Harrison, and Grover Cleveland, created forest reserves and possessed other conservation-related credentials, they lacked long-term vision. Roosevelt was different. His personal interest in natural history and the outdoors is the subject of countless biographies and several of Roosevelt's own autobiographies. As historian Ian Tyrell explains, "Roosevelt is well known as an advocate of the masculine and strenuous life, a nationalist, an instigator of American empire, a lover of nature and the American west, a hunter, and yet a conservationist without par among American presidents."[24] Conservation was more than a political concept to Roosevelt; it was also a deeply personal and moral issue.[25] Nature was Roosevelt's "rock and salvation."[26]

Also, unlike other presidents, Roosevelt's support for conservation was closely intertwined with empire-building. Resource conservation was a means of satisfying the Rough Rider's military and expansionist impulses. In his 1908 annual message to Congress, he conveyed a stern warning about empires that had collapsed due to a failure to conserve their forests, soil, watersheds, and wildlife. Roosevelt illustrated his point with photographs of denuded mountainsides, severely eroded soils, and debris-clogged rivers in the Shanxi Province of China.[27]

In Roosevelt's mind, only national conservation policies and initiatives could transcend trans-boundary turf wars, ensure the efficient and sustainable use of resources, and, consequently, strengthen America's geopolitical stature.[28] And only by strengthening America's geopolitical stature could the prosperity of the next generations of Americans be secured.

---

[23] *Id.* at 4-5.

[24] *Id.* at 4.

[25] Robert L. Fischman, *The Significance of National Wildlife Refuges in the Development of U.S. Conservation Policy,* 21 J. Land Use & Envtl. L. 1, 10–11 (2005).

[26] Brinkley, *supra* note 19, at 14.

[27] Tyrell, *supra* note 22, at 18.

[28] *Id.* at 171.

Roosevelt's Chief Forester, Gifford Pinchot, agreed that "conservation had to go global."[29] Cutting down forests on both sides of the boundary line between Canada and the U.S. adversely affected international streams, fisheries, and the economy. But North American conservation initiatives were not enough. The two men aspired to create a World Conservation Congress to meet at the Hague after Roosevelt left office in 1909. Pinchot was bitterly disappointed when Roosevelt's successor, President Taft, called it off, thereby thwarting resource conservation "as a primary means of insuring a permanent peace."[30]

Peace, prosperity, and inter-generational equity are recurring themes in Roosevelt's work. Several of Roosevelt's declarations invoke duties to "the people unborn," and the people's "children and their children's children forever."[31] The quotation inscribed on his monument at Theodore Roosevelt Island in Virginia proclaims, "The nation behaves well if it treats the natural resources as assets which it must turn over to the next generation increased and not impaired in value."[32] In his remarks to the Conference on the Conservation of Natural Resources, Roosevelt cautioned:

> [W]e have thoughtlessly, and to a large degree unnecessarily, diminished the resources upon which not only our prosperity but the prosperity of our children must always depend. We have become great because of the lavish use of our resources. But the time has come to inquire seriously what will happen when our forests are gone, when the coal, the iron, the oil, and the gas are exhausted, when the soils have still further impoverished and washed into the streams, polluting the rivers, denuding the fields and obstructing navigation.[33]

The sustainable use of the nation's and even the world's natural resources required scientific management. Roosevelt's curiosity about the natural world and his staunch support for science can be seen most vividly through his legacy in wildlife conservation.

---

[29] Brinkley, *supra* note 19, at 804.

[30] M. Nelson McGeary, Gifford Pinchot 108 (1960).

[31] Brinkley, *supra* note 19, at 21.

[32] Theodore Roosevelt Conservation Partnership, http://www.trcp.org/2012/01/14/treat-natural-resources-as-assets/ (visited Sept. 9, 2019) (quoting Theodore Roosevelt, Speech before Colorado Livestock Association, Denver, Colo., Aug. 29, 1910).

[33] Theodore Roosevelt, Remarks to the Conference on the Conservation of Natural Resources (May 13, 1908), in Roosevelt's Writings: Selections from the Writings of Theodore Roosevelt 208 (Maurice Garland Fulton, ed.) (MacMillan 1920).

Wildlife Protection and Scientific Management

At the young age of eight years old, Teddy created a natural history museum in his bedroom, and filled it with specimens of insects, mice, shrews, birds, and one snapping turtle, described as "an aggressive pond-dweller covered in algae and decorated with a gruesome frill of leeches."[34] Teddy came by his passion for animals and taxonomy naturally. His father, Theodore Senior, was one of the founders of the American Museum of Natural History, which was situated near the Roosevelt home in Central Park, New York. Theodore Senior was among many men of that era who considered himself a "muscular Christian." To these men, spending time outdoors, hiking, swimming, rowing, and hunting, built both moral and physical strength.[35] Teddy's frail constitution and frequent bouts with asthma troubled his father deeply. Theodore Senior challenged his son to overcome his boyish weakness and to "make your body." Teddy set out to do just that, in the gym and in the mountains of the Adirondacks and beyond, where camping, fishing, hunting, and collecting specimens of all sorts fit neatly into his self-improvement regimen.[36]

By the time he was a teenager, Teddy had developed an obsession for birds.[37] Douglas Brinkley observes that, more than any prayer book or psalm, songbirds were "liberators" of Roosevelt's very soul.[38] To Roosevelt and others, the senseless slaughter of brown pelicans and other nongame birds symbolized "industrialization run amok."[39]

Feathers and other bird parts were sought for fashionable hats worn by upper-class women of the Gilded Age. The proliferation of fashion magazines heightened the demand, while the advent of semiautomatic rifles facilitated a steady supply of birds. By the late 1800's, over fifty species of birds were being slaughtered for their feathers, and the snowy egret and other species were threatened with extinction.

New York City and London were at the epicenter of the millinery trade. As the situation became more dire and more widely publicized, Queen Victoria issued a proclamation denouncing the use of ornamental feathers in the British Empire.[40] Around the same time, Congress passed the Lacey Act of 1900, which Roosevelt, then-governor of New York, supported. The Lacey Act, named for long-time Iowa congressman John Lacey, prohibits transport across state lines of

---

[34] Lunde, *supra* note 15, at 17.

[35] *Id.* at 11, 34-35.

[36] *Id.* at 37-38.

[37] *Id.* at 43.

[38] Brinkley, *supra* note 19, at 14.

[39] *Id.* at 8.

[40] *Id.* at 10-11.

birds taken in violation of state or foreign laws, thereby closing a loophole that allowed poachers to sell birds and other wildlife by taking their catch outside of the jurisdiction where it had been illegally taken.[41]

The Lacey Act did not solve the problem. It was poorly enforced, and did little to slow the plume trade. After he became president, a particular rookery in Florida came to Roosevelt's attention. Pelican Island had a reputation for such an abundance of avian activity that, to Roosevelt, it was nothing short of a "biological hymnal" where "[e]xuberant streams of birds congregated ... like figures in a timeless dream."[42] When it was threatened by development, proponents of federal protection found an attentive audience in Teddy Roosevelt.

President Roosevelt was not only sympathetic to the cause, he was in a position to deliver, wielding unilateral executive power. Upon learning that there was no law that would prevent him from making Pelican Island a Federal Bird Reservation, Roosevelt issued his now-famous statement, "I So Declare It." With that, on March 14, 1903, Roosevelt created the first unit of the National Wildlife Refuge System. He subsequently followed up by declaring fifty more wildlife reserves and refuges during his time in the White House.[43]

The establishment of Pelican Island was the first time that the federal government set aside land for the sake of wildlife. It also created a new kind of "dominant use" system governed by the philosophy that all activities on refuges should be compatible with wildlife protection. The modern-day management of national wildlife refuges follows this principle, with science as a basis for decision making. Roosevelt bestowed authority over Pelican Island upon the U.S. Biological Survey, headed by Dr. C. Hart Merriam, a long-time friend of Roosevelt.[44]

The U.S. Biological Survey was created by Congress in 1885. Even before he became President, Roosevelt championed the Survey's creation and continued viability "like a fight promoter."[45] At first, the Survey's scope was limited to "economic ornithology," with mammals being added to its repertoire the following year. Its mission was to promote birds and other wildlife "helpful" to farmers and sportsmen while eradicating "injurious" pests. Prior to Roosevelt's presidency, the Survey was a "struggling, dispirited bureaucratic waif, far from the centers of power."[46] In 1905, Roosevelt renamed it the Bureau of Biological Survey, and expanded its mandate to include mapping the nation's wildlife resources. With Roosevelt's support, the Bureau's authority grew. Eventually,

---

[41] 16 U.S.C. §§3371-3378. *See* William Souder, *How Two Women Ended the Deadly Feather Trade*, Smithsonian Magazine, Mar. 2013, at https://www.smithsonianmag.com/science-nature/how-two-women-ended-the-deadly-feather-trade-23187277/.

[42] Brinkley, *supra* note 19, at 7.

[43] *Id.* at 14.

[44] *Id.* at 13.

[45] *Id.* at 75.

[46] Boyce Rensberger, *Biological Survey an Orphan at 100,* Wash. Post, July 1, 1985.

the Bureau was transferred from the Department of Agriculture to the Department of Interior, and then it merged with the Bureau of Fisheries in 1940 to create the U.S. Fish and Wildlife Service.[47]

President Roosevelt's work on behalf of birds was far from over. He was particularly concerned about the effect of deforestation on migratory birds. Cognizant of the fact that "nature didn't recognize artificial boundaries," Roosevelt invited representatives of Canada and Mexico to Washington, DC for the North America Conservation Congress in 1909.[48] His effort laid the groundwork for the Migratory Bird Treaty Act of 1918.[49] Congress had passed a migratory bird preservation act in 1913, signed by Roosevelt's successor, President Taft, but some feared that it stood on shaky ground, constitutionally. To strengthen the bill, Senator Elihu Root, former secretary of state under Roosevelt, suggested making it a treaty with Canada, which is precisely what transpired in 1918.[50]

Roosevelt's wildlife conservation agenda went well beyond birds. In his mind, wild bison were "incalculably valuable to the collective psyche of the nation."[51]

By the time Roosevelt became president, media reports of carnage of bison, particularly in Yellowstone Park, were widespread. If Yellowstone was not protected, one of the last herds of wild bison could go extinct.[52] The editor of *Forest and Stream* magazine, fellow New Yorker George Bird Grinnell, shared one of his articles on the devastating impact of market hunters with Roosevelt.[53] With this, Grinnell, who had founded the New York Audubon Society and was deemed the "father of American conservation" by the New York Times, gave Roosevelt his first real education in wildlife conservation.[54] The two naturalists recognized a need for a more organized effort, and they set forth to form an association of powerful men bound together by their interests in outdoor adventure, hunting, and wildlife conservation. The Boone and Crockett Club was launched in Roosevelt's Madison Avenue apartment in 1887. In Roosevelt's own words, the Club was for men who believed that "the heartier and manlier the sport ... the more attractive it is."[55]

---

[47] *See* David J. Schmidly, W. E. Tydeman, and Alfred L. Gardner, U.S. Biological Survey: A Compendium of its History, Personalities, Impacts, and Conflicts 116 (Texas Tech. 2016), available at https://repository.si.edu/bitstream/handle/10088/29758/SP%2064.pdf?sequence=1&isAllowed=y; Fischman, *supra* note 25, at 10–11.

[48] Brinkley, *supra* note 19, at 790.

[49] 16 U.S.C. §§703–712.

[50] PJ DelHomme, *A Century of Saving Birds,* Montana Outdoors 20 (July-Aug. 2018).

[51] Brinkley, *supra* note 19, at 14.

[52] Lunde, *supra* note 15, at 142.

[53] *Id.* at 131.

[54] Brinkley, *supra* note 19, at 186.

[55] *Id.* at 138.

According to Douglas Brinkley, "Many historians now believe that the Boone and Crockett Club—Roosevelt's brainchild—was the first wildlife conservation group to lobby *effectively* on behalf of big game."[56] With Roosevelt's guidance, the Club fostered a "fair chase" hunting ethic; without that ethic, "hunters would have been forever the enemies of wildlife, but Theodore Roosevelt made it possible for them to rejoin the ranks of naturalists."[57]

As for the indiscriminate slaughter of bison and other big game in Yellowstone, Congressman Lacey, who was a Boone and Crockett Club member, introduced the Yellowstone Protection Act and pushed it through Congress.[58] Until then, park administrators had next to no power to punish poachers of bison and other wildlife. The Act, which gave the Department of Interior authority to prosecute violators of the law, became the cornerstone of future law enforcement in the park.[59]

The Yellowstone Protection Act was essential to bison conservation in the park, but it was by no means the limit of Roosevelt's aspirations. He dreamed of creating a "buffalo common" in the Great Plains and the West.

When Roosevelt met William Temple Hornaday in 1888 at Hornaday's Buffalo Group exhibit at the Smithsonian Museum, he recognized another kindred spirit. Hornaday, the Smithsonian's chief taxidermist, was known as a conservationist, though he killed as many or more "endangered animals world-wide than any other single person of his generation."[60] Despite their zeal for hunting, both men feared that birds and game species were being slaughtered much more rapidly than they could reproduce, and that the "natural world was careening toward disaster."[61]

Hornaday and Roosevelt founded the American Bison Society (ABS) in 1905 to prevent the extinction of the Plains bison. That same year, Oklahoma politicians campaigned widely for a national park in their territory. Meanwhile, the New York Zoological Park (now known as the Bronx Zoo) offered the federal government fifteen bison to create a herd at the Wichita Forest Reserve in Oklahoma if the government agreed to fence the reserve. Wielding his presidential power, Roosevelt designated the Wichita Forest and Game Preserve by Proclamation of June 2, 1905.[62] Unlike Pelican Island, this time, Roosevelt had

---

[56] *Id.* at 206 (emphasis supplied).

[57] *Id.* at 251.

[58] 28 Stat.73 (May 7, 1894).

[59] Lunde, *supra* note 15, at 141.

[60] Gregory J. Dehler, The Most Defiant Devil: William Temple Hornaday and His Controversial Crusade to Save American Wildlife (2013).

[61] Stefan Bechtel, Mr. Hornaday's War: How a Peculiar Victorian Zookeeper Waged a Lonely Crusade for Wildlife That Changed the World 51 (2012).

[62] *See* Jan. 24, 1905, ch. 137, §1, 33 Stat. 614 (Jan. 24, 1905) (codified at 16 U.S.C. §684) ("The President of the United States is authorized to designate such areas in the Wichita

Congress's blessing to make the Wichita declaration. After an eventful train trek across the country, the bison arrived in 1907, and their descendants populate the renamed and expanded Wichita Mountains Wildlife Refuge.[63]

The creation of a bison preserve in Montana was more challenging, and more disturbing, from an ethical and racial standpoint. In 1908, the ABS convinced Congress to seize over 16,000 acres of the Flathead Indian Reservation to create the National Bison Range. When tribal leaders told the U.S. Indian Agent that they did not want to give up their best hunting grounds, the Agent said they had no choice in the matter and a price for the land was dictated to the Tribes.[64]

The statute, passed by Congress and signed by Roosevelt, explicitly stated that the Range would be populated with bison provided by ABS.[65] Prior to 1908, there had been an existing herd of 400-500 bison on the Flathead reservation.[66] Roosevelt and others urged Congress to appropriate funds to purchase the herd, but they were unsuccessful in arousing support and their efforts failed. The owner, Michel Pablo, sold the herd to the Canadian government when the U.S. failed to accept his offer of sale. Eventually, funding was secured, and the ABS purchased some of the Pablo bison back from the Canadian government to form the initial herd at the National Bison Range.[67]

For Roosevelt, the conservation of bison and other wildlife and birds went hand-in-hand with his fascination with science. By the late 19th century, natural history was a rapidly advancing, cutting edge science.[68] Roosevelt and other conservation leaders at the turn of the century were filled with optimism that science

---

National Forest and in the Grand Canyon National Forest as should, in his opinion, be set aside for the protection of game animals and birds and be recognized as a breeding place therefor.").

63 FWS, Wichita Mountain Wildlife Refuge, https://www.fws.gov/refuge/Wichita_Mountains/wildlife.html (Sept. 29, 2014).

64 *See* Confederated Salish and Kootenai Tribes of the Flathead Reservation v. United States, 437 F.2d 458, 465 (Ct. Cl. 1971) (finding that the taking of the land for the National Bison Range constituted a taking under the Fifth Amendment of the U.S. Constitution).

65 16 U.S.C. §671.

66 The herd descended from animals brought to the Flathead Reservation by a Pend d'Oreille man, Latati, in the 1870's. They were sold to Michel Pablo and Charles Allard in 1884. Alyssa Kelly, *Telling the Story of the National Bison Range*, Charkoosta News, Dec. 6, 2018, available at http://www.charkoosta.com/news/telling-the-story-of-the-national-bison-range/article_3c1eefe8-f9a7-11e8-8449-4beca69422f6.html.

67 Brian Upton, *Returning to A Tribal Self-Governance Partnership at the National Bison Range Complex: Historical, Legal, and Global Perspectives*, 35 Pub. Land & Resources L. Rev. 51, 72-75 (2014) (citing Bon I. Whealdon, I Will Be Meat for My Salish 113 (Robert Bigart, Salish Kootenai College Press/Montana Historical Society Press 2001), and *All But Outlaws of Great Buffalo Herd Moved from Flathead to Make Room for the Settler*, The Daily Missoulian 1 (July 4, 1909)).

68 Lunde, *supra* note 15, at 113.

and technology would secure their hope of "an abundant future."[69] Along with his Chief Forester, Gifford Pinchot, Roosevelt became a staunch proponent of science-based land management to promote orderly resource development.

Roosevelt's brand of resource development, be it orderly or otherwise, included harvesting wildlife. John Muir attempted to shake Roosevelt out of his machismo view of experiencing the outdoors through hunting. On a backpacking trip in Yosemite, Muir asked, "Mr. President, when are you going to get beyond the boyishness of killing things ... are you not getting far enough along to leave that off?"[70]

Roosevelt did not, in fact, "get beyond the boyishness of killing things." For many conservationists today, "Roosevelt's brand of naturalism seems so alien to us ... that we can legitimately question his bona fides." After all, author Darrin Lunde asks, "How many naturalists shoot animals and make museum specimens today?"[71] He explains that to understand Roosevelt as a naturalist, "we need to locate him in the naturalists' world that he knew—a world that wholeheartedly embraced guns, hunting, and taxidermy as equally important to a naturalist's craft."[72] Lunde points out that modern society's separation from wild nature comes at a cost, just as killing wild creatures did in Roosevelt's era:

> Today we are so conditioned not to disturb nature that the mere thought of actually collecting specimen seems taboo.... We tend to see ourselves more as interlopers rather than valid members of the animal kingdom. By today's ethics, nature has become something to protect empathetically or observed from a distance *and nothing more.*[73]

Roosevelt and other naturalists of his era were more—one part explorer, one part scientist, and one part machismo outdoorsmen. The three elements are difficult if not impossible to separate and compartmentalize.

The explorer-scientist elements of naturalists like Roosevelt were satisfied by collecting animals by the thousands. For Roosevelt, "The real joy of nature ... was the chance to engage with it."[74] Not passively, but actively, and often with blood-stained hands.

The machismo aspect of hunting may seem like an outlier among the three elements of naturalists like Roosevelt, but it was mainstream in the late Victorian

---

[69] Hays, *supra* note 16, at 2-3.

[70] J. Baird Callicott, *Contemporary Criticisms of the Received Wilderness Idea*, in The Wilderness Debate Rages On 355, 369 (2008) (citing Roderick Nash, Wilderness and the American Mind (3d ed. 1982)).

[71] Lunde, *supra* note 15, at 247.

[72] *Id.* at 2, 255.

[73] *Id.* at 254 (emphasis added).

[74] *Id.* at 76.

age, when manliness "was an idea of exceptional importance to contemporary males and to Roosevelt in particular."[75] Far more than merely "a reaction to the well-known sexually repressive Victorian mechanisms for cataloging and regulating male desire," Sarah Watts explains how, "in the context of the late Victorian crisis of cultural authority ... Roosevelt represented a stratum of elite white leaders who, feeling the enervating effects of modernism, created ideologies of social and political power based on whiteness and manhood."[76]

More existentially, Roosevelt believed that hunting was essential to the conservation of American culture, wildlife, and wild land. Absent a deeply intimate and death-defying connection with wilderness, future Americans would lose their "great fighting masterful virtues."[77] Protecting wild landscapes was imperative for protecting American heritage and dominance, and Roosevelt vowed to do just that.

National Monuments and Roosevelt's Public Lands Legacy

Under Roosevelt's presidency, the National Forest Service was founded, the Antiquities Act was passed, and 230 million acres of national parks, national forests, and federal game and bird preserves were protected.[78] In addition, Roosevelt's presidential withdrawals reserved vast quantities of coal and other natural resources.

According to a yearbook issued shortly after Roosevelt's presidency, the public had become "seriously concerned with the abuses in the acquiring of public lands by which the government and the people were being defrauded of their chief asset."[79] Ill-conceived dispositions to homesteaders and railroads were especially troublesome. Wielding the presidential pen, Roosevelt withdrew large tracts of coal- or oil-bearing lands from "compulsory seizure ... for alleged agricultural purposes" by private interests under the homestead acts.[80] In just one year, 1906, he withdrew 66 million acres of land from homestead disposition because the land probably contained "workable deposits of coal."[81] Roosevelt

---

[75] Richard Abrams, Theodore Roosevelt: The Man and His Times, https://www.presidentprofiles.com//Grant-Eisenhower/Theodore-Roosevelt-The-man-and-his-times.html#ixzz5vU2IPn7c (visited July 31, 2019).

[76] Sarah Watts, Rough Rider in the White House 11, 13 (2003).

[77] Callicott, *supra* note 70, at 363.

[78] National Park Service, Theodore Roosevelt and Conservation (Nov. 16, 2017), https://www.nps.gov/thro/learn/historyculture/theodore-roosevelt-and-conservation.htm.

[79] The New International Yearbook: A Compendium of the World's Progress 411 (ed. Frank More Colby) (1910).

[80] *Id.*

[81] John W. Lowe, *Withdrawals and Similar Matters Affecting Public Lands,* 4 RMMLF-INST 2 (1958).

also urged Congress to retain in perpetuity "all the coal, oil, and gas lands still remaining in the possession of the government," and to place them under a leasing program "under proper regulations."[82] Congress acquiesced in subsequent enactments.[83]

One of Roosevelt's most widely acclaimed legacies is the National Park System, but he did not, in fact, create either the System or the National Park Service. Both were creations of Congress, through legislation signed by President Woodrow Wilson.[84] Even so, during Roosevelt's administration, the network of national parks grew substantially. When the National Park Service was created to manage them as a National Park System in 1916, 35 sites came under its jurisdiction. Roosevelt had a hand in creating 23 of them.[85]

Only five national parks existed when Roosevelt became President—Yellowstone, Sequoia, General Grant, Yosemite, and Mount Rainier. During his presidency, Roosevelt signed legislation establishing five more: Crater Lake; Wind Cave; Sullys Hill (later re-designated a game preserve); Mesa Verde; and Platt, Oklahoma (now part of Chickasaw National Recreation Area).[86] Another Roosevelt enactment had a more wide-sweeping effect on the mosaic of federal conservation lands: the Antiquities Act of 1906.[87] Sponsored by Congressman Lacey, the Act was passed by Congress and signed by Roosevelt with no recorded opposition and very little comment. The Antiquities Act enabled presidents to proclaim historic landmarks, historic or prehistoric structures, and other objects of historic or scientific interest in federal ownership as national monuments. Roosevelt did not hesitate to take advantage of this new executive authority. By the end of 1906 he had proclaimed four national monuments: Devils Tower (Wyoming); El Morro (New Mexico); Montezuma Castle (Arizona); and Petrified Forest (Arizona).

Roosevelt's most celebrated monument is the Grand Canyon.[88] He was inspired by the art of Ansel Adams and Thomas Moran, and by the bravery of John Wesley Powell, an explorer-conservationist who traveled the length of

---

[82] Charles Richard Van Hise, The Conservation of Natural Resources in the United States 10 (1918).

[83] Sam Kalen, *Where Do We Go from Here?: The Federal Coal Leasing Amendments Act—Past, Present, and Future,* 98 W. Va. L. Rev. 1023, 1026 (1996) (citing the 1910 Pickett Act and the 1920 Mineral Leasing Act).

[84] National Park Service Organic Act of 1916, 16 U.S.C. §1, as amended, Pub. L. 113–287, §3, Dec. 19, 2014, 128 Stat. 3096 (codified at 54 U.S. Code §100101).

[85] Nat'l Park Service, Theodore Roosevelt and Conservation, https://www.nps.gov/thro/learn/historyculture/theodore-roosevelt-and-conservation.htm (updated Nov. 16, 2017).

[86] Brinkley, *supra* note 19, at 450.

[87] 16 U.S.C. §431.

[88] Nat'l Park Service, Theodore Roosevelt and the National Park System (Apr. 5, 2019), at https://www.nps.gov/thrb/learn/historyculture/trandthenpsystem.htm.

the Colorado River through the treacherous rapids of the Canyon.[89] Roosevelt wanted the Grand Canyon to be a new national park, but Congress refused to act, in large part because powerful interests in the Arizona territory had staked claim to the minerals, the rangelands, the water rights, and recreational access.

Territorial governor Nathan Oakes Murphy, "an antigovernment zealot," lobbied against the Grand Canyon reservation, and for that matter all of Roosevelt's public irrigation and forest initiatives.[90] For Roosevelt's part, if Congress and the Arizona contingent "were confused about the Grand Canyon's irreplaceable aesthetic value, he would *make* them see it."[91] His approach was to "just declare something and let the chips fall where they may."[92] First, Roosevelt enlarged the existing forest reserve, which had been created by President Harrison in 1893, and then, in 1906, he provided more protection by designating most of the area as a game preserve to protect wildlife and to prevent the establishment of future mining claims.[93]

Despite these protective overlays, the environmental and scenic values of the Canyon remained vulnerable. Once again, Roosevelt stepped into the breach. Wielding the authority of the Antiquities Act, he bestowed national monument status on the Grand Canyon in 1908. By proclaiming that over 800,000 acres in and around the Canyon was an "object of historic or scientific interest," the monument became off limits "from appropriation and use of all kinds under all of the public land laws subject to all prior valid adverse claims."[94]

The Arizona delegation was incensed. Ralph H. Cameron, an entrepreneuring businessman-politician with interests on the South Rim, sued. Cameron had been charging tourists a toll for the use of the Bright Angel Trail, including, possibly, Roosevelt himself when Roosevelt visited the Canyon for the first time in 1903.[95] Cameron had also filed numerous mining claims on the South Rim and within the Canyon under the General Mining Law of 1872.[96] The Department of Interior determined that his claims within the newly created Monument were invalid, but Cameron contested the determination, and continued to obstruct public access while insisting on his right to hold onto his claims. When

---

[89] Brinkley, *supra* note 19, at 450.

[90] *Id.* at 451.

[91] *Id.* at 755 (emphasis supplied).

[92] *Id.* at 754-55. See *supra* notes 42-43 and accompanying text (discussing Roosevelt's Pelican Island Bird Reserve).

[93] John Copeland Nagle, *What If the Grand Canyon Had Become the Second National Park?,* 51 Ariz. St. L.J. 675, 693 (2019).

[94] Douglas H. Strong, *Ralph H. Cameron and the Grand Canyon (Part I),* 20 Arizona and the West 41, 52 (1978).

[95] *Id.* at 47. *See* Bob Ribokas, Grand Canyon Explorer, http://kaibab.org/kaibab.org/gcps/teddy.htm (visited Oct. 1, 2019).

[96] 30 U.S.C. §21 *et seq.*

the United States sued to enjoin Cameron's interference with public access, Cameron responded by arguing that Roosevelt had no authority to designate the Grand Canyon as a national monument. Cameron lost the battle when the U.S. Supreme Court issued its decision that the Grand Canyon, "one of the greatest eroded canyons in the world," was undoubtedly an object of scientific interest and therefore came within the specifications of the Antiquities Act.[97]

In 1919, just one month after Roosevelt's death, Congress finally passed a statute creating Grand Canyon National Park.[98] As for Ralph Cameron, he continued to attempt to monopolize the South Rim and Bright Angel Trail through political means when he was elected as a U.S. Senator in 1920. Roosevelt's legacy withstood Cameron's efforts to control access to the Canyon, however, and Cameron failed to block appropriations for its management or to oust the director of the National Park Service, Stephen Mather.[99] By 1926, the Department of Interior, the Forest Service, and the federal courts had vanquished Cameron's dream of striking it rich in the Grand Canyon.[100]

Roosevelt's efforts to protect the Grand Canyon have had lasting effects that go well beyond the Canyon itself. Using the precedent set by Roosevelt in his ambitious use of the Antiquities Act, almost every subsequent president has proclaimed new national monuments, many of which were elevated by Congress into some of the nation's most beloved national parks. Not content to limit their proclamations to small historic or scientific objects, presidents of both parties have created much larger national monuments, including 56 million acres of federal lands in Alaska for seventeen monuments (Carter), 1.9 million acres in Utah for Escalante Grand Staircase (Clinton), 90 million acres off the coast of Hawaii for Papahanaumokuakea Marine Monument (George W. Bush), and 1.4 million acres in Utah as Bears Ears National Monument (Obama).[101] Several of these monuments are now under attack by President Trump, who has dramatically diminished their size under the theory that what a president can declare he (or his successor) can also dismantle.[102] Although the federal courts have yet to sort out the merits of this theory, it seems clear that the power of the Antiquities Act as envisioned and utilized by President Roosevelt is to protect the public's land and resources, not to destroy or privatize them. After all, as Professor Mark

---

[97] Cameron v. U.S., 252 U.S. 450 (1920).

[98] Act of Feb. 26, 1919, ch. 44, §1, 40 Stat. 1175 (codified as amended at 16 U.S.C. §§221-228j).

[99] Douglas H. Strong, *Ralph H. Cameron and the Grand Canyon (Part II)*, 20 Arizona and the West 155, 156-158 (1978).

[100] *Id.* at 169, 172.

[101] National Park Service, Archeology Program; Antiquities Act, https://www.nps.gov/archeology/sites/antiquities/monumentslist.htm (last updated Oct. 15, 2019).

[102] Hopi Tribe v. Trump, No. 17-CV-2590 (TSC) (D.D.C. Sept. 30, 2019) (denying defendant's motion to dismiss).

Squillace points out, the Act "has given our nation and its people a conservation legacy that is the envy of other nations."[103]

In addition to the preservation of scenic monuments and wildlife reserves, Teddy Roosevelt believed that working lands should be retained in federal ownership and managed sustainably. Acting upon the advice of Gifford Pinchot, Roosevelt proclaimed 32 new forest reserves and enlarged several other existing reserves.[104] The 1891 General Revision Act authorized the President to "set apart and reserve ... any part of the public lands wholly or in part covered with timber or undergrowth, whether of commercial value or not, as public reservations." In all Roosevelt and his predecessors withdrew over 194 million acres of forest lands under this statute. Congress largely repealed it in 1907, but only after Teddy had made a huge batch (16 million acres) of "midnight reserves" the eve before the repeal.[105]

The U.S. Forest Service, which was created by Roosevelt in 1905, with Pinchot as the nation's first Chief Forester, has had a lasting impact on national conservation policies as well. By implementing a centralized management system based on Progressive Era ideals, the use of science to achieve sustainable yields of forest products has assumed a more prominent role in forest uses, and the influence of raw politics has been diminished somewhat.[106] Because of this foundation, for at least the first fifty years of its history, the Forest Service enjoyed a degree of public support and respect seldom given government agencies.[107]

Roosevelt's Use of Executive Power

By the early 1900s, the majority of media outlets and leaders across the political spectrum agreed that measures needed to be taken to prevent the waste of natural resources, but public opinion was deeply divided as to *who,* exactly, should take those measures. That said, there was no question in Teddy Roosevelt's mind—federal intervention was not only justified but was absolutely imperative. State and local approaches could allow public resources to "fall

---

[103] Mark Squillace, *The Monumental Legacy of the Antiquities Act of 1906,* 37 Ga. L. Rev. 473, 582 (2003).

[104] Sandra B. Zellmer, *The Devil, the Details, and the Dawn of the 21st Century Administrative State: Beyond the New Deal,* 32 Ariz. St. L.J. 941, 1049 (2000) (citing Paul W. Gates, History of Public Land Law Development 580 (1968)).

[105] David H. Getches, *Managing the Public Lands: The Authority of the Executive to Withdraw Lands,* 22 Nat. Resources J. 279, 286 (1982) (citing 16 U.S.C. §471 (1970) (repealed 1976).

[106] Hays, *supra* note 16, at 122-146.

[107] Charles Wilkinson & Daniel Cordalis, *Heeding the Clarion Call for Sustainable, Spiritual Western Landscapes: Will the People Be Granted A New Forest Service?,* 33 Pub. Land & Res. L. Rev. 1, 4 (2012).

haphazardly into private hands," and that simply would not do.[108] Moreover, to Roosevelt, the exercise of federal power over wildlife use and habitat protection, river basin development and transboundary water management, hydropower generation and distribution, and fossil fuel reserves was emblematic of the country's status as a rising world power.[109]

Roosevelt's presidency stood at the crossroads. At the end of the nineteenth-century, American politics were decidedly Jeffersonian. National power was seen as a direct threat to democratic priorities and processes, which many believed ought to reside primarily in the state legislatures.[110] Opponents of strong federal control of public lands claimed that the federal government was the worst of all arbitrary despotisms, prone to denying common people the right to make a living on the land. Roosevelt's conservation initiatives experienced push-back from western ranching, mining, and logging groups who loathed the ever-expanding scope of federal interference.[111]

But at the dawn of the twentieth century, Roosevelt rose above those political currents by putting both national and presidential power in a new and different light. After all, this was the age of Darwinism, which preached the gospel of the fit and the survival of the fittest. Charles Darwin's publication, *On the Origins of Species by Means of Natural Selection,* created a growing awareness of evolutionary biology and its conservation implications. Darwin influenced many of Roosevelt's policies, "including his pro-expansionist sentiments, when he flat-out stated that 'the rivalry of natural selection' was 'one of the features of progress.'"[112] Fitness entailed both physical and moral superiority, and thus Darwin's theories, to Roosevelt, justified vigorous use of centralized power.[113]

Not only did Roosevelt believe in a strong national government, he also believed in the forceful use of executive power. Roosevelt was so utterly confident of his own grasp of the truth and of his steadfast devotion to the public's interests that he felt like a righteous crusader when carrying out his stewardship mission through unilateral measures, especially executive orders. He issued over

---

[108] Daniel Pollak, *S.D. Warren and the Erosion of Federal Preeminence in Hydropower Regulation,* 34 Ecology L.Q. 763, 771 (2007).

[109] Tyrell, *supra* note 22, at 171. Although his impact on federal water policy is beyond the scope of this chapter, it is worth noting that Roosevelt secured the creation of the first National Waterways Commission, 35 Stat. 818 (1909), which urged that the federal government undertake unified development of river systems through multi-purpose projects, and signed the Reclamation Act of 1902, 43 U.S.C. §§ 371 *et seq.*, which delivers water to irrigators through federal projects.

[110] Richard Abrams, Theodore Roosevelt: The Man and His Times, https://www.presidentprofiles.com//Grant-Eisenhower/Theodore-Roosevelt-The-man-and-his-times.html#ixzz5vU2IPn7c (visited July 31, 2019).

[111] Tyrell, *supra* note 22, at 6.

[112] Brinkley, *supra* note 19, at 302.

[113] Abrams, *supra* note 110.

1,000 of them, which was nearly ten times more than his predecessor in office.[114] Many of his executive orders were relatively insignificant or clerical, but others had a profound impact on the country, especially the conservation of public lands and resources. The creation of national monuments, wildlife refuges, and forest reserves stand among them.

Roosevelt's hand-picked successor, President William Howard Taft, agreed on the need for resource conservation, but intended to accomplish it in very different ways. In contrast with Roosevelt, Taft was more comfortable with state and private control. If federal involvement was warranted, Taft tended to seek legislation instead of issuing executive orders.[115]

According to Taft, Roosevelt's notion that presidents possess broad residual power was "unsafe," and could lead to unwarranted and even dangerous results, "doing irremediable injustice to private right."[116] Ironically, during his presidency, Taft himself withdrew a vast swath of public lands in Wyoming and California from disposition to reserve oil for the U.S. Navy, and in *U.S. v. Midwest Oil Co.*, the Supreme Court upheld the withdrawal as a long-standing type of executive action having the tacit agreement of Congress.[117] The Court observed that Taft's order was in the public interest and did no harm to existing private rights. Yet arguably Taft's oil withdrawal was at least as bold, and as anti-democratic, as any order Roosevelt had ever made. As the dissenting opinion pointed out, to the extent that there were any congressional acts relevant to Taft's withdrawal, it was the 1897 Oil Placer Act, which *opened* the public lands to the free extraction of mineral oils.[118] Yet there is no doubt that Taft's withdrawal was necessary. Otherwise, the United States would have been required to purchase back, at great cost, the oil that had been produced from the public lands by private companies, who had paid virtually nothing for that oil, to fuel the Navy in the years leading up to World War I. In this instance, at least, Taft agreed with Roosevelt that the ends—conservation of public resources for the public good—justified the means.

---

[114] Lorraine Boissoneault, *The Debate Over Executive Orders Began With Teddy Roosevelt's Mad Passion for Conservation,* Smithsonian Magazine, Apr. 17, 2017.

[115] Paolo E. Coletta, William Howard Taft—Legislative Affairs and Tempestuous Politics, https://www.presidentprofiles.com//Grant-Eisenhower/William-Howard-Taft-Legislative-affairs-and-tempestuous-politics.html#ixzz5vU17ReiN (visited July 31, 2019).

[116] John P. Roche and Leonard W. Levy, The Presidency 23-25 (1964).

[117] U.S. v. Midwest Oil Co., 236 U.S. 459, 471 (1915).

[118] *Id.* at 511-512.

Trump's Conservation Policies and Use of Executive Power

The distinctions between the conservation policies and impacts of Roosevelt and Trump are stark, from forest management to national monuments to wildlife. However, there is a common thread—the use of unilateral executive power to accomplish presidential ends.

President Roosevelt's aggressive approach to the use of executive power continues to shape how presidents make their mark on the nation. All but one president since George Washington have issued executive orders, but since Roosevelt the number and scope of orders have increased dramatically. Many have been mundane, such as requiring flags to be flown at half-mast upon the death of a dignitary, but some have had profound effects, both negative (*e.g.*, Franklin Roosevelt's World War II internment camps) and positive (*e.g.*, Harry Truman's desegregation of the military).[119]

Before taking office, Trump disparaged his predecessor's executive orders as disastrous power grabs. Since then, in each year of his presidency, Trump has issued more executive orders than did President Barack Obama during the same time span.[120] The quantity of Trump's orders is less notable than the content, which includes sweeping directives for energy development, wildlife killing, a border wall between the U.S. and Mexico, and immigration bans and deportations.[121]

Perhaps the starkest contrast between Trump's orders and Teddy Roosevelt's orders is illustrated by their use of the Antiquities Act authority to designate national monuments. Instead of designating new or expanded monuments, President Trump ordered drastic reductions to two national monuments in Utah and recommended significant management changes for others. Specifically, Trump shrank Bears Ears National Monument, a remarkable landscape filled with red rock canyons, archaeological resources, and sites that are sacred to numerous Native American tribes, by 85 percent.[122] He slashed another monument, Grand

---

[119] *See* Kevin M. Stack, *The Statutory President*, 90 Iowa L. Rev. 539, 548-549 (2005); William G. Howell, Power Without Persuasion: The Politics of Direct Presidential Action 7 (2003) ("[U]nilateral policy making has become an integral feature of the modern Presidency."). William Henry Harrison is the only president who did not issue any executive orders, but he died just 31 days after taking office.

[120] Kevin Freking, *Trump Once Called Executive Orders 'Power Grabs,' But His 3-Year Total Outpaces Obama*, Global News, Oct. 19, 2019.

[121] *See* Kevin R. Johnson, *Immigration and Civil Rights in the Trump Administration: Law and Policy Making by Executive Order*, 57 Santa Clara L. Rev. 611, 629 (2017); David M. Driesen, *President Trump's Executive Orders and the Rule of Law*, 87 UMKC L. Rev. 489, 497-512 (2019).

[122] Proclamation No. 9681, Modifying the Bears Ears National Monument, 82 Fed. Reg. 58,081 (Dec. 8, 2017).

Staircase-Escalante, in half.[123] By reversing the protections put in place by previous presidents, Trump's orders facilitate extensive development on the public lands and privatization of the public's resources.

In another notable departure from Roosevelt's conservation agenda, the Trump Administration rolled back a 40-year-old interpretation of a policy aimed at protecting migratory birds under the MBTA. First it announced that it would not enforce an interpretation of the MBTA that prohibited "incidental takes" that kill birds.[124] "Incidental takes" caused by wind turbines and other major industrial activities are not specifically directed at migratory birds but can have more deleterious effects than hunting, even though, in many cases, the effects could be avoided by relatively modest and inexpensive measures.[125] Subsequently, Trump's Department of Interior issued an order stating that "incidental" takings did not violate the MBTA.[126] In response, seventeen high-ranking officials from previous Republican and Democratic administrations sent a letter to Trump's Secretary of Interior opposing the change, and legal challenges are pending.[127]

Fossil fuel development is another Trump Administration priority that has been effectuated through unilateral executive measures. At the direction of President Trump, the U.S. State Department approved the transboundary Keystone XL pipeline to transport tar sands oil from Alberta to refineries in the United States. The proposed pipeline had been analyzed extensively and ultimately rejected by the Obama Administration. When Trump's State Department changed course, a federal judge blocked the pipeline from going forward because it lacked an adequate environmental analysis.[128] Trump later side-stepped the

---

[123] Proclamation No. 9682, Modifying the Grand Staircase-Escalante National Monument, 82 Fed. Reg. 58,089 (Dec. 4, 2017).

[124] Memorandum from K. Jack Haugrud, Acting Sec'y, to Acting Solicitor, U.S. Dep't of Interior, *Temporary Suspension of Certain Solicitor M-Opinions Pending Review* (Feb. 6, 2017), https://www.doi.gov/sites/doi.gov/files/uploads/temp_suspension_20170206.pdf.

[125] Complaint, Nat'l Audubon Soc'y v. U.S. Dep't of the Interior, No. 1:18-cv-04601 ¶¶ 1, 7 (S.D.N.Y. filed May 24, 2018), https://perma.cc/MUX3-ZHFK.

[126] Memorandum from Principal Deputy Solicitor to Sec'y, U.S. Dep't of Interior, *The Migratory Bird Treaty Act Does Not Prohibit Incidental Take* (Dec. 22, 2017), https://www.doi.gov/sites/doi.gov/files/uploads/m-37050.pdf.

[127] Jennifer A. Dlouhy, *Trump Administration Reverses Obama-Era Policy on Accidental Bird Deaths*, Bloomberg (Dec. 22, 2017), https://www.bloomberg.com/news/articles/2017-12-22/trump-is-said-to-reverse-strict-obama-era-policy-on-bird-deaths-jbi84akp; Nat. Res. Def. Council, Inc. v. U.S. Dep't of the Interior, 397 F. Supp. 3d 430 (S.D.N.Y. 2019) (denying defendant's motion to dismiss).

[128] Indigenous Envtl. Network v. United States Dep't of State, 347 F. Supp. 3d 561 (D. Mont.), order amended and supplemented, 369 F. Supp. 3d 1045 (D. Mont. 2018), and appeal dismissed as moot, No. 18-36068 (9th Cir. June 6, 2019).

ruling by issuing a presidential permit, which he claims is not subject to judicial review under the Administrative Procedure Act.[129]

Fossil fuel development deserves special attention here. In contrast to Roosevelt's 1906 coal withdrawal and President Taft's oil withdrawal, the Trump Administration has dramatically ramped up fossil fuel production on the federal lands through executive fiat.[130] Specifically, with regard to coal, the United States owns an approximately 570-million-acre mineral estate. Over forty percent of the coal produced in this country comes from federal land. Despite the broad sweep of the federal coal-leasing program, the BLM has not undertaken a comprehensive environmental review for the federal coal program since 1979.[131] To assess the climate change implications and environmental, economic, and social externalities of federal coal production, in 2016, former Secretary of Interior Sally Jewell issued a Secretarial Order directing BLM to prepare a programmatic environment impact statement (EIS). Jewell's Order also imposed a moratorium on new coal leasing pending completion of the EIS. In 2017, shortly after taking office, President Trump issued an executive order directing his Secretary of Interior Ryan Zinke to "take all steps necessary and appropriate to amend or withdraw" the Jewell Order. Zinke subsequently issued a secretarial order, which lifted the moratorium, ended the EIS process, and directed BLM to "process coal lease applications and modifications expeditiously." A federal district court set aside Zinke's decision to lift the environmental protections and forego environmental analysis as arbitrary and capricious.[132]

Several other environmentally destructive measures are being implemented through federal agency notice-and-comment rule making, but even these measures are directed by the Trump White House. One rule, in particular, deserves comment. The National Park Service, at the direction of Trump's Secretary of Interior, proposes to rescind a regulation that barred hunters from using cruel and unsportsmanlike practices on certain public lands. In marked contrast to Roosevelt's "fair chase" ethic, the Trump rule would allow hunters on public lands in Alaska to bait brown bears with bacon and doughnuts, use spotlights to

[129] Presidential Permit, TransCanada Keystone Pipeline, Mar. 29, 2019, available at https://www.whitehouse.gov/presidential-actions/presidential-permit/. Reviewability is being tested in Indigenous Action Network v. Trump, 428 F. Supp. 3d 296 (D. Mont. 2019) (denying defendant's motion to dismiss).

[130] Presidential Executive Order on Promoting Energy Independence and Economic Growth, Mar. 28, 2017, available at https://www.whitehouse.gov/presidential-actions/presidential-executive-order-promoting-energy-independence-economic-growth/.

[131] Citizens for Clean Energy v. U.S. Dep't of the Interior, 384 F. Supp. 3d 1264 (D. Mont. 2019).

[132] *Id.* at 1271–72.

shoot mother black bears and cubs hibernating in their dens, and kill wolves and pups in their dens.[133]

Professor David Driesen asks whether we should see President Trump's executive orders as an extraordinary affront to the rule of law, or merely as the normal practice of a President taking discretionary measures as is his due. Driesen concludes that, taken together, Trump's actions "send a message that the President unilaterally controls policy," which not only erodes the public's faith in the rule of law, but also blatantly flies in the face of separation of powers, especially legislative prerogatives and judicial review.[134] Driesen ultimately concludes that Trump's executive orders "systematically and very deliberately . . . undermine the law's goals."[135]

Arguably, the same could be said of Roosevelt's executive orders. But there is a key distinction between the orders issued by Roosevelt and those issued by Trump. Roosevelt's orders conserved the federal public lands, natural resources, and wildlife, leaving the door open to Congress and future administrations to change course if the public interest demanded mineral extraction or other forms of use or development. By leaving the land intact, wildlife habitat and other ecosystem services, including climate change mitigation and adaptation, can continue to be provided to the public. Trump's orders, by contrast, deplete or destroy the lands and resources, and foreclose future opportunities. The battle over national monuments demonstrates this principle most directly. By designating the Grand Canyon and other federal public lands as national monuments, Roosevelt protected them for future generations to manage in a fashion that best serves the public interest.[136] By diminishing Grand Staircase and Bears Ears, and opening the excluded areas to extraction and development, Trump is eliminating conservation options and impoverishing future generations.

Conclusion: Teddy Roosevelt's Conservation Legacy

More than places of recreation, reflection, or solitude, and more than habitat for wildlife species, Roosevelt viewed national monuments, wildlife refuges, and forest reserves as essential resources to be shared in common by the people as a whole. Roosevelt himself justified his use of executive power to conserve remarkable places like the Grand Canyon in terms of intergenerational equity

---

[133] National Park Service, Hunting and Trapping in National Preserves, Proposed Rule, 83 Fed. Reg. 23621 (May 22, 2018) (to be codified at 36 C.F.R. Part 13).

[134] Driesen, *supra* note 121, at 518.

[135] *Id.* at 514.

[136] *See* Sandra B. Zellmer, *A Preservation Paradox: Political Prestidigitation and an Enduring Resource of Wildness*, 34 Envtl. L. 1015, 1087 (2004) (concluding that "both preservation goals and democratic values are well served through monument declarations").

and America's rich natural heritage: "Our people should see to it that [these places] are preserved for their children and their children's children forever with their majestic beauty all unmarred."[137]

Roosevelt's successful effort to protect the nation's public lands and resources at a crucial time in America's political and economic history takes its place beside the Emancipation Proclamation issued by his hero, Abraham Lincoln. Even during his lifetime, to many Americans, like Lincoln, Roosevelt was a folk hero. In just seven years and sixty-nine days, President Roosevelt protected over 234 million acres of public lands, ranging from oddities like a wind cave and a petrified forest to ancient cliff dwellings to giant sequoias and the greatest eroded canyon on earth. His vision and his bold actions provide an enduring legacy for his generation, those that have followed, and those yet to come.

It is true that, in contrast to Lincoln's efforts to end slavery and to bridge racial divides, the effects of Roosevelt's actions on American Indian people and communities are mixed, at best. By putting Roosevelt's actions and views in the context of their time, and by learning from Roosevelt's mistakes, perhaps a step towards a buffalo commons for all, and towards the reconciliation that such a commons may represent, can be made. We honor Teddy Roosevelt's legacy, and enhance democratic ideals, when we continue to cherish the public lands and the wildlife that subsists on them, and to protect them for present and future generations of all Americans.

---

[137] Theodore Roosevelt, Outdoor Pastimes of an American Hunter 317 (1905).

Part II

Creators and Saviors

The True Pioneers of Part I educated us on the importance of the natural and physical environment, and pointed out that humans were threatening the integrity and sustainability of parts of this natural world. Eventually, the human-caused damage to natural systems and natural resources became so acute that certain far-sighted individuals recognized that specialized laws and legal institutions needed to be created in order to address this looming issue. These individuals, in effect, "invented" the new legal doctrine of environmental law. One of the chapters in Part II identifies some of the key players and "creators" of environmental law. They met during a conference in 1969, and this gathering of first generation environmental law avatars turned out to be the incubator for this new area of law about to emerge throughout the late 1960s and early 1970s.

Once the new environmental laws were initially in place, criticisms emerged which challenged the staying power of these relatively new and unprecedented protections of natural resources and systems. Certain individuals in important government positions stepped up and "saved" some environmental protection laws under siege. One of those individuals is the topic of another chapter in Part II. Secretary of Interior Bruce Babbitt is recognized as an official who saved one of the most ambitious of these new environmental laws—The Endangered Species Act.

The creators and saviors discussed in the chapters that follow are also pioneers. The first chapter in Part II recounts how some pioneered a new, and now universally accepted, legal doctrine – environmental law. And, in Part II's other chapter, a pioneer helped to ensure the future viability of an important preservation law, one that demanded the restoration and protection of threatened and endangered species.

Chapter 4

The Airlie House Conference and the Dawn of Environmental Law

Anthony Dan Tarlock[1]

Introduction

This chapter focuses on a small group of legal academics and activist lawyers who helped to create environmental law as a distinct field of teaching, scholarship, and practice in the late 1960s, and a seminal conference that helped to create a community of scholars and practitioners. The group consisted of a few senior scholars, whose important contributions are largely forgotten today, and a group of young scholars who grasped the importance of the need for a legal framework to prevent persistent environmental degradation. As a participant in this latter group, I have delved deep into the recesses of my memory to try to recreate the zeitgeist of the 1960s and some of the important people who influenced us through their writing or actions. I have deliberately tried to convey both the naïve optimism and intellectual excitement of the 1960s. This chapter is being written as environmental protection laws and the science behind them are

[1] Dan Tarlock is University Distinguished Professor Emeritus at the Illinois Tech Chicago-Kent College of Law. He was born and raised in the San Francisco Bay Area and holds both an A.B. and L.L.B. from Stanford University. Prior to joining the Chicago-Kent faculty, he was a member of the law facilities at the University of Kentucky and Indiana University, Bloomington. He has visited at numerous law schools including the universities of Chicago, Kansas, Michigan, Pennsylvania, Southern California, and Utah. In 2018, he was the Distinguished Visitor in Residence at the Lewis and Clark College of Law. His career has been focused on the intersections among domestic and international environmental regulation, water allocation, energy production, and land use regulation. He has authored numerous articles, book chapters, casebooks, a treatise and treatise chapters on these subjects. He is also the co-author, with Professor Holly Doremus, of Water Wars in the Klamath Basin: Macho Law, Combat Biology, and Dirty Politics. In addition to consulting widely with law firms and government agencies, he has severed as a member of the Water, Science and Technology Board of the National Academies of Science, a Special Legal Advisor to the Submissions Unit of the NAFTA Environmental Side Agreement, and the Technical Advisory Committee of the Global Water Partnership.

being systematically dismantled and rejected by the administration of President Donald J. Trump in a way that was previously unimaginable. Should there be a rebirth of environmental law in the United States, my hope is that those involved in the project will find the lessons of the initial construction of the field, both negative and positive, useful.

The first part of the chapter sketches the early "rational," as opposed to the now mythic, 1960s. The early 1960s laid the foundations for the environmental decade (1969-1980) that produced the basic legal framework of environmental protection. The chapter then sketches the biographies and early contributions of the small group of scholars, with apologies to the memories of those omitted, who were primarily interested in the "conservation" of natural resources, the pre-environmental term for the concern over the degradation of nature. Finally, I revisit a path-breaking event that has an on-going legacy for environmental law, the September 1969 Airlie House Conference. The Conference played a major role in making environmental law both an academic discipline and practice field, and it helped to create a vibrant community of academics and scholar-practitioners. Most of the profiled group participated in the conference, either as authors of background papers or as invited guests. The background papers and a full transcript of the deliberations, along with bibliographical material, were published in 1970 as Law and the Environment, edited by Malcolm Baldwin and James K. Page.

The Rise of Environmentalism in the Rational and Mythic 1960s

For most people in the twenty-first century, the 1960s are seen as a mythic, radical, boundary-breaking time that began around 1964-1965 and ended in the early 1970s. But free love, drugs, the Beatles, anti-Vietnam War protests, the demand for racial and sexual equality, and political environmentalism that emerged from this heady and still contested time was preceded by the rational 1960s. During this time enlightened public officials and a few non-legal academics laid out the case for environmental protection. Environmental law is primarily rooted in the rational 1960s, although the political environmentalism that arose in the mythic 1960s, in part fueled by the release of energy from the anti-Vietnam War movement, helped to create the political pressure that led to a legislative framework for what was hoped to be permanent, effective environmental protection.

The Kennedy Legacy and Stuart Udall

John F. Kennedy's 1960 election as president laid the groundwork for environmental protection as a major public policy objective. It is hard for most people in the second decade of the twenty-first century to appreciate the intellectual excitement created by the Kennedy Administration. To those of us who invested our energy in the 1960 campaign, it seemed that the new, dynamic administration was bringing the best of American thinking and culture to bear on a host of domestic and international problems that had been festering for several decades. The primary problems were racial and economic inequality and the need to confront aggressively the Soviet Union in Africa, Asia, and Latin America. But, pressure for what came to be called environmental protection also was building in the 1950s. Post World War II America created a measure of affluence for millions of Americans, many of whom were moving from large cities into the suburbs. The new affluence and suburban migration produced diffuse demands for more open space for recreation, a more beautiful landscape, less visible pollution, and better control of science and technology, especially atomic energy. These forces slowly emerged as a political priority during the Kennedy and Lyndon B. Johnson Administration, which followed President Kennedy's tragic assassination in 1963 (1960-1968).

The seminal idea of respecting and protecting nature first appeared on the political agenda during the administration of Theodore Roosevelt (1901-1908). As described in Chapter 3, President Theodore Roosevelt's commitment to the conservation of natural resources through public ownership and efficient use included a nature preservation element. But, the early twentieth-century fight over the construction of Hetch Hetchy dam in an equally beautiful valley immediately north of Yosemite National Park in Californian created a split in the conservation movement. One branch stressed the public control of public resources to promote efficient development, and the other advocated the preservation of scenic wonders and natural beauty by withdrawing public land from almost all use except enlightened enjoyment and rugged recreation. Both branches' appeal faded during the rapacious and corrupt 1920s, but they had a partial rebirth in the 1930s during the New Deal. President Franklin Roosevelt's deep interest and commitment to natural resource stewardship remains underappreciated to this day. By the 1950s, conservation had again lost its widespread appeal, but natural resource preservation again reemerged in the mid-1950s, first over fights to prevent dams on the upper tributaries of the Colorado River and then to set aside large amounts of public land as perpetual wilderness.

Walling off large areas of public lands is usually attributed to the now iconic naturalist Aldo Leopold. In 1924, he persuaded the United States Forest Service to designate administratively three-quarters of a million acres of mountains, rivers, and desert in New Mexico as the Gila Wilderness, the first area in the world to be managed as a wilderness area. Four decades later and eight years of Congressional debate due to Western states opposition, Congress enacted the Wilderness Act of 1964. Four years later, the wilderness system was completed by the Wild and Scenic Rivers system. However, early exploitation-preservation fights were primarily political and had limited legal or law school curricular implications as did the wilderness and wild and scenic rivers legislation.

Environmental as a science-based, comprehensive lens to which to view a series of problems from visible pollution to species loss emerged in the early 1960s, largely due to two books, Rachael Carson's 1962 *Silent Spring* and Aldo Leopold's 1949 *A Sand County Almanac.* The book was the culmination of the great naturalist's thinking about nature. Leopold's elegant land ethic suggested a broader scientific and ethical basis for protecting nature from human intrusion. The book was little noticed when it was initially published, but it became a best seller in the 1960s and had a seminal influence on environmentalism and ultimately environmental law.

Ideas, however, need implementation through champions with power and influence. In the Kennedy-Johnson administrations, America was blessed to have a champion who redefined and expanded conservation of natural resources to include environmental protection. Steward Udall, a Congressman from Tucson, Arizona, served as Secretary of the Interior from 1961 to 1969. Udall grew up in northern Arizona in a powerful political family and was steeped in the conservation tradition of the Theodore and Franklin Roosevelt. During his stewardship of the Department of Interior, the United States preserved some 4 million acres of land that included the Canyonlands, Guadálupe Mountains, North Cascades and Redwood national parks in addition to numerous other monuments, seashores, wildlife refuges and recreation areas.

Udall's enduring legacy is that he reinterpreted the conservation-preservation tradition to include the broader idea of environmental protection. During his stewardship of the Department of Interior, environmental protection first emerged as a rational dialogue among a few cabinet officials, legislators (and their staffs), and representatives of the old-line conservation groups and then spread outward from there. Udall was deeply influenced by Carson and Leopold. When Silent Spring appeared in 1962, he immediately recognized that her thinking was a paradigm shift in this about the way that we used the "natural" or Edenic world. Udall immediately befriended Carson and followed closely the bitter reaction to her critique of pesticide use. He also recognized the profound implications of A Sand County Almanac.

Secretary Udall's response to these two seminal books immediate and far-reaching was to use them as the foundation to reinterpret the conservation-preservation tradition. In 1963, he published The Quiet Crisis (yes, government officials actually read and wrote serious books in the rational 1960s). The book told a wide audience that Silent Spring "spurred new lines of thought about resources and the limits of technology that began to alter the thinking of my generation." Leopold's land ethic became the foundation of Udall's plea for a new conservation ethic beyond "walling off" nature from humans based on a much more holistic and scientific vision of the environment emerged compared to the aesthetic and spiritual justifications for preservation used in the past.

The popularization of Carson and Leopold's thinking and provided many of those interested in natural resource conservation with what seemed to be a powerful theoretical framework to justify the need for the regulation of all forms of resource use. On a personal note, as a sophomore at Cornell University in 1959, I attended a lecture by then Congressman Stuart Udall. He was introduced by the eminent presidential scholar, Clinton Rositer, as a likely star there was to be a Kennedy Administration. A few years later, as a still stressed (a word that was never used in the 1960s) second-year law student, I still remember getting a call from my mother that I had to read a wonderful new book that she has just purchased. The first edition of *The Quiet Crisis* still sits on my bookshelf next to a first edition of Edward Albee's *Desert Solitaire*, another must-read gift from my mother. They played a large role in the subsequent course of my academic career, as I am sure they did for others of my generation.

Secretary Udall's thinking had a deep impact in the Kennedy Administration. In the introduction to *The Quiet Crisis*, President Kennedy wrote (and I think fully understood what he was saying):

> We must do in our own day what Theodore Roosevelt did sixty years ago and Franklin Roosevelt thirty years ago: we must expand the concept of conservation to meet the imperious problems of the new age. We must develop new instruments of foresight and protection and nurture in order to recover the relationship between man and nature and to make sure that the national estate we pass on to our multiplying descendants is green and flourishing.

From Paradigm Shift to Law: Senator Henry Jackson

Secretary Udall did much to raise the consciousness of the executive branch, but as was clear in the 1960s, Congress had the primary responsibility to enact legislation to address new social problems. For this, we are greatly indebted to Senator Henry (Scoop) Jackson of Washington state that took the next step and inadvertently did much to create modern environmental law. Both Secretary Udall and Senator Jackson saw environmental policy and environmental protection primarily as an extension of the New Deal state. In the 1960s, the main players were to be Congress and reformed "expert agencies" rather than lawyers and judges. However, ironically, Senator Jackson laid the foundation for the rejection of the New Deal state and a vastly expanded role for the judiciary.

In the mid-1960s, Senator Jackson was the chair of the Senate Committee on Interior and Insular Affairs, and he sponsored numerous Congressional studies and colloquia on environmental policy that brought the thinking of leading academics, mainly scientists, and others into the public eye through a series of committee publications. Their work played a major role in fundamentally changing our view of our natural heritage. As the historian Richard N. L. Andrews, was "[t]he most revolutionary element of the new public consciousness was the powerful new awareness of the environment as a living system—a 'web of life' or ecosystem—rather than just a storehouse of commodities to be extracted or a chemical machine to be manipulated."

One academic was my colleague and friend at Indiana University, Bloomington, and Lynton Keith Caldwell. Caldwell, a political scientist interested in policy implementation and an early advocate of environmental protection. Caldwell believed that ecology would be a unifying force in the public administration and that an understanding of science would lead the Execute Branch to take the necessary protection decisions. Frustrated by Executive Branch claims that agencies and cabinet departments lacked the legal authority to protect the environment, Caldwell and Jackson's staff set out to correct the problem in one fell-swoop by the passage of what ultimately became the National Environmental Policy Act in 1969 (NEPA).

Caldwell and Jackson hoped to create a new federal policy that would be internalized by the Executive Branch, a plausible idea at the time. Neither Caldwell nor the staff envisioned that the statute would be primarily enforced by the courts. Their assumption was that agencies and cabinet departments would either take the necessary protection decisions, or if they lacked the authority to do so, they would ask Congress for the necessary additional authority. Caldwell wanted NEPA to change outcomes, not just be another ignored legislative declaration of policy and wanted to correct what he saw as the major defect in an earlier act that articulated a new federal policy, the Employment Act of 1946. The Act, generally known as the Full Employment Act of 1946 rejected the creation of a right to a job but did declare that "Congress hereby declares that it is the continuing policy and responsibility of the federal government to use all practicable means consistent with its needs and obligations.... in a manner calculated to foster and promote free and competitive enterprise and the general welfare, conditions under which there will be afforded useful employment for those able, willing, and seeking work, and to promote maximum employment, production, and purchasing power.

To Caldwell, the problem with the Full Employment Act was that there was no "action-forcing" mechanism to ensure compliance. Thus was born Section 102 of NEPA, the duty to prepare an environmental impact statement. The evolution of NEPA as a litigation tool to challenge all manner of federally-related actions is another multi-volume story. For my narrative of pre-1070 environmental law, the point is that the actions of Udall, Jackson, and experts such as Caldwell helped to legitimize environmental protection as a subject worthy of serious study by law students.

The Search for Law to Complement Environmentalism

Environmentalism but Not Environmental Law

In the mid-1960s, environmental protection, or conservation of natural resources management as it was then called, began to enter the legal academy thanks to a small group of law professors who became interested in protecting natural resources from human degradation. There were few legal guideposts. Science, economics, and philosophy created the need for protection, but in the mid-1960s, it was hard to envision dealing with environmental degradation as a legal discipline and practice area. Environmental law, as we now know it, simply did not exist; it was hardly even an aspiration in the academy or practice. A legal subject must have four characteristics to thrive specialty area, and none of these existed in the mid to late 1960s. First, it must have a distinct core of principles to avoid being dismissed as just "law and...." Principles are usually drawn from statutes, cases, or the constitution, despite strenuous but unsuccessful efforts to convince the Supreme Court to recognize a right to environmental quality. Save for the law of nuisance, the idea of respecting "nature" had almost no roots in the Anglo-American legal tradition or in any other major legal system. The seemingly simple imperative of environmentalism, leave nature alone to the maximum extent possible, did not reflect the Holmesian evolution of centuries of human experience which had shaped the law. Second, it must be a sustainable area of practice that provides job opportunities for interested law school graduates. Third, it must have a group of dedicated teachers and scholars and outlets for their research and writing. Finally, the subject must have a firm place in the law school curriculum.

None of these conditions in the early 1960s, and those of us interested in environmental protection had to take a different route to develop first principles. We turned to scientists, economists and philosophers. The intellectual foundations of environmentalism and environmental law can be traced to the 19th-century, as described in Chapter 1, or beyond, but the more contemporary writings of Aldo Leopold and Rachael Carson provided a what seemed to be a powerful but straight-forward philosophical and scientific justification to justify government regulation of pollution and what later became the conservation of biodiversity. Economists soon chimed in and added a more elegant and powerful justification for the regulation of waste discharges and other activities which degraded the environment: the internalization of external costs. Kenneth Boulding's chapter, The Coming Spaceship Earth, in Environmental Quality in a Growing Economy and, Garret Hardin's, The Tragedy of the Commons that appeared in Science in 1962. Barry Commoner's now largely forgotten 1971 book, The Closing Circle seemed to a complete intellectual framework. I included excerpts from these writings in the first chapter of an environmental law casebook that I published in 1974 with Eva and John Hanks, Environmental Law and Policy. They seemed to tell the students all they needed to know about the rationales for environmental law.

The history of earlier concerns with natural resources provided some precedent, mainly with respect to water resources. The closest antecedent seemed to be the early 20th-century Conservation Movement. For example, the first course with conservation in the title is Joe Sax's Conservation and the Law which he taught in 1966 when he visited the University of Michigan. When I first started teaching, I tried to see what influence the Conservation Movement had on legal scholarship, but I could find very few articles and cases. There were a couple of exceptions mining and water law. Professor Richard Lazarus has traced the history of environmental law at Harvard to a 1911-1912 course in Mining and Irrigation Law taught by Nebraska-born Roscoe Pound before he became dean. Water law had some legs; it became an established course in the 1950s at several Western Schools and the University of Wisconsin. This course spawned several early environmentalists as Section IV describes. But, for the most part, the Conservation Movement was primarily a political one.

And, the New Deal administrative state seemed to choke off any possibility of challenging federal actions that degraded the environment. During the New Deal, administrative law was founded on the principle that the agencies formed to govern the use of natural resources, as were all agencies, such as the then Federal Power Commission were expert agencies entitled to great deference. Thus, they were shielded from effective judicial review. The statutory regimes which promoted the degradation of the landscapes, rivers, and airsheds that NGOs and their lawyers were trying to reverse were all enacted before environmental values were widely understood, and these statutes conferred almost unlimited discretion on administrative agencies to choose among a wide range of resource use options from the rarely considered complete preservation to full development. Access to the courts was limited because standing was thought to be confined to common law or statutory rights or the clear legislative creation of non-common law legal interests. Thus, there was law but not "real law" as Justice Holmes defined it: a prediction of what a court would do. At Airlie House, a young attorney on the verge of a major career as an environmental lawyer, James Moorman presented a 52 page paper entitled, Outline of Federal law for the Practicing Lawyer, but the references were almost entirely statutes and administrative regulations.

Real law had to wait for the rise of political environmentalism. In the mid-1960s, the rational debates within the Kennedy-Johnson Administration, described in Section II, had not yet morphed into political environmentalism, although a sense of urgency was slowly building. Post World War II urban growth increased the public's taste for beauty and recreational opportunities. The link between smog and the internal combustion engine was clear by the end of the 1950s. Scientists were trying to validate Silent Spring by linking DDT and other synthetic pesticides to suspected health and ecosystem damages. However, it was not until 1968-69 that political environmentalism emerged. The February, 1969 Santa Barbara oil spill and the Cuyahoga River fire in Cleveland shortly thereafter suggested that the degradation of the natural world would increase. These seminal events were helped by the release of social reform energy from the anti-Vietnam War movement. The result was widespread and non-partisan support for new laws to protect the environment.

The first indication that there could be real environmental law was the 1965 second circuit decision, Scenic Hudson Preservation Conference versus the Federal Power Commission, 354 F.2d 608 (2nd Cir. 1965). The court remanded an FPC license for a pumped storage plant at an iconic mountain on the Hudson River (which was ultimately ironically killed by political action). To do this, the court first granted an ad hoc citizen group gained unprecedented standing to represent non-economic and aesthetic interests, and it then created an agency duty out of whole cloth to consider less environmentally damaging alternatives to the planned project. James Moorman described the case as "an exciting breakthrough in the law of standing to sue." On the merits, the plaintiffs convinced the court of appeals to read a broad regulatory statute, which at best conferred discretion on the agency to consider aesthetic values (a then much-contested idea), to impose mandatory duties on an agency to consider environmental values, and to justify more fully decisions not to protect them. Scenic Hudson opened up the possibility for the first time that public agencies could be sued for failing to take environmental impacts and values into account.

Environmental law owes an immeasurable debt to one of *Scenic Hudson's* attorneys, David Sive who helped to create environmental law almost out of whole cloth. Sive followed the great common law tradition left open to socially marginal groups and of out of necessity turned to the courts. He pursued a "rule of law litigation" strategy without the constitutional foundation that those challenging racial discrimination enjoyed. He created the fiction that the recognition of new environmental protection duties merely required courts to perform their traditional and constitutionally legitimate function of applying and enforcing, rather than creating, pre-existing rules. David Sive used his victory in *Scenic Hudson* to upend New Deal administrative law. The then-dominant legal process school posited that legislatures and agencies, not courts, were the best institutions to make environmental decisions. In a widely read 1970 law review article, Some Thoughts of an Environmental Lawyer in the Wilderness of Environmental Law, 70 Columbia Law Review 612, Sive reclassified New Deal expert agencies as ossified, concrete-pouring mission agencies. He argued that to discipline them, environmental enforcement had to be shared between the agencies and citizens operating through non-governmental organizations.

Another equally influential, fiery young lawyer was Victor Yannacone, Jr., who was suing the chemical companies which manufactured DDT. Yannacone's contribution was less theoretical but equally fundamental. He first coined the term environmental law and succinctly articulated its fundamental norm then and now: "Sue the Bastards." Yannacone was able to create a special environmental section in the American Trial Lawyers Association in 1969. Two years later, the august American Bar Association quickly followed suit. The first American Bar Association committee, which is the forerunner of the current Section on Environment, Energy, and Resources (SEER), was formed in 1971. Both lawyers were present at Airlie House.

Things moved quickly after *Scenic Hudson*. Lawsuits challenging administrative agency decisions such as pipeline and powerline routes, interstate route locations, and the failure to include national forest land in the newly created wilderness system. The academy responded quickly to these developments, which helped to lay the foundation for the explosion of environmental law in the 1970s. Law and the Environment included a bibliography of 221 law review articles written between 1965 and 1968.

From the Courtroom to the Classroom

Who were the small group of established teachers that responded to a growing quasi-environmental problem, atomic energy, by introducing courses in its regulation? One group consisted of a few senior scholars interested in the control of potentially dangerous technology as well as nature protection. A second group consisted of young teachers interested in air and water pollution, pesticide use reduction and the preservation of scenic areas. The two paths came together at Airlie House. In this section, I single out three senior forerunners who helped bring environmental issues into the classroom and then on six scholars on the cusps of their careers who made major subsequent contributions to the field after Airlie House, with apologies to others whom I have excluded. The senior forerunners are Jacob Beuscher of the University of Wisconsin, David Cavers of the Harvard and Harold Green of George Washington University My candidate pioneers are N. William Hines, James Krier, Arnold Reitze, William Rogers, Joseph Sax and myself. Bill Hines, Joe Sax and I came to environmental law from an interest in natural resources, primarily water use. Joe Sax and I came from an interest in western water law and Bill came from an interest in Midwest water issues affecting agriculture. Jim Krier and Arnold Reitze focused on air pollution and Bill Rogers first introduced the regulation of pesticides into the curriculum. All but Reitze and Rogers were at Airlie House.

We in the first generation were isolated intellectually within our law schools and chaffed at teaching basic courses. With no disrespect for generations of property law scholars, many of us were more concerned with worrying about what was happening around us than the difference between contingent remainders and executory interests. We were often the only persons with such an interest in the faculty, and not all schools were enthusiastic about putting resources in this area. For example, in 1971, the University of California, Berkeley's School of Law founded the Ecology Law Quarterly. The impetus came from a suggestion of a few San Francisco attorneys, and the journal was launched despite the skepticism of the dean. Fortunately, Airlie House re-enforced our belief that environmental law was a subject worth dedicating our careers to developing.

The Senior Forerunners of Environmental Law

There are always antecedents to new developments, and a small group of older, established scholars had been interested in the social costs of the exploitation of natural resources and the application of new technologies since the 1950s. Three names stand out, Jake Beuscher of Wisconsin, David Cavers of Harvard, and Harold Green of George Washington University.

Professors Cavers and Green came at environmental issues through an interest in the regulation of modern technology, primarily atomic energy. David Cavers was perhaps the first environmental law teacher. He taught at Harvard between 1942 and 1968 and made two major contributions to environmental law. While a member of the Duke Law School faculty in 1932, he persuaded the law school to start Law and Contemporary Problems. This interdisciplinary journal published a number of influential inter-disciplinary symposia on natural resources and land use issues. At Harvard, he became interested in the regulation of atomic energy, an interest of then-President James Conant. This led Cavers to a broader interest in the social costs of technology. In 1964-1965, he taught a seminar in Government Regulation and Environmental Hazards, and before his retirement, he taught a course in the regulation of atomic energy and air and water pollution generally. After he retired, he and the eminent administrative law scholar, Louis Jaffe, who described himself as an "unmitigated environmentalist," jointly taught an environmental law seminar. Both Cavers and Jaffe attended the Airlie House Conference. Jaffe contributed a short chapter in the Airlie House conference proceedings, Standing to Sue in Conservation Suits, that set out an elegant defense of private attorney generals. As a footnote to history, their course was briefly taught as Legal Process and Technological Change by Lawrence Tribe in the Spring of 1969. Professor Tribe had worked in the Office of Technology Assessment before joining the Harvard Law School faculty and becoming the leading constitutional law scholar of his generation.

Jacob Beuscher was one of the leaders of the Wisconsin "law-in-action" movement which focused on the on-the-ground application of law and the economic and social forces that contributed to its evolution. In the 1950s he conducted a pioneering analysis of Midwestern states water law in the 1950s and published a pioneering set of water law materials in 1964 shortly before his death in 1967. The book covered public trust and pollution issues in depth. Beuscher was represented at Airlie House by a protégé, James McDonald of the University of Wisconsin School of Law.

The Water Group

Between 1966 and 1967, law schools began teaching courses about environmental management from several different perspectives. Three of us, N. William Hines of the University of Iowa, Joe Sax at the Universities of Colorado and Michigan, and myself at Indiana University, Bloomington came at environmental protection largely through an interest in water.

Bill Hines

Bill Hines was an early, influential leader in environmental law scholarship and curriculum development before he was sucked into law school administration. Although born in Chicago, Bill was raised on a dairy farm outside of Kansas City. After finishing first in his class at the University Of Kansas School Of Law in 1961, he began a two-year teaching fellowship at Harvard. In an early sign of how quickly his career would develop, shortly after arriving in Cambridge, Bill was offered a position at the University Of Iowa College Of Law which included a reduced teaching load and a position in the newly created Agriculture Law Center. He was almost immediately was named director. His interest in agriculture's water quality and quantity problems led to a series of monographs on these issues and laid the foundation for his rapid emergence as a leading environmental scholar and curriculum innovator.

Between 1966 and 1971, Bill published six major articles on water and air pollution. His three Iowa Law Review articles on the history of federal, state, and interstate water pollution regulations remain the leading analysis of water pollution law prior to the enactment of the Clean Water Act in 1972. He also did pioneering work on what came to be known as non-point source pollution. In the mid-1960s, the University Of Iowa College Of Law reformed its curriculum to include a greater public law component to reflect the growing role of government in addressing a number of pressing social problems. Bill's contribution was to develop materials for a Property II course, Resource Planning, first taught in 1967. It started with private land-use governance, servitudes, and covered a range of topics that came be the core of early courses in environmental law including regulatory takings, planning, water allocation systems, pollution prevention stormwater management, federal and state laws to protect natural resources and a topic opened up by *Scenic Hudson*, litigation strategies to protect sensitive environmental resources.

Bill attended the Airlie House Conference, and prepared a background paper, quoted extensively in my chapter, describing his course. He continued to make major contributions to the new field, including his work on water pollution control for one of the last gasps of the rational 1960s, the 1973 report of the National Water Commission, Water for the Future. Unfortunately for environmental law, his equally impressive administrative talents were immediately recognized, and he was named dean in 1977. He served with great distinction until 2004, securing a new building and guiding Iowa to a top 30 law school. As a footnote, Bill resumed his environmental scholarship after retiring as dean and even after retiring from the faculty, continues to teach an elective version of the property course he created.

Joseph Sax

Joe Sax's monumental career is fully covered in Chapter 6, but I want to trace out his early and fast route to environmental law. Joe's introduction to water law was initially involuntary. A native Chicagoan, Joe came to know and love the West through family car trips to the western National Parks. Five years after graduating from the University of Chicago Law School, Joe landed a job at the University of Colorado and was assigned water law even though he had no experience or prior interest in the field. In typical Joe fashion, he quickly mastered the subject, produced a complete set of bound photocopied materials by 1965, and in 1968 published the first modern water law casebook with a full coverage of water pollution law. Simultaneously, his deep dive into the fascinating history of California's alienation of its tidelands in the 19th and early 20th-centuries and subsequent efforts to reassert public rights in them led him to write his path-breaking public trust article.

A. Dan Tarlock

After my first year of law, to my total shock, I was elected to the Stanford Law Review. After a failed attempt to write a note on some obscure Federal Trade Commission rule, I asked for a replacement topic and was given a recent Colorado water rights case that no one else wanted. Learning about western water law dovetailed nicely with my long interest in the history of the region, and my case comment had brought me to the late Charlie Meyers as a research assistant on his landmark work on the Colorado River. A long hospital stay during my third year allowed me to read books such as John Wesley Powell's *Report on the Lands of the Arid Regions of the United States* which led to a half-baked idea of linking the conservation movement to law. I decided to join the Sierra Club. In those days, one had to have a member letter to join the elite Sierra Club, and Charlie told me that a "relatively" well-known author and member, Wallace Stegner, taught in the English Department. I made an appointment to meet with him; he agreed to write the letter and wished me luck with my idea. When I took water law in the winter of 1965, I asked Charlie if I could write a paper on the legal ways to protect free-flowing rivers. I still remember his terse, Texas-twang response: "I don't think there's much there but OK." It only earned me a B plus, but it became my first published article and launched by teaching career.

The Air and Pesticide Group

James Krier

Jim Krier, an Airlie House participant, entered environmental law by chance. After two years in private practice in Washington, D.C., he took a position at the UCLA School of Law. The school had recently received a Ford Foundation grant to develop an environmental law curriculum, and the dean asked Jim if he would teach a course in environmental law. After first telling the dean that there was no such thing, Jim began to prepare a course after being offered a rare benefit in those days, summer compensation. Before moving to Los Angeles, Malcolm Baldwin, one of the organizers of the Airlie House, heard of his plans and invited Jim to the conference, and asked him to write about the burden of proof in environmental litigation, in keeping with the litigation theme of the conference. In contrast to the water people, air pollution was a natural focus for someone living in smoggy Los Angeles. Jim's 1971 casebook, *Environmental Law and Policy*, takes the prize as the first environmental law casebook issued by a major law school publisher.

Jim quickly became a leading environmental law scholar and was a leader in applying the insights of the then new law and economics movement to environmental law. After UCLA, he taught at Stanford before joining the University of Michigan Law School Faculty in 1983. Jim continued to publish major environmental articles into the 1990s before switching his focus to property where he made major theoretical contributions.

Arnold Reitze

Arnold Reitze is a classic example of someone following a youthful passion to become one of the nation's leading experts on the Clean Air Act and environmental law generally. He grew up in Jersey City, New Jersey and developed a love of the outdoors and hiking through the Boy Scouts. By age 14, he began hiking the Appalachian Trail and ultimately became an accomplished mountaineer. After graduating from Rutgers Law School, he joined a defense litigation law firm which did toxic tort litigation, including asbestos cases. This experience led to his interest in air pollution. In 1965, he joined the Case Western Reserve Law School faculty.

One year later, Arnold became a pro bono environmental lawyer in addition to teaching natural resources, water law, pollution control, and administrative law with a focus on energy issues. He represented the Izaak Walton League, the American Lung Association, and Ohio's Citizens for Clean Air and Water, becoming an expert in the early, weak air and water statutes, including the air pollution conference process under the 1963 Clean Air Act. He also participated in the efforts to clean up the Great Lakes under the International Joint Commission and to establish stream quality standards under the 1965 Federal Water Pollution Control Act.

In 1969, the Ford Foundation funded three law school programs in environmental law. In 1969 and in 1970 Arnold became the founding director of George Washington University Law School's environmental law program. In addition to his prodigious clean air scholarship, informed by advanced degrees in environmental science and technology, he directed an environmental L.L.M program educating a number of civilian US Army Corps of Engineers Lawyers and JAG officers. He retired from George Washington University in 2008 and taught for another decade at the University of Utah Law School.

Bill Rogers

Bill Roger's extraordinary career, which combined prodigious scholarship with what came to be called environmental justice activism, deserves a separate chapter, if not book. Fortunately, a partial summary is available in a tribute organized by the University of Washington School of Law in 2007 and published in 82 Washington Law Review, Vol. 3. Bill offered one of the pioneer environmental law courses at the University of Washington School of Law in 1967. Like some of us, influenced by the Law in Action movement of the University of Wisconsin, he looked around him and focused on local conflicts. Shortly after that, he added pesticide regulation to the core environmental law curriculum, although pesticide overuse remains an understudied subject. William H. Rodgers, Jr., The Persistent Problem of the Persistent Pesticides: A Lesson in Environmental Law, 70 Columbia Law Review 567 (1970).

Airlie House: From Law of the Environment to Environmental Law

The Road to Airlie House

In the Fall of 1968, I was sitting in my office at Indiana University, Bloomington when I received a phone call from Sheldon Plager of the University of Illinois College of Law, whom I knew by reputation from a book, Florida Water Law, co-authored with Dean Frank Maloney published that year. Sheldon invited me to a conference on law and environment in the Virginia hunt country scheduled for the next Fall, and he asked me to prepare a paper on the state of environmental law teaching in law schools. As a young law teacher, starting my third year of teaching, I was thrilled and surprised to learn that besides the conference expenses; there was money for me to interview people who were developing courses. Of course, I said yes.

The Airlie House Conference was a seminal moment in the development of environmental law, more important for its aftermath than for the two days of deliberations. Environmental law developed rapidly after Airlie House and all four conditions for a sustainable area, real law, a specialty practice, a core of academics to synthesize the rapidly developing law and a place in the law school curriculum, were in place. As one of the many memorials to the pioneering "environmental" lawyer, David Sive put it, at Airlie House, "[h]is essential argument was that "environmental law" needed to exist." It was the first major gathering of those us already doing environmental law and trying to figure out how to teach it. It also brought to together many of the lawyers, primarily working for Congressional committees or environmental organizations were creating environmental law out of whole cloth. The conference helped to create the two communities and joined them together. It would be pretentious to compare to Airlie House to the 1787 Constitutional Convention. However, I think no other modern legal subject can trace its origins to a specific event. And, in my 48 years of teaching that followed Airlie House, I never attended a gathering whether people were aware of the importance of what they were considering.

Airlie House is an 1899 mansion and farm in Warrenton, Virginia outside of Washington, D.C. It became a conference center in 1961 and was dubbed, according to its website, an "Island of Thought." In the 1960s, one of the major environmental organizations was the Conservation Foundation supported by the Conservation and Research Foundation. The Foundation had funded a conference in 1965 on the Future Environments of North America, which produced one of the early and influential collection papers by of scientists and public policy students concerned with environmental quality. The Foundation's main focus was land acquisition, but it had a young lawyer on the staff, Malcolm Baldwin, who had the vision that environmental law should be a field of teaching and practice because more needed to be done to protect the environment beyond land acquisition. With support from the parent research foundation, he formed a committee consisting of Russel Train, the head of the Conservation Foundation from 1965-1969 and the Administrator of the EPA from 1973-1977, three law professors, George Lefcoe of Yale, Sheldon Plager of Illinois and Joseph Sax of Michigan. They were joined by William Van Ness, Jr. Special Counsel to the Senate Committee on Interior and Insular Affairs who would shortly become famous as the chief draftsman of NEPA, and Wallace Bowman of the Environmental Policy Division of the Library of Congress.

The participants were already leaders in the conservation field, established or rising academics and Congressional staff members who would help draft much of the legislation that still forms the core of environmental law and practice. In addition to the law professors discussed earlier, among the participants who would play major roles in the field were: (1) David Currie of the University of Chicago. David was one of the first teachers at an elite law school to embrace the subject. He had drafted the Illinois Environmental Protection Act and served as the first chair of the newly formed Illinois Pollution Control Board. (2) Thomas Jorling, Minority Counsel to the Senate Committee on Public Works. Along with Leon Billings, Jorling led the bi-partisan drafting of the Clean Air and Water Acts. (3) J. Michael McCloskey was the Executive Director of the Sierra Club between 1969 and 1985, and, along with the fiery David Brower, helped move the Sierra Club into the forefront of environmental advocacy and litigation. (4) James Moorman was the first head of the Sierra Club Legal Defense Fund and later Assistant Attorney General for Lands and Natural Resources during the Carter Administration. (5) Nicholas Robinson was perhaps the youngest attendee having just finished his second year at Columbia University Law School. He went on to a distinguished teaching career at Pace University Law School and became one of the major figures in international and comparative environmental law. Anthony Roisman was a member of a small law firm doing Federal power Commission (now FERC) work. Along with his two partners, Edward Berlin and Gladys Kessler (one of the two women at the conference) wrote a paper Law in Action: the Public Trust Doctrine, and (7) Victor Yannacone, Jr., whose "sue the bastards" strategy developed in the DDT litigation remains the pillar of environmental law. Finally, a shy young activist who had made a name for himself in automobile safety and whose organization would soon make major contributions to environmental protection, Ralph Nader, stopped by for cocktails.

The Consequences of Airlie House

The most lasting consequence was the creation of Environmental Law Institute, which celebrated its golden anniversary in 2019, and the Environmental

Reporter that the Institute was established to create. The Environmental Reporter was the first systematic collection of the flood of litigation and laws that followed NEPA and the Clean Air and Air Acts. As ELI's website explains:

> The major proposal presented at the conference was a prospectus for an Environmental Law Reporter. A monthly publication was proposed that would collect environmental statutes, regulations, court decisions and other documents, and would carefully analyze developments in the field. The conferees warmly endorsed the prospectus, signaling the beginning of a successful effort to secure Ford Foundation funding for the Environmental Law Reporter, within the framework of a new institute.

Environmental and related courses grew rapidly after Airlie House and specialized journals followed. An environmental law program started in 1969 at Lewis and Clark law School in Portland, and by 1970, environmental law was being offered at several schools. Specialty journals soon followed. The weekly updates were essential reading for all environmental law teachers and practitioners.

Another lasting impact of Airlie House is the synergy it created among participants. For example, a meeting David Cavers and David Currie at Airlie House led to the funding of a study of the control in Los Angeles led by Jim Krier. His book, Pollution and Policy, co-authored with Edmund Ursin and published in 1978, remains a classic study of the intersection between science and politics in the establishment of environmental quality regimes.

For me, the conference's most important legacy was the creation of unique community of scholars and practitioners. Before email and the internet gave birth to virtual communities, Airlie House created a "pre-virtual" community by helping to shift the focus of environmental law scholarship outward from the legal academy. We in the first generation had little in common with most of our colleagues other than personal ties and the same non-specialized legal education that we had been given. Environmental law came not from the corpus of existing law school libraries, but from a variety of outside sources. And, it was relentlessly focused on innovation and reform, not simply the synthesis and marginal adjustment of existing cases and statutes. It soon became apparent that we needed considerable scientific and technical knowledge to understand the issues and to suggest effective legal responses. As well as reading widely in ecology, economics, philosophy and history, we had to go out the law school to find "tutors" in the university. We also had to go outside the academy to keep abreast of the cascade of new developments that began in the 1970s such as legislation, administrative regulations, and National Academy of Sciences studies.

Travel also became a way of life. Continuing Legal Education providers began to organize conferences as did other organizations. Our community expanded to include not just other law professors but those working major conservation and wildlife protection organizations, the names of which would begin to appear as plaintiffs in key cases (the term non-governmental organization had not yet been coined), and the lawyers who soon developed major environmental practices. We saw colleagues with increasing frequency which led to collaboration and the exchange of ideas as well as last friendships.

Conclusion: Why Did Environmental Law Flourish?

Despite, the rapid emergence of environmental laws and scholarship in the 1970s, it was not inevitable that environmental law would sustain itself as a curricular and practice specialty. Not all the political movements that arose in the 1960s found a permanent place in law school curricula. Nor did they all morph into lucrative practice areas. The activist 1960s created four new political movements with important legal ramifications: civil rights for disenfranchised, first for racial minorities and then for other oppressed minorities such as the LGBT community, environmental feminism, poverty reduction, and environmental protection. All four resulted in new courses and scholarships. But, only two, environmental law and civil rights also generated substantial practice opportunities. All areas have all had a significant influence on diverse areas of the law and legal scholarship, but only environmental law sustained itself as a vibrant area of teaching, scholarship and practice.

The simple answer to the survival of environmental law is that environmental problems have only been partially solved at and continue to worsen both in the United States and worldwide. However, I like to think that Airlie House gave those of us trying to grapple with legal solutions, and the many talented academics and lawyers who soon followed, a sense of legitimacy and urgency and laid the foundation for the community that exists to this day.

Chapter 5

Bruce Babbitt: The Man Who Saved the Endangered Species Act

J.B. Ruhl[1]

On a warm spring morning in 1994, cars began pulling in to the parking lot of Matt's El Rancho, an iconic Mexican restaurant in Austin, Texas, that has been serving up tacos and tamales from 1956 to this day. For anyone familiar with Austin politics at the time, the stream of patrons walking through the front door was an unlikely, odd assembly of landowners, politicians, environmental activists, and real estate developers not usually seen in the same room without an argument arising. They gathered in the large patio room in the front of the restaurant, where tables and chairs had been arranged in a large square open in the middle. The guests started heaping the sumptuous buffet offerings on their plates and finding seats near friends.

At the time, I was an attorney practicing as a partner in Fulbright & Jaworski, a staid Houston-based law firm with offices spread throughout Texas

[1] J. B. Ruhl is the David Daniels Allen Distinguished Chair of Law at Vanderbilt Law School in Nashville, TN. He is an expert in environmental, natural resources and property law, and also studies the legal industry and legal technology. He was named director of Vanderbilt's Program on Law and Innovation in 2014 and serves as the Co-director of the Energy, Environment and Land Use Program. Before he joined Vanderbilt's law faculty in 2011, he was the Matthews & Hawkins Professor of Property at the Florida State University College of Law, where he had taught since 1999. His influential scholarly articles relating to climate change, the Endangered Species Act, ecosystems, governance, and other environmental and natural resources law issues have appeared in the California, Duke, Georgetown, Stanford and Vanderbilt law reviews, the environmental law journals at several top law schools, and peer-reviewed scientific journals. His works have been selected by peers as among the best law review articles in the field of environmental law twelve times from 1989 to 2018. Over the course of his career, he has been a visiting professor at Harvard Law School, George Washington University Law School, the University of Texas Law School, Vermont Law School, and Lewis and Clark College of Law. He began his academic career at the Southern Illinois University School of Law, where he taught from 1994 to 1999 and earned his Ph.D. in geography. Before entering the academy, he was a partner with Fulbright & Jaworski (now Norton Rose Fulbright) in Austin, Texas, where he also taught on the adjunct faculty of the University of Texas School of Law.

and elsewhere (now known as Norton Rose Fulbright, it was one of the largest law firms in the world then and still is). I had been invited to the breakfast on behalf of my client, the Austin Home Builders Association. I found a seat between a newspaper reporter and another local attorney, exchanged some small talk, and dug in to my huevos rancheros. A few minutes later an attorney for a local environmental interest group sitting a few seats away got my attention and wagged his finger at me, threatening that his organization was going to sue one of my clients and the federal government to challenge a permit the government had issued under the Endangered Species Act (ESA) authorizing my client's proposed subdivision development. He described the permit as, "deeply flawed." My response was something to the effect of, "Bring it on, it's bulletproof."

That exchange captures the tension in the room that day. Austin had been ensnarled for several years in controversy over how much the ESA restricted land development in the region and how to solve the problem. Section 4 of the ESA requires the Department of the Interior, through its U.S. Fish and Wildlife Service (FWS), and the Department of Commerce, through its National Marine Fisheries Service (NMFS), to identify species that are threatened or endangered with extinction. When a species is so "listed," Section 7 of the statute requires federal agencies to consult with FWS and NMFS to ensure activities they carry out, fund, or authorize do not jeopardize the continued existence of the species. Also, under Section 9 of the ESA all persons, public and private, must avoid "taking" any individuals of the species. Take includes the obvious, such as killing or trapping, but also sweeps in activities that impair the species' habitat to the point of causing death or injury to any individuals of the species. That would be real estate development. With all the species that had recently been listed with habitat in Austin and surrounding Travis County—in the air, on the ground, and underground—the combined effect of these two restrictions was to pose significant and costly compliance problems for almost any land development project in the area. We had gathered that day to hear about a solution.

Our guest of honor was Bruce Babbitt, whom President Clinton had appointed as Secretary of the Department of the Interior (Interior), and he was there to tell us there was a better way. The ESA includes provisions for permitting land development projects that otherwise would violate the take prohibition, provided the project is designed to meet certain conservation standards. ESA compliance in Austin and elsewhere had been handled on a project-by-project basis under these permitting provisions, one of which is found in Section 7 of the statute for projects carried out, funded, or approved by federal agencies, and the other of which is found in Section 10 for projects without that federal agency connection. Having represented dozens of public and private clients seeking both kinds of permits, I knew how expensive and protracted the permitting process could be and the costly impact the conservation conditions could have on their projects. A proposed local public road or school might need to be redesigned, or a proposed private subdivision development might have to set aside dozens of acres as conservation. To be sure, the goal of protecting endangered species is paramount, but it comes at a cost and the costs were building up in Austin. As much as the local real estate industry was squawking, however, the local environmental activist community was calling for even more species listings and tougher restrictions in ESA land development permits.

The solution Secretary Babbitt had come to Austin to promote was called a "multi-species regional plan." The idea was to pool resources to purchase and conserve a 10,000 acre expanse of prime species habitat. This chunk of habitat would serve as the mitigation for future development in the area that degraded habitat of the protected species. Land developers in those areas would need only to pay a fee—albeit a costly one—and follow pre-set conditions and they would be clear to go under the ESA. In fact, work on designing the regional plan had begun a year earlier, led by FWS and staff at the City of Austin. I had been involved in the stakeholder group, so I had a sense of where the plan was headed. The purpose of Secretary Babbitt's visit was to get the various interests behind a local bond referendum Travis County had placed on the ballot for the following month's election.

The key to making the regional plan work was to purchase the preserve lands up front, with the fees imposed on future land development used to pay off the bonds over time. Austin city voters has approved a $22 million bond referendum two years earlier to support habitat acquisition within the city limits. Now it was the county's turn to pony up. As straightforward as that sounded, $49 million was a big ask, and not everyone in the room was on board. Babbitt was in town to pump up support for the plan and the bond referendum.

When the time came for the Secretary to address the crowd, he laid out the options with a commanding grasp of the facts and the practicalities. Continuing with the case-by-case permitting approach was fraught with problems, he argued. The costs were high for each project, and the mitigation habitat required to offset the projects' impacts wound up in a less effective "postage stamp" pattern rather than in big tracts. The investment in the preserves would pay off for the entire community many times over, as an expanse of open space that size near the central city would not only protect the species more effectively but also promote recreation and water quality. The regional plan approach was the way to go, and the bonds would allow us to assemble the preserve lands in one push rather than in bits and pieces over time, if ever. I became convinced, as were others.

As it turned out, the bond referendum failed. It was competing with other bond proposals that enjoyed broader support. Given that the preserve lands were to be located in the affluent western part of the city and county, the regional plan bond proposal failed to attract support in the lower-income and minority communities of the east side. But the regional plan did not die. The energy and unity Secretary Babbitt had sparked lived on, and we found a way to finance the plan over time. To be sure, not everyone was happy with the plan—that is true even to this day—and the region's ESA woes have by no means abated. But the breakfast at Matt's El Rancho that day was a turning point, thanks largely to Secretary Babbitt.

Living through the Austin ESA experience was the highlight of my legal practice career, but what makes Bruce Babbitt's cameo appearance at a Mexican restaurant breakfast worthy of a chapter in a book on the pioneers of environmental law? Why should law students and lawyers learn about what Babbitt did? The short answer is, he saved the Endangered Species Act. The Austin regional plan effort was just the tip of the iceberg on that score.

But there is more to it than that, as if that weren't enough. Babbitt did not just fend off assaults from Congress against the ESA, he did so by transforming the way the ESA works, designing and instituting programs that have become models for the balance between conservation and development. He was the architect of a vast agenda of administrative reform—an end-run around Congress—that responded to complaints about the ESA's impact on property rights and economic development. Whether those complaints were valid or not, they were fueling discontent in Congress, putting the ESA in the bullseye of Representative Newt Gingrich's "Contract with America." The unthinkable had become a real possibility—Congress might move to amend the ESA, and not to strengthen it. Babbitt's counter-punch strategy was not to pitch a fit—he simply made the ESA work better and thereby took the wind out of Congress's sails. The ESA made it through unscathed.

Babbitt's maneuvering, recounted in detail in this chapter, offers a profound lesson in administrative law and the exercise of Executive Branch power. Although it is widely regarded as having some of the sharpest teeth among the environmental statutes, the ESA is remarkably brief compared to the Clean Water Act, Clean Air Act, and its other kin. It is brimming with undefined terms and open-ended authorities. Babbitt and his team at Interior tapped into that opportunity, taking full advantage of the wide berth courts give agencies to interpret the statutes they implement. Wisely, the reform agenda had a core theme—make the ESA work better *for landowners* without sacrificing the protections it extends to imperiled species. Under his watch the Department of Interior rolled out program after program with that as the goal, and public and private landowners, as well as state and local governments, came on board. Ironically, it was hard-line environmental groups who felt like outsiders looking in through the window. But it had to be done, and Babbitt—who had impeccable "green" credentials—was the one to do it.

It has been said that "only Nixon could go to China," meaning it took a staunch Republican president to open relations with the Communist regime. In much the same way, only a solid Democrat beloved by conservationists could pull off sweeping reforms of the ESA programs designed to embrace landowner interests and incentives. In short, only Babbitt could go to ESA reform. This is the story of how he got there, and much more.

The Big Picture

Twenty-five years after I first met Secretary Babbitt at the Matt's El Rancho meeting in Austin, I spent two hours chatting with him in the sun-filled conference room of the Wyss Foundation, a nonprofit conservation organization housed in a classic brownstone just off of Dupont Circle in Washington, DC. I had not seen or spoken with him since the Austin meeting—by no means were we personally acquainted other than knowing about each other's work on the ESA—but I wanted to interview him for this chapter. Our mutual friend John Leshy, a preeminent natural resources law professor now on the faculty at UC-Hastings, had taken an eight-year hiatus from legal academia to serve as Solicitor of Interior during Babbitt's administration. I explained this book's focus and asked John if he would be willing to connect me with Babbitt for an interview. He generously did so, and I was gratified when Secretary Babbitt quickly emailed me saying he'd be happy to meet. I was even more gratified when, learning of the interview, the Rocky Mountain Mineral Law Foundation approved a grant request to cover my travel expenses—evidence of how much Babbitt's work on the ESA continues to resonate.[2] This chapter draws extensively from our meeting and from the pleasant talk we had over lunch afterwards at a nearby Italian restaurant.

To prepare for the interview, I re-read numerous law journal articles I and other legal academics and practitioners published about the ESA, particularly those covering events surrounding the Austin experience and Babbitt's administrative reform agenda.[3] Binge-reading the articles brought back many (mostly fond) memories, as well as renewed admiration for what Babbitt accomplished.

---

[2] I am indebted to the Foundation for their support and to Jan Laitos for assistance in securing the grant.

[3] For my work focused in particular on the Austin experience and ESA reform, see J.B. Ruhl, *Endangered Species Act Innovations in the Post-Babbittonian Era—Are There Any?*, 14 DUKE ENVIRONMENTAL LAW & POLICY FORUM 419 (2004); J.B. Ruhl, *Who Needs Congress? An Agenda for Administrative Reform of the Endangered Species Act*, 6 N.Y.U. ENVTL. L.J. 367 (1997-1998); J.B. Ruhl, *Biodiversity Conservation and the Ever-Expanding Web of Federal Laws Regulating Nonfederal Lands: Time for Something Completely Different?*, 66 COLO. L. REV. 555 (1995); J. B. Ruhl, *Regional Habitat Conservation Planning under the Endangered Species Act: Pushing the Legal and Practical Limits of Species Protection*, 44 SW. L.J. 1393 (1990). For the work of others I consulted on those themes, see John D. Leshy, *The Babbitt Legacy at the Department of Interior: A Preliminary View*, 31 ENVTL. L. 199 (2001); Joseph L. Sax, *Environmental Law at the Turn of the Century; A Reportorial Fragment of Contemporary History*, 88 CAL. L. REV. 2375 (2000). I also am co-author of a law school casebook that deeply explores the history and context of the ESA and several other case studies included in this chapter. *See* JOHN

I also read the book he published in 2005, *Cities in the Wilderness*, which offers a sweeping account of his time as Interior Secretary as well as a vision for the future of conservation in an urbanizing world.[4] The book opened my eyes to other accomplishments Babbitt chalked up as Secretary, many of which I had not seen through my ESA glasses.

After the interview—in truth, while working on this chapter—for background and context I got in touch with several people who worked closely with Secretary Babbitt at Interior, as well as some "ESA wonks" heavily involved in ESA work at the time. Without exception, when I told them why I was getting in touch each person responded immediately with eagerness to tell their story about Babbitt and his influence on their careers.[5]

More than an account of my sources,[6] I offer this background to frame the big picture about Secretary Babbitt before going through the history in detail. Based on what I saw as an ESA practitioner and later as an academic closely studying ESA developments, and drawing from all the sources I used for this chapter, three themes underlie Babbitt's pioneering impact. The first is that he was a hands-on Secretary, going into the field to understand context and help solve problems. The Austin trip was not an isolated exception to an office-based administration. Quite the opposite, as Babbitt explained to me (and I can confirm first hand), the ESA was mired in collision conflicts and bureaucratic impasse around the nation when he took over at Interior. He quickly concluded that the only pathway out was for him to be on the ground, personally talking and listening to scientists, policy-makers, and community stakeholders. He did so in Texas, the Pacific Northwest, California, Arizona, Nevada, Florida, and countless other places during his eight years at Interior. And he was effective. Marc Ebbin, who served six years as one of several Special Assistants to the Secretary, was with Babbitt on many of these trips and told me Babbitt was able to talk seamlessly across the political and economic spectrums.

The second theme is that Babbitt was also hands-on in Washington and well-versed in the details of statutes and policies under Interior's domain. He did not delegate the important points of ESA reform to deputies and wait for their reports, or send representatives for congressional testimony on matters critical

---

Nagle, J.B. Ruhl & Kalyani Robbins, The Law of Biodiversity and Ecosystem Management (4th ed. 2019).

[4] Bruce Babbitt, Cities in the Wilderness: A New Vision of Land Use in America (2005).

[5] I am thankful especially to Don Barry, Marc Ebbin, and David Hayes, from whose interviews I draw extensively.

[6] I have not burdened this chapter with footnotes in "law journal" extent or style. All content can be found in my interview notes, the law journal articles and my casebook cited above, Babbitt's book, and a few online biographical accounts accessible by searching for "Bruce Babbitt."

to Interior—he inserted himself personally in the processes and came with a lawyer's knowledge of the law and policy. As Marc Ebbin put it, Babbitt was a technician when it came to his grasp of the statutory and regulatory text Interior was charged with administering.

Lastly, Babbitt was able to innovate because he envisioned opportunities where others did not and was willing to step out of politics to enter public policy making in its pure form. Don Barry, who served as Assistant Secretary for Parks and Wildlife under Babbitt, told me that the day after the Democrats lost both Houses of Congress in the 1994 mid-term elections, the mood was glum in Interior's executive suite. When Secretary Babbitt arrived, however, he was positive. As he put it to them in his pep talk, the challenge of dealing with a hostile Congress was an opportunity to do things they would have been uncomfortable doing before. Ironically, in other words, he couldn't have sold ESA reform and his many other innovations to the conservation community had the environment not been up against the ropes in Congress.

Following some brief biographical material on Secretary Babbitt's early days and his road to Interior, I use five case studies to drive home these three attributes of the Babbitt run at Interior: (1) the Northwest Forest Plan; (2) ESA administrative reform, which receives the bulk of my attention; (3) National Monument designations under the Antiquities Act; (4) a 1997 legislative overhaul of the National Wildlife Refuge System; and (5) a series of "water war" resolutions Babbitt orchestrated. In each case you will see that Babbitt was hands-on in the field, hands-on in Washington, and a pioneering innovator of environmental law.

Early Days

Bruce Babbitt entered the world on June 27, 1938, and grew up in Flagstaff, Arizona. The Babbitts were a prosperous ranching family, and young Bruce naturally enjoyed the hiking and skiing the Flagstaff area offers. He developed a strong affinity for nature and conservation values in his formative years.

Babbitt left Arizona in 1956 to attend the University of Notre Dame, where he majored in geology with the intent of returning to Arizona to work in the mining industry. After graduating with honors in 1960, he received a scholarship to earn a Master of Science degree in geophysics from the English University of Newcastle. Along the way, however, Babbitt's interests turned to public service, and after graduating from Newcastle he entered Harvard Law School. After graduating from Harvard in 1965, he worked with the Volunteers in Service to America (VISTA) for two years before returning to Arizona to work with a Phoenix law firm. He and Harriet (Hattie) Coons wed in 1968 and have remained together ever since.

The Road to Interior

Babbitt entered the public service sphere in 1974, when he was elected Arizona's attorney general. While taking on high-profile land sale fraud, price-fixing, and insurance cases as attorney general, Babbitt was unexpectedly thrust into the governor's office. The elected governor at the time, Raul Castro, resigned in 1977 to become ambassador to Argentina, and Arizona's Secretary of State, Wesley Bolin, was next in line to become governor by succession. Bolin died the next year, however, and Babbitt as attorney general was next in line. He became the youngest governor in Arizona history, at age 39, on March 4, 1978, and after finishing out Castro's remaining term was elected to two full terms as governor with overwhelming voter support.

Babbitt described his agenda as governor to me as "pretty conventional," and he was perceived as a moderate that balanced fiscal restraint with progressive social and environmental policies. On the environmental front, his focus was on expanding state parks, planning for state lands, and water management. He oversaw adoption of a landmark groundwater management plan and, in June 1980, a comprehensive state water bill that was hashed out in negotiations with water users, with little input from environmental interests. That was not because Babbitt was insensitive to environmental concerns. It was because giving them seats at the table would have killed the bill, so Babbitt relied on his internal conservation compass to ensure the environment was represented. This brand of pragmatic politics would surface often in Babbitt's career, including as Interior Secretary.

While eminently qualified for the position, serendipity helped put Babbitt in the Secretary's office at Interior. While Babbitt was governor, in 1985 he and another young governor named Bill Clinton helped found the Democratic Leadership Council. The Council focused on moving the party towards more centrist agendas at the national level, pulling back from the leftward turn it took beginning in the 1960s. He also served as chair of the Democratic Governors' Association. Both of these positions gave Babbitt national exposure, and the connection with Clinton grew strong, as the two families became good friends. That combination proved game-changing in his career.

Babbitt sought the Democratic Party's 1988 nomination—the first to declare—but dropped out early in the race. His soft-spoken manner and generally humble style did not match up well with modern presidential campaigning. He returned to law practice in Phoenix and also became president of the League of Conservation Voters. In the 1992 election, however, his friend Bill Clinton won the White House and the Democrats easily held on to both Houses of Congress. A favorite of conservationists and a known political moderate with a national reputation, President Clinton's nomination of Babbitt for Interior Secretary took less than a day of Senate hearings and was confirmed by unanimous consent. Bruce Babbitt walked into his first day as Interior Secretary on January 22, 1993, where he served until January 2, 2001. His Assistant Secretary Don Barry described Babbitt to me as the "finest conservation Secretary of the twentieth century." In the pages that follow we see why.

Learning to Love the Spotted Owl

I asked Secretary Babbitt what he was thinking on that first day—where was he going to steer Interior? He knew that the environmental portfolio is scattered all over the place in the federal system and asked himself where he could move the needle. EPA, he sensed from the start, would be making water its centerpiece, and Vice President Gore claimed climate change. Within Interior, the National Park Service was in good shape, and the National Wildlife Refuge System was as well, although the latter came under fire later in his tenure. He could make a difference, he thought, with the ESA, which was under siege by landowner and property rights interests. Also there was the Bureau of Land Management (BLM), which in the federal public lands domain inherited the "leftovers" after choice federal lands had been allotted to parks, refuges, forests, and other uses. BLM was essentially in the business of granting cattle grazing permits and had for all practical purposes been left out of the federal conservation family, and Babbitt had ideas for how to change that. Alas, he did not have long to scope out these agendas before reality struck. Babbitt was about to learn a lot about a majestic bird—the northern spotted owl—and how incendiary the ESA had become.

The northern spotted owl is believed to have historically inhabited most forests throughout southwestern British Columbia, western Washington and Oregon, and northwestern California as far south as the San Francisco Bay. Loss and degradation of its nesting, roosting, and foraging habitat due to timber harvesting, land conversions, natural disturbances such as fire and windstorms, as well as competition with encroachment by the larger, more generalist barred owl, had led to a decline of spotted owls throughout much of their historic range. The FWS listed the owl as a threatened species in 1990, providing it all the ESA protections against "take" and "jeopardy" mentioned above, then designated a vast area in the region as its "critical habitat" in 1992. Then, not long before Babbitt took office, a federal judge issued an order halting all timber sales on National Forests. Perfect timing for a new Interior Secretary.

The problem for the owl is that forests with late-successional and old-growth characteristics the species prefers are also preferred for timber harvesting to meet the demand for all types of forest products. As the amount of suitable habitat declined from timber harvesting, so did the number of spotted owls. Listing the owl gave it protections under the ESA designed to help it recover, but those protections necessarily also severely restricted timber harvesting throughout the region. Many communities within the owl's range, particularly in rural areas, depended on timber harvesting as their economic base. Timber harvesting employs workers who buy trucks, go with their families to local shops, and so on. The owl increasingly was seen as the enemy, as restricted timber harvesting in turn restricted local economies. And they blamed "the feds." One can debate the true causes and extent of economic decline in the area, but that was the perception, and by the time Babbitt walked into his office at Interior the owl was a big problem.

The owl was Babbitt's first high-profile challenge at Interior and he knew he had to get it right. President Clinton helped kick off the process in April 1993 by convening a town-hall meeting in Portland. This heightened expectations, but after Clinton left Babbitt says what he saw everywhere was "bewildering complexity."

Given his hands-on nature, he realized immediately that it would require his personal involvement and that he could not manage the problem from his office in Washington. He would have to go into the field to talk and listen. But he had to manage an issue in Washington as well. Forests in the owl's range are a mix of private, state, and federal land. The vast majority of the federal land was part of the National Forests System, with additional land in National Parks, Wildlife Refuges, and BLM land. The U.S. Forest Service (USFS) manages the National Forests and sells leases for the timber harvesting that takes place on them, which is extensive. The problem for Babbitt was that USFS is an agency within the Department of Agriculture, meaning that he as Interior Secretary was about to tell another Cabinet officer how to run things.

Babbitt told me the mess he inherited in the Northwest was the catalyst for two important lessons that would help carry him through his tenure at Interior. The first was that it is about *landscapes.* He knew the problem could not be solved one National Forest at a time—he needed to develop a region-wide approach. It came to be known as the Northwest Forest Plan (NWFP). The second lesson was that he needed to gain the confidence of the scientists to help the agencies make science-based policy judgments. The biologists at FWS working on the owl's recovery did not trust the USFS bureaucrats in charge of National Forest timber harvesting. Babbitt needed to give the scientists time to develop a strong science-based plan for forest management, then to get them talking with the policy people.

But being on the ground talking and listening, having a plan, taking a landscape focus, and using a science-based approach wasn't going to be enough—Babbitt needed something to trade. It turned out to be the federal lands. As Don Barry explained, to defuse the controversy on the ground, the federal government agreed to shoulder more of the burden for owl management and recovery so the ESA's timber restrictions could ease off on private and state forests. Ultimately, the NWFP covered over 24 million acres of federal lands in the region, managed by four different federal agencies. The agencies agreed to implement cooperative planning, improved decision making, and coordinated implementation of the NWFP on federal lands, as well as to improve coordination and collaboration with state, tribal, and local governments for management approaches that support or complement the goals of the NWFP.

The details are too extensive and complex to recount here, but the centerpiece of the plan was to drastically reduce timber harvesting on the federal lands and replace that with a network of conservation reserves managed by using an ecosystem-scale strategy. It has succeeded for the most part, though wildfires have become an increasing threat and climate change is disrupting the entire ecological region. Even so, it is clear that Babbitt was instrumental in turning around the timber harvest culture that permeated the USFS, thus making recovery of the owl a real possibility rather than a pipe dream.

Overhauling the ESA to Save the ESA

As complex and controversial as the NWFP was for Babbitt, he had one big advantage on his side—the federal government owned a whole lot of owl habitat, meaning it could impose restrictions on itself. But the ESA applies to state, local, and private lands as well. In those contexts Interior looks like it is telling others what to do, and they don't usually take kindly to that. It did not take long for three other birds to cause Babbitt this kind of heartburn.

Two months after Babbitt took office as Secretary, the FWS listed the coastal California gnatcatcher as a threatened species. A small gray songbird, the gnatcatcher is a resident of scrub dominated plant communities from southern Ventura County southward through Los Angeles, Orange, Riverside, San Bernardino, and San Diego Counties, California into Baja California, Mexico. There is a lot of private land in that swath of California, and the ESA hammer was about to come down on it thanks to the gnatcatcher. As Babbitt puts it in his book, "then the storm broke."

When FWS proposed listing the gnatcatcher, Babbitt received a briefing memo and the supporting scientific materials. The ESA requires that listing decisions be based solely on the biological science—economic impacts cannot be considered—so the memo was pure science. Babbitt was convinced and the gnatcatcher was listed. What Babbitt concedes blindsided him, however, was the land use implications, which he described as a blanket development moratorium on the fastest growing real estate market in California. Media coverage was relentless, telling story after story of delayed and failed subdivision projects, tightened construction lending, and lost jobs. Babbitt told me this was the only time he got heat from the White House—California, after all, had fifty-four electoral votes.

Fortunately for Babbitt, California had enacted the Natural Community Conservation Planning Act in 1991. This provided the platform for the kind of landscape-scale approach Babbitt believed was the future of the ESA. In fact, the state NCCP process had begun to founder under Republican Governor Pete Wilson's administration, which emphasized voluntary landowner participation. The gnatcatcher listing, which a heavy regulatory impact, resuscitated Wilson's political motivations to make the NCCP a solution.

Also fortunate was that San Diego County and, more significantly, the Irvine Company, which owned large tracts of land in gnatcatcher country, were interested in using the NCCP as the mechanism for solving their ESA compliance issues. The Irvine Company was instrumental in going forward. Its sole shareholder, Donald Bren, was a staunch Republican who for all practical purposes owned and ran Orange County, where the not coincidentally city of Irvine is the economic center. Bren preferred negotiation to litigation, and Babbitt agreed to meet with him in Phoenix. Babbitt explained that large tracts of suitable habitat would be needed. Somewhat to his surprise, Bren did not disagree. The question was how much? The two agreed to have their respective biologists teams meet and hammer it out.

Babbitt saw the opportunity for an unprecedented ESA win on private land and assigned his Special Assistant Marc Ebbin to get on the ground in southern California and work with stakeholders to find solutions. Ebbin shuttled between California and Washington, reporting weekly to Babbitt about progress and obstacles. Ebbin told me that Babbitt was as involved in the process as one could ever imagine a Cabinet officer could be, even to the point of taking the process out of FWS leadership's control. Babbitt was also willing to experiment with innovations that had never been used before in ESA programs, doing so largely through contract-like agreements with the state, San Diego County, and the Irvine Company. Many of those innovations, Ebbin explained, were the genesis for the administrative reforms Babbitt began rolling out later. They also concerned FWS leadership. But over time they broke down barriers and ultimately both San Diego County and the Irvine Company agreed to and obtained NCCP/ESA regional plan permits setting aside hundreds of thousands of acres for the gnatcatcher. Babbitt saw this as a defining moment in the transformation of the ESA into an agent of federally-led land use planning guided by a balance between species management and economic development.

While Babbitt was gaining traction in southern California with relative success, however, the picture was not as rosy in other parts of the nation where the ESA had landed on urbanizing landscapes. Many cities could provide examples. I will use Austin, Texas, as the case study, not only because of my personal familiarity with the events but also because it was an early testing ground for transporting ESA innovations from California.

As the opening paragraphs of this chapter explained, things were not going well for the ESA in Austin when Babbitt arrived for the Tex-Mex breakfast. The FWS had listed a small migratory songbird, the black-capped vireo, in 1987. During its breeding season, the vireo inhabits scrubby mid-successional habitat—the kind one might find five or ten years after a wildfire on the way to maturing into a forest landscape not preferred by the vireo. Fire control and urban development reduced the availability of such habitat, leading to the listing. Another migratory songbird species, the golden-cheeked warbler, inhabits woodlands with tall ashe juniper trees during its breeding season. Both species find their breeding season habitat in only one place in the world—central Texas. In effect, between the vireo in scrubby areas and the warbler in woodlands, much of the so-called Texas "Hill Country" was covered.

The hitch is that the two birds winter in parts of Mexico (the vireo) and Central America (the warbler), meaning that one could destroy their habitat in the winter without directly killing any birds. That started to happen a lot, especially for the warbler. In the late 1980s FWS began rattling its sword about the warbler, threatening to list it under the ESA. Indeed, I personally attended one meeting at which an FWS employee made such a threat, which only accelerated habitat destruction as landowners sought to get rid of the problem before the species was listed. Eventually, the FWS had enough of that and listed the warbler in May 1990, warning that habitat destruction in the winter was prohibited if it impaired the species' nesting in the spring. This ignited pitched battles between the agency and landowners in the region.

Austin was entering a boom period in the early 1990s, and the two songbirds were gumming it up. As was happening in southern California because of the gnatcatcher, commercial real estate lenders were wary of the ESA, and development project loans were harder to come by. The situation became so contentious that the FWS, which had its District Office in Fort Worth, opened a field office in Austin. The mood started to improve as the new office began working with landowners to find solutions.

One early innovation the Austin office designed was known as the "bird letter." Working with biologists and lawyers like me, a development project would put together a plan to stay away from identified warbler/vireo habitat, thus avoiding prohibited take of the species. FWS would review the plan and, if satisfied take would not occur, would issue what was essentially a no-action letter that lenders took comfort in. This helped take some heat off the ESA.

Sam Hamilton, who later rose to become Director of the FWS and shortly thereafter tragically died of a heart attack, took over the Austin Field Office and began pulling in the Babbitt reforms one-by-one. The first was the Habitat Conservation Plan (HCP) program. As discussed in the opening of the chapter, the ESA provides two ways to obtain permit approval for otherwise prohibited take, one under Section 7 for project with a federal agency connection (funding or permitting) and one under Section 10 for all other projects. The Section 10 process had only been used a few times when Babbitt took office, most notably for a development in California. Yet many development projects have no federal connection—they need a Section 10 permit. The Austin Field Office became a crucible for designing these HCP permits, and the experience there became the template for designing habitat mitigation as the condition for take approval. In essence, FWS would approve a development in or near warbler/vireo habitat in exchange for conservation of prime habitat elsewhere. But as also discussed in the opening, Babbitt was not satisfied with this "postage stamp" approach, which did not lead to landscape-scale mitigation habitat. This is why he pushed the regional HCP for Austin.

It's possible that ESA innovations might have stopped there—with regional plans the preferred approach and smaller HCPs used to fill in the gaps. Then the mid-term election disaster happened, and Babbitt knew he needed to do more or else the ESA would be on the chopping block in Congress. His strategy was to make the ESA work for landowners like those in Austin and other cities on the hunch that, if it worked for them—if they could get their developments through the ESA with clear rules of the game and reasonable conditions—real estate industry support for dismantling the ESA would diminish. It worked.

As both Don Barry and Marc Ebbin explained to me, after the post-election pep talk, Babbitt formed a team at Interior to brainstorm ESA reforms the agency could implement without congressional involvement. He knew he'd get no help from Congress, so he planned to take advantage of every opportunity the ESA, as it existed, gave the agency to innovate. And Babbitt was hands-on in the process. The team met with him formally every week to vet ideas, discuss progress, and seek input. Don Barry told me the process was completely devoid of political strategizing—it was about making good public policy, even if it made Democrats and conservationists uncomfortable. There were times when he felt euphoric to be part of the process, to see public policy form the way it is supposed to.

To a large extent, Babbitt was able to take this approach because of his relationship with President Clinton. They had been equals, were cut from the same moderate Democrat mold, and remained good friends. Clinton had delegated most oversight on environmental policy to Vice President Gore, whose focus was primarily on climate change, not on gnatcatchers and warblers. Babbitt told me the White House, as a result, was essentially laissez-faire with him, trusting him not to mess things up. This gave Babbitt the space to focus his ESA energy on making landowners rather than conservationists feel better about the statute. Indeed, Babbitt did not feel at all compelled to run his team's ideas by the conservation community. The one exception was Michael Bean, a prominent figure at the Environmental Defense Fund who was widely known for his deep grasp of the ESA and ability to find creative approaches for building incentives that led landowners to pursue conservation-friendly development solutions. Babbitt's team actively sought and benefited from Bean's input.

The reforms that rolled out of Babbitt's office are detailed in the many articles I cited previously as sources. The point for these purposes is that they changed landowner incentives substantially. As Sam Hamilton put it, if a landowner finds gold on the property, it's a good thing, but if the landowner finds a golden-cheeked warbler, it's a bad thing. It doesn't have to be that way.

The new approach was signaled in a 1995 policy called *Protecting America's Living Heritage: A Fair, Cooperative and Scientifically Sound Approach to Improving the Endangered Species Act (Fair Approach)*. The fact that the given short name explicitly was *Fair Approach* spoke volumes. The three most important incentive-altering reforms that came out of this umbrella policy in the form of agency regulations or policies included:

- *Candidate Conservation Agreements (CCA)*: Candidate species include those not yet listed but headed that way if measures are not take. The CCA approach allows a landowner with habitat of such a species to implement conservation measure that would help the species recover if it should be listed, and then if the species is listed the CCA automatically would convert to a Section 10 HCP.
- *Safe Harbors*: Landowners with habitat of a species that is listed have no legal duty to improve the habitat for the species' benefit, or even to prevent natural degradation of the habitat. Under Safe Harbors, a landowner who does allow the habitat to improve can receive a permit to bring the habitat back to the prior "baseline" at a later date. This proves useful for species that depend on a particular stage of vegetative growth.
- *No Surprises*: In what may have seemed to landowners as an obvious measure, Babbitt (with a lot of encouragement from Michael Bean of EDF), developed the No Surprises policy to assure landowners seeking HCP permits that a deal is a deal. If in the future the species continued to decline due to foreseeable circumstances identified in the permit (e.g., climate change, spread of an invasive species, drought), the landowner would not be liable to provide anything more than what the HCP permit required.

Of course the details of each of these reforms is far more complex than is described here, but this gives a flavor of their orientation. They were not popular with the far left conservation groups, to say the least, but all have survived the litigation such groups brought to challenge them and all have remained embedded in the ESA program through the subsequent Bush, Obama, and Trump administrations. Indeed, it is hard to imagine how the ESA would work without them.

While these and many other reforms in the same vein were being invented, Babbitt inundated congressional hearings on the ESA with Interior officials touting the *Fair Approach* and the merits of the reforms for landowners. The grassroots call for ESA reform in the landowner community was not silenced by any means, but the local real estate groups in Austin, Southern California, and other cities were more interested in working with the new rules, if they worked, than lobbying Congress. Other factors certainly led to the ESA escaping damage in Congress, but no one familiar with the events of the day would argue against the proposition that Babbitt's vision and his determination to put politics aside and craft good policy was a necessary and significant force.

Repurposing the Bureau of Land Management Through the Antiquities Act

There are National Parks, National Forests, National Wildlife Refuges, and a long list of other national treasures on federal public land. Then there are the BLM lands. Known as the western rangelands, they are the vast, dry grasslands and deserts that stretch from Nebraska, Kansas, and Texas westward to the Sierra Nevada mountains. Prior to the Civil War, ranchers freely grazed their livestock across the private, state, and federal lands in the region, moving herds from place to place. After the war, the cowboy era of long cattle drives took hold, with ranchers herding cattle from the plains to railheads leading eastward. The demand for beef rose steadily as the nation entered a long period of economic expansion, and ranchers put more and more cattle on the grasslands. Some ranchers introduced sheep to the picture, and eventually the competition for grass and water became so fierce that violence and small-scale wars broke out. The grasslands were being depleted, and the severe drought of the early 1930s, which led to the apocalyptic dust storms of the Dust Bowl, finally led Congress to intervene.

Congress enacted the Taylor Grazing Act of 1934 to bring order to grazing on federal public lands. The law delegated responsibility to Interior to divide the rangelands into grazing districts, limit the amount of grazing that can take place in each district, and charge fees for grazing permits. Offices within Interior developed rules for administering the program, and the grazing practices of the West were transformed. The job of administering the program fell to the newly-created Bureau of Land Management in 1946. BLM now manages 247 million acres of land—one-eighth of the country's land mass—all of it west of the Mississippi River. It has spent 75 years since then embroiled in battles between ranchers and conservationists. But that is a different story than the one for this chapter.

Although I have painted a bleak picture of BLM lands, there are areas within the vast expanse that are every bit as gorgeous as any National Park, and many areas have deep cultural significance for Native Americans given their use of the grasslands before European settlement. Areas like these became the way

Secretary Babbitt worked to inject a conservation mission into BLM's grazing culture. He chose an obscure but powerful statute as the mechanism.

On June 8, 1906, President Theodore Roosevelt signed the Antiquities Act into law. The short statutory text authorizes the president "in his discretion, to declare by public proclamation historic landmarks, historic and prehistoric structures, and other objects of historic or scientific interest that are situated upon the lands owned or controlled by the Government of the United States to be national monuments." Congress was concerned about rampant "pot hunting" by private collectors scouring the BLM lands for Native American artifacts, and designed the Antiquities Act as a way to remove certain areas from access for such purposes. Congress got that, but a lot more it didn't see coming as well.

Have you heard of the Grand Canyon National Park? It started out as the Grand Canyon National Monument. President Roosevelt designated it a National Monument under the Antiquities Act in 1908. He had been pressing Congress to designate the Grand Canyon a National Park since visiting it in 1903, but Congress was not budging. The Antiquities Act was his end-run opportunity. The statute is unusual in the federal public lands realm in that it allows the president to designate monuments without so much as consulting with Congress. All of the other units in the federal domain—parks, forests, refuges, and so on—require an Act of Congress. So, with the stroke of a pen, Roosevelt carved over a million acres of land out of the rangelands and into National Monument status. Congress enacted the Grand Canyon National Park Act in 1919. The end-run worked. And that kind of Executive power to leave a legacy on the landscape has proven irresistible—the Act has been used over 100 times by all but four presidents since its enactment.[7]

When the Grand Canyon became a National Park, its management fell to the National Park Service (NPS), which was established as an agency within Interior in 1916. Over time this became the practice even for National Monuments on BLM lands not converted into National Parks—management responsibility was given to the NPS. After all, the BLM did grazing, the NPS did parks. Babbitt saw a problem in that. He found a solution in Utah.

The federal lands in southern Utah are among the most remote in the nation—the last to be mapped in the contiguous 48 states. In 1996, President Clinton designated over 1.8 million acres in the area as the Grand Staircase-Escalante National Monument. It was the nation's largest National Monument. It is not managed by the NPS—Babbitt convinced President Clinton to give it to the BLM.

---

[7] Those four are Presidents Richard Nixon, Gerald Ford, Ronald Reagan, and George H.W. Bush. President George W. Bush designated a vast National Monument in the ocean off of Hawaii. President Obama designed more National Monuments than any president before him, with 26 under his signature. President Donald Trump ordered several National Monuments to be reduced in size.

The BLM had long been under fire from conservationists for putting grazing over all else. Congress had intervened in 1976 with enactment of the Federal Land Policy and Management Act (FLPMA), which imposed a "multiple use" mandate to manage the BLM lands for uses beyond grazing, and to ensure "sustained yield" of the resources. BLM adopted rules in 1995 to emphasize "rangeland health" under its FLPMA mandate, but the agency was still perceived, both from inside and outside, as being mostly about grazing. Babbitt considered the practice of handing National Monuments to the NPS as perpetuating BLM's grazing culture, so he parted from that practice with the Grand Staircase-Escalante.

As Don Barry put it, when Babbitt made that announcement, everyone in the BLM and NPS thought he'd lost his mind, but it turned out to be a brilliant move. It gave the BLM a conservation mission it could not subsume under grazing. The idea caught on. In 2000, the BLM created the National Landscape Conservation System, better known as the National Conservation Lands, with the mission to conserve, protect, and restore nationally significant landscapes on BLM lands that have outstanding cultural, ecological, and scientific values for the benefit of current and future generations. Babbitt is credited by many with starting this mission turn through the Grand Staircase-Escalante proclamation. In effect, he leveraged presidential power to perform an end-run around his own Interior Department. It worked so well that the National Landscape Conservation System Act was signed into law in March 2009, permanently unifying the individual units as a public lands system, protecting them by statute so that their continued goals would not be subject to diversion by a future president or Interior secretary. It was the first new congressionally authorized public lands system in decades. By 2016, the system included over 870 designated areas covering a total of 35 million acres.

There is a cautionary tale in this story of Executive power, however. The Grand Staircase-Escalante National Monument was not popular with Utah state and local officials and communities, and has remained a point of contention. BLM's newfound conservation goals also did not sit well with many of the industries that use BLM lands. In addition to grazing, BLM also manages extractive uses such as mining and oil and gas production. When President Trump began his administration, the BLM and the monument were in his crosshairs. He could not unilaterally undo the BLM's Conservation System, as it is now protected by statute. But in 2017 he ordered a reduction in size of Grand Staircase-Escalante by almost half, and in 2019 Interior Secretary David Bernhardt ordered the headquarters of BLM to be moved from Washington, DC, to Grand Junction, Colorado, ostensibly to put it closer to the lands it manages. As of this writing, the Grand Staircase-Escalante order is mired in litigation over the question whether the Antiquities Act allows a president to undo a predecessor's proclamation, and Senate budget proposals have thus far included no funds for moving the BLM.

Working with Congress on Wildlife Refuge Legislation (After Another End Run)

The National Wildlife Refuge System comprises 520 different refuges covering a total of 93 million acre—an area larger than the National Parks System—all of which today is managed by Interior's Fish and Wildlife Service. Dating back to 1869, each refuge has been created by an Act of Congress, and over time this ad hoc process led to a wide variety of missions for different refuges. Wildlife conservation, of course, has been a consistent theme. So has hunting. Babbitt happened to be running Interior when the two collided.

Through legislation in 1962 and 1966, Congress attempted to transform the "bunch" of refuges into a system. The 1966 legislation allowed FWS to permit any uses in a refuge that were "compatible with" the major purposes for which the refuge was established. FWS implemented this standard with regulations that were not especially demanding, and a series of lawsuits and damning reports eroded the agency's standing as a refuge steward. Senator Bob Graham introduced several bills in the early 1990s to shore up the system, but they were perceived by "hook and bullet" fishing and hunting interests as not sufficiently open to those uses.

When the Republicans took back Congress in 1994, Representative Don Young took up the banner for hunting and fishing and introduced a bill in 1996 that would substantially have elevated them as refuge system use priorities. Being an election year, the Clinton camp did not stage a strong opposition, counting on the bill to die in the Senate, which it did. The 1996 election also did not go well for the Democrats in Congress, so Babbitt saw a return of Representative Young's bill on the horizon. He decided to head the bill off at the pass.

Much as he and President Clinton did with the Antiquities Act, Babbitt turned first to raw Executive power in the form of an executive order. Clinton issued Executive Order 12,996 on March 28, 1996. The order leveraged what power the president has to act unilaterally in coordinating refuge management, which is considerable. The key feature of the order was to make wildlife conservation the primary purpose of the entire system but to allow hunting, fishing, and other "wildlife-dependent recreational uses" that would not interfere with wildlife conservation or the other purposes of the refuge. This gave hunting and fishing what they wanted, but drew the line at "wildlife-dependent" to limit what other kinds of uses could slip in.

When Representative Young re-introduced his bill, the executive order proved extremely useful to Babbitt. As Don Barry explained, rather than send a high-level official to testify on Young's bill, Babbitt went himself. Young's bill was unnecessary, Babbitt testified—the executive order was working and gave hunting and fishing the security they sought. The executive order and having a Cabinet officer deliver the testimony was a major blow to the bill. Perhaps sensing the bill would surely die again in the Senate, Young agreed to work with Babbitt on a consensus bill. Babbitt's condition was that he would personally oversee negotiations in his Interior conference room.

The negotiators were hand-picked by various, often-combating interests who were not used to "getting along." Had they met in a conference room on Capitol Hill, Babbitt knew the discussions would get nowhere. Thus was the brilliance of Babbitt's condition to personally oversee the negotiations in his offices. As Don Barry put it, each meeting was like the estranged siblings going to grandmother's house for Thanksgiving—you put on your friendly faces and don't get testy in front of Grammy. Eight weeks later, the group had hammered out what became the National Wildlife Refuge System Administration Act of 1997. By no coincidence, it looked a lot like Executive Order 12,996. It passed in the House of Representatives by 407 yes votes to 1 no vote. No one believes that would have happened without Babbitt's personal commitment, pioneering vision, and eye for the end run.

Water Legacies

I describe myself as working at the intersection of environmental law and land use, which is why the previous four case studies focus on the terrestrial. But Babbitt, who identified his groundwater and surface water management plans as key gubernatorial accomplishments, did as much in the aquatic sphere while at Interior as he did on land. I would have been remiss to leave out that dimension of his administration and thank David Hayes, who served two years as Babbitt's Deputy Secretary (and again in that position during the Obama administration), for telling me so when I described where I was headed with the chapter.

Hayes walked me through several of Babbitt's major water-related initiatives that have had lasting effect in the West, all of which, as Hayes put it, are characteristic of his "big picture" vision for problem-solving. One was Babbitt's effort to resolve the pressing problem's arising from California's persistent use of more water from the Colorado River than it had been allocated through historic apportionment processes. It was able to do this because of a water surplus in the river—more water flowed into California than it was allocated. But the upstream states were developing and climate conditions were depleting the river. Arizona and Nevada were growing weary of California's unquenchable thirst, and Babbitt saw a train wreck in the making. Babbitt brokered the deal in the late 1990s by giving California 15 years to devise a plan to wean itself off of its overconsumption, but also assuring the up-river states that it was going to happen. Hayes was deeply involved in forging the plan that emerged, known formally as the Colorado River Water Use Plan but referred to as the "4.4 Plan" due to California's annual 4.4 million acre-feet basic apportionment of the river.

The plan was a complex assemblage of conservation measures, water transfers (agricultural to urban), canal seepage recovery, groundwater banking, conjunctive use, and other initiatives designed to reduce water use from the river by 800,000 acre-feet annually. The key to it working was an internal state water allocation quantification plan that fixed various water user rights. The plan was finalized in 2003 and upheld in the courts in 2013.

Hayes recounted similar feats in California, where Interior was instrumental to formation of plans for dealing with the Bay-Delta and its growing problem with water use impacts on endangered species, and in Arizona, where Babbitt pursued water rights claims on behalf of the Gila River Indian Community that led to a major settlement with the state in 2004. Neither of these, nor the 4.4 Plan, has been without continuing controversy, but none would have been put in place without Babbitt's hand in play.

Babbitt's fingerprints on water are not limited to the West. Indeed, the opening chapter of his book is devoted to one of the most controversial water systems in the East—the Everglades. Elegantly written and filled with historical detail, the chapter offers a window into Babbitt's ability to both grasp the big picture but find solutions that operate at the field level. To put it mildly, the Everglades ecosystem was in crisis when Babbitt took over at Interior, the victim of over a century of human re-plumbing of the vast "river of grass" that had little tolerance for tinkering, much less wholesale upheaval. The story of how Babbitt got the Corps of Engineers, the Florida sugar industry, and the Republican Congress on board for a 30-year, $8 billion restoration plan is too long and rich to recount here—you'll much more enjoy reading about it in *Cities in the Wilderness*. Suffice to say that in November 2000, while the Supreme Court was deciding *Bush v. Gore*, President Clinton signed the Everglades restoration bill into law. That would not have come to pass without Babbitt's vision and masterful command of the facts and the politics.

After Interior

Bruce Babbitt walked out of his Interior Secretary's office on January 2, 2001, never to return to politics, at least not directly. He took a five-year "time out" to establish the Amazon Conservation Foundation, an NGO based in Lima, Peru, to purchase and secure protected areas in the Amazon Basin. In 2016 California Governor Jerry Brown asked him to provide counsel on the continuing travails in the Bay-Delta area, which eventually involved so much time and effort that it led to him going on the state payroll until Brown left office. And he continues to provide effort and input on National Monument affairs, particularly on those President Trump has ordered reduced in size. He is, at age 81, a free agent as he puts it, a floater not on anyone's payroll and free to choose his next environmental project. As we wrapped up our lunch, he shared that he would soon be back in the Amazon, where no doubt he will leave more of his fingerprints on what will later be seen as lasting progress.

Reflections

When Jan Laitos and the late John Nagle asked me to contribute a chapter to this book, I agreed on one condition—that I could write about Bruce Babbitt as a pioneer of environmental law. Bear in mind that I was not a Babbitt "insider" like John Leshy, David Hayes, Don Barry, and Marc Ebbing. They worked at his side for years, whereas I have only met him twice, once for breakfast and once twenty years later for lunch. They surely could have told his story more ably than I have. And bear in mind as well that for the entire time he was Interior Secretary, he and I were on opposite sides of "the v," as lawyers put it—as in I was involved in litigation against Interior on several occasions, always on behalf of land users. My clients in Austin didn't particularly like Bruce Babbitt—or at least the agency he led—to say the least. Until they met him. Until they came to appreciate what he was doing with the ESA, and why. He certainly turned me around that day at Matt's El Rancho. In short, I was a convert, not an acolyte, which may make an admiring word from me that much more difficult for detractors of Babbitt's vision for the ESA and Interior's broader mission to dismiss.

But why would I take the time and effort to write a whole chapter about him? It was to correct the record. Without fail, when I wrapped up my one-on-one interviews with Babbitt's aides, we agreed that he simply has not received as much credit as he deserves. Indeed, I did not realize how much credit he deserves for so many accomplishments outside my field of vision. So this has been my way of correcting that injustice, my way of thanking the man I consider to have saved the Endangered Species Act. Three cheers for Bruce Babbitt, a true pioneer of environmental law!

Part III

The Innovators

Another kind of pioneer in environmental law is one who takes a fresh look at an existing, accepted legal doctrine, and argues that the doctrine should be, and in fact can be, expanded and broadened to include environmental protection. These pioneers are innovators because they see that standard thinking about an area of law can be viewed differently, and interpreted in a way that better accommodates the notion of environmental protection of natural resources. The chapters of Part III identify three such innovative pioneers. One individual pioneer pointed out how the staid and limited "public trust" doctrine could be massaged and expanded to establish a specialized trust relationship in various natural resources within states. Another saw that standard energy law contained within it an environmental component. One chapter discusses the individuals who saw in the conservative water law prior appropriation doctrine an ingenious way to protect environmentally-friendly instream flows of water.

There is another type of environmental pioneer who is an innovator because the pioneer challenges a prevailing assumption about natural resources use. If the assumption is not entirely accurate, then there may be another view that can arise that may be more conducive to protecting the resource, or that suggests different legal means of managing the resource. One chapter in Part III addresses the revolutionary thinking of an innovator who challenged the assumption, grounded in standard neoclassical economics, that individuals make resource use decisions based primarily on individual welfare maximization. As such, regulatory systems needed to be imposed that forced self-maximizers to consider others. This pioneer suggested that *cooperation* may also occur among competing resource users, which does not require such stringent legal oversight. Another chapter in Part III considers a pioneer-innovator who took a fresh look at agriculture, and realized that environmental demands need to be incorporated in standard agricultural practices.

Chapter 6

Joseph Sax: The Public Trust in Environmental Law

Gerald Torres[1] and Mary Christina Wood[2]

Introduction

Most Americans born after 1980 do not remember the time before there were systematic legal efforts to protect the environment. They may have heard of the mobilization of 20 million Americans who took to the streets on the inaugural Earth Day in 1970, but most do not really know why their fellow Americans

[1] Gerald Torres is Professor of Environmental Justice, Yale School of Forestry and Environmental Studies and Professor of Law, Yale Law School. Professor Torres is former president of the Association of American Law Schools (AALS). He has served as deputy assistant attorney general for the Environment and Natural Resources Division of the U.S. Department of Justice in Washington, D.C., and as counsel to then U.S. Attorney General Janet Reno. In addition to his numerous publications, he has served on the board of the Environmental Law Institute, on EPA's National Environmental Justice Advisory Council. He served on the National Petroleum Council. He was Board Chair of the Advancement Project, the nation's leading racial and social justice organization. He is Chair of Earth Day Network and serves as a Trustee of the Natural Resources Defense Council. He is a board member of the Bauman Foundation. He is a member of the Council on Foreign Relations and the American Law Institute and has taught at Cornell, Yale, Harvard, and Stanford Law Schools.

[2] Mary Christina Wood is Philip H. Knight Professor of Law at the University of Oregon and the Faculty Director of the law school's nationally acclaimed Environmental and Natural Resources Law Center. She is an award-winning professor and the co-author of a leading textbook on public trust law. Her book, Nature's Trust: Environmental Law for a New Ecological Age (Cambridge University Press), sets forth a new paradigm of global ecological responsibility. She originated the legal approach called Atmospheric Trust Litigation, now being used in cases brought on behalf of youth throughout the world, seeking to hold governments accountable to reduce carbon pollution within their jurisdictions. She has developed a corresponding approach called Atmospheric Recovery Litigation, which would hold fossil fuel companies responsible for funding an Atmospheric Recovery Plan to draw down excess carbon dioxide in the atmosphere using natural climate solutions. Professor Wood is a frequent speaker on climate issues and has received national and international attention for her sovereign trust approach to global climate policy.

were marching to demand action on the environment. They may have heard of or even read Rachel Carson's *Silent Spring* that laid out the likely effects of our profligate use of pesticides and herbicides and other commercial toxins. Or perhaps they are familiar with the Aldo Leopold's clearly stated reasons to conceive of the world we live in as a biotic community and be guided by what he called a land ethic. Almost certainly, they would not know of a young Department of Justice lawyer who, in the early 1960's, first asked questions about how the law could be used to protect the environment.

Joseph L. Sax began his career in the Justice Department and there he learned how the administrative state functioned and how citizens might engage and challenge its decisions. He also understood through his defense of the actions of the government that the government was the agent of the people and that the mechanism of the state had to labor for the common good. These goals all depended on a clear understanding of the role of the government and how its decisions affecting broadly held resources needed to be closely scrutinized, not just for regularity, but to ensure that they were doing the work of the people in the way that took full account of their fiduciary responsibility in regards to those resources.

He believed deeply in citizen activism. His book *Defending the Environment* was subtitled "*A Strategy for Citizen Action*." The book does not minimize the difficulty of taking on entrenched interests, but it offers moments of hope that those in the middle of protracted disputes can look to for reassurance. There is one bit of irony in the book that even Joe had forgotten about. In the discussion of the effort to stop the landfill at Hunting Creek, a young Deputy Assistant Secretary of the Interior got an earful. That Deputy Assistant Secretary was Jim Watt. When Joe was asked, "*the* James Watt?"—the official who, during the Reagan administration, was bent on dismantling environmental protections—Joe reflected briefly and said with a laugh, "yes, I think it was." They were adversaries even then, but the victor was the one who believed in the people and their right to protect their environment rather than the apologist for the despoilers.

This chapter highlights Joseph Sax, a legal pioneer who rediscovered the public trust principle in modern American law and who then applied it to environmental decision making. His scholarly excavation through legal materials dating back to ancient Rome revealed the public trust as a principle of property law that operated as an inherent limitation on governmental power. It was not dependent on any statutory enactment. Its roots are ancient, and he traced the principle back to the Roman laws expressed in the Justinian Institutes. The trust principle holds that some resources are simply so crucial to society that government cannot "alienate" them by giving them away to private interests, nor can it allow their destruction. Resources that are crucial to the proper functioning of society and which are incapable of either public (in the sense of governmental) or private ownership are said to be held "in trust" by the state. The government, as a trustee, must manage them as a fiduciary for the benefit of the present and future generations of citizens. This public trust principle charges officials with a strict obligation to protect those elements of ecosystems that are not reducible to public or private commodities as generational inheritance for all citizens. Joe Sax's work spelled out the proper legal incorporation of this principle as a public trust mandate that necessarily included intergenerational equity.

This ancient legal obligation has existed like an essential strand of legal DNA in all forms of government, but especially in those that claim legitimacy through consent. Importantly, Professor Sax demonstrated that consent was not the genesis of the obligation but just the clearest expression of the duty that binds all government. The importance of the public trust idea in American law was not obvious until Professor Sax wrote a seminal article on the subject in 1969. *The Public Trust Doctrine in Natural Resource Law: Effective Judicial Intervention*, published in the Michigan Law Review, became the most cited article in the field of environmental law.

Countless decisions both in the United States and internationally have relied on its reasoning to apply the trust to protect society's crucial resources. Professor Sax pointed out the need for a reinvigorated trust idea in our legal system, and he explored the decisions that had invoked the trust since the founding of the nation. Writing at the dawn of modern environmental law, he observed that the power of government must be to act in the best interests of the people and future generations and to resist private profiteers in bending policy that would betray that fundamental obligation. Sax understood that, while some problems in society arise because of majorities oppressing minority interests, in the realm of environmental law virtually the opposite occurs: politically powerful minority interests constantly pressure governmental agencies to alienate resources and allow pollution even when doing so harms the public interest. The power of well-organized interests against a diffuse public interest is a well-recognized political liability in democratic systems, but that inherent hazard cannot be permitted to change the basic orientation of public law. As Sax recognized, "For self-interested and powerful minorities often have an undue influence on the public resource decisions of legislative and administrative bodies and cause those bodies to ignore broadly based public interests." He therefore concluded that public trust protection is needed in "a wide range of situations in which diffuse public interests need protection against tightly organized groups with clear and immediate goals."

In suggesting that the trust would be a necessary constraint on government, Sax had to wade into the matter of judicial enforcement. Summarizing a wide range of trust cases, he suggested standards by which it would be appropriate for a court to halt agency action. We describe them more fully below. He also explored the judicial interface with legislatures, noting that if a legislature violated the trust, a court could order a "legislative remand" sending the matter back to the legislature for reconsideration. In that manner, Sax observed, each branch would observe its constitutionally appointed role. His observation of the implications of the trust duty were to show how it not only was fully consistent with the idea underlying the system of separation of powers, but more importantly it was a critical part of the proper functioning of that system.

Sax's trust scholarship gained significant attention in the academic world decades before attaining a similar impact in the broader world of judicial and public policy debate. He published the article immediately prior to passage of a multitude of laws by Congress in the early 1970s. Those laws ushered in a new era of environmental law—one dominated by the new statutes and regulations passed to implement them. When that happened, American lawyers and most law professors focused almost singularly (and perhaps properly) on what the statutes said. That narrowness of focus obscured the underlying trust obligation that was at the heart of the statutes and at the root of the administrative process.

For four decades, most lawyers and judges simply assumed environmental law was working and for limited purposes of the most obvious pollution reduction, it was. There is no question that the Clean Water Act reduced water pollution in significant ways or that the air, as measured by pulmonary health, is markedly cleaner than before the Clean Air Act. But the assumption of unvarnished success was increasingly belied by the science showing that the effects of pollution were pervasive, systemic, and threatened ecosystem destruction and collapse.

The failure of the basic environmental statutory scheme is manifest in the broad ecological challenges now facing humanity, but the field also suffers from a volatility that can no longer be ignored. Regulations implementing the statutes undergo wrenching change with nearly every administration, and the few protective ones that have been passed are later invalidated by administrations allied with industry interests. What this volatility reveals is that environmental law has come unmoored from its foundation. The focus on the cost internalization function of pollution control caused those tasked with environmental protection to forget that the justification for environmental regulation was based on the trust principle as much as tort law.

The United States has more pages of environmental law than any other nation on Earth. Congress passed the Clean Water Act, Clean Air Act, Endangered Species Act, and a host of other laws in the 1970s to protect and restore the environmental systems that were threatened by the unregulated industrial activity that was guided by the goal of shifting costs to others. That strategy was reflected in the political pressure relentlessly exerted by the regulated community, and it eroded the will of state and federal officials to administer the statutes' protections as vigorously as the statutes might allow. The constant tug and pull of the politics surrounding enforcement and the reach of the core environmental statutes resulted in much of the destruction the statutes were designed to prevent. Agencies are not immune from the politics of the environmental protection, and in times when enforcement was undervalued, the permit systems and other provisions in these statutes were used to open vast public lands to coal mining and oil drilling, log the national forests, harm already endangered or threatened species, increase toxic groundwater pollution, and perhaps most crucially, permit massive carbon emissions to destabilize the atmosphere. A transformational approach was needed to reorient environmental enforcement in the public interest and to see clearly that the public interest, and not just baseline health measurements, were at the root of the statutes.

This confluence of phenomena brought a renewed focus on the work of Joe Sax as a legal pioneer who illuminated the public trust principle in modern American environmental law. The duty embedded in the trust runs not just to the living, but to their descendants. The duty is captured by President Theodore Roosevelt's famous speech given at the rim of the Grand Canyon in 1903 where he declared:

> We have gotten past the stage, my fellow citizens, when we are to be pardoned if we treat any part of our country as something to be skinned for two or three years for the use of the present generation, whether it is the forest, the water, the scenery. Whatever it is, handle it so that your children's children will get the benefit of it.

As citizens face continual battles with their own government to protect scarce and crucial resources, more and more lawyers are now crafting cases that invoke the public trust, and the principle is coming out of a long period of dormancy to bear on modern ecological crises. Courts have repeatedly made clear that the trust stands apart from statutes, and some have made clear that the trust is at bottom a constitutional obligation binding governmental agencies at the state or federal level. In significant measure, the Sax scholarship poised this remarkable doctrine to transform environmental law and bring about a fundamental change in the underlying assumptions animating the law. Youth facing the prospect of runaway climate change have invoked the trust principle in a series of cases known as Atmospheric Trust Litigation, described more below. Others have invoked it to protect groundwater and wildlife that was otherwise subject to destruction under permit systems.

The potential of the trust revolves around the logic of democracy. Joseph Sax understood that to have any impact the trust would have to be enforced in courts against the other branches of government. He grappled deeply with the trust's role in American democracy, and his writings today continue to illuminate a path forward. In many respects, the trust scholarship of Sax leaves a legacy far greater than the environmental realm. It urges us to examine the essential role and purpose of government.

The Constitutional Trust and Democracy: A Saxian Vision

As we have pointed out, most legal observers would agree that credit for the resurrection of the modern public trust doctrine ought to be placed at the feet of one scholar: Professor Joseph Sax. Of course, even if the only contribution Professor Sax had made was either to the public trust doctrine or to the reconceptualization of property law's takings jurisprudence, his place in the scholarly firmament would be secure. But he did much more. There are few people about whom it could be said-certainly in the law-that they were there at the beginning, when environmental law emerged as a field. Joe was one of those people.

His arguments all rely on a firm grounding in democratic political theory. He argued for an understanding of law that supports the democratic legitimacy of lawmaking. Professor Sax understood the relationship of property to the legitimate functioning of the state. Moreover, his work had a direct effect on the discursive field that defined the environmental movement. Aside from his explicitly scholarly work, more popular books like *Defending the Environment* and *Mountains Without Handrails* gave a theoretical framework and a language to the claims that environmentalists were making. His work also insulated environmentalism from the charges of elitism by rooting protection of the environment in our democratic tradition and by reaffirming the public content of private rights.

A theory of law must justify the substantive conclusions as well as the process for resolving disputes over ends. By focusing on property-especially the constitutional dimension of property-Professor Sax had to immediately engage a particularly troublesome intersection of public and private law. The history of the common law shows that property ideas had as much to do with conceptions of the state as they did with the development of the market. Because of this, the changing conceptions of property constituted us as much as the overt political charters we adopted to regulate government or to secure rights. We occupy a seat at the end of a very long train of events that make up our understanding of the social functions of property. The democratizing currents in American social life could not help but influence our understanding of legal categories.

What Professor Sax did was to identify and question the role of the state in creating, defending, and regulating property-both private property in his analysis of the limits of regulation and public property in his work on the public trust. Yet he did not assert a normative vision of his own; instead, he excavated the traces of his argument from our legal and cultural traditions. Thus, he notes the Roman law and early English law roots of the public trust doctrine. In his book, *Playing Darts With a Rembrandt*, for example, he shows how a durable public claim to important cultural artifacts arose in the response to the revolutionary Terror in France of 1794.

This constitutive archeology is one of the foundations of Professor Sax's work, and while his arguments are commonly characterized as "novel," in fact they are faithful to the democratizing forces that balanced the private needs of an emerging market economy with the continuing solidary functions of property. They are, in an important way, illustrations of the ways in which the social function of property constitute us as a people and as a polity. Of course, law-making reflecting as it does continuing struggles over power does not trace a straight line, but that is not the point of Professor Sax's work. He locates families of principles as a method of inquiry.

In exploring Professor Sax's contribution to environmental law, it is important to note that his article on the public trust doctrine focuses on "effective judicial intervention." While it is in the field of constitutional theory that the question of whether judicial intervention in controlling legislative prerogatives is legitimate, Professor Sax has illustrated that the role of the courts is often dispositive and often the only meaningful restraint on what would otherwise be illegitimate legislative action. He demonstrates that the checking function of courts increases the democratic legitimacy of the popularly elected branches of government. If the public trust doctrine is part of our constitutional tradition, the state has an obligation to create a mechanism to attend to that duty. What Professor Sax shows is that environmental law is the structural expression of that duty.

Professor Sax suggests that the public trust doctrine is a species of constitutional law. The exact method for protecting those natural resources that are part of the inalienable assets of the public is within the legislative domain, but the courts have a specific and important role to play in superintending that duty's actual fulfillment.

The claim that some public trust issues are not justiciable is untenable. The checking function that courts play in limiting overreach by the political branches of government is part of the proof of that. Reluctance to intervene in the administrative process is a common default position, but Sax provides a test for courts to apply to ensure that the resources that are endowed with the public interest are protected. Because the fundamental function of courts in the public trust area is one of democratization, the court must inquire, at a minimum, whether the processes that produced an administrative or legislative outcome are a function of political imbalance.

As he painstakingly demonstrates, the question of political imbalance is not one that merely reflects any particular judge's preference; it requires a searching inquiry into the process that produced the decision, and consideration of whether the public had an adequate opportunity to have its interest represented. This can also include an inquiry into the appropriate decisional authority. The proper constituency to decide is thus part of the review, and the remedy can include a movement from one level of decision-making to another. As mentioned earlier, Professor Sax suggests a remedy that has come to be described as a "legislative remand." This is the capacity for courts to influence the legislative agenda in order to take better account of the public interests at stake in the management or protection of resources that are clothed with the public trust. Environmental challenges could have been characterized, as many commentators have suggested, by highlighting the gravity of the threat posed by environmental degradation, but that physical threat is as much a function of political and democratic degradation as it is a function of inattention to the external costs associated with modern industrial life. According to Sax, environmental law and the commitment to protect our natural resources and wild spaces are expressions of our commitment to a robust democratic life. It is a reaffirmation of our obligation as citizens who stand in relation to each other and to the future.

Essential attributes of sovereignty can be particularly imperiled by legislative inaction. This is true in the public trust context, where government's role as a trustee depends on the condition of essential natural resources. Natural resources, like the atmosphere, are complicated and delicate. Without proper care, these resources can deteriorate to a point where restoration is no longer possible. If the substance of the public trust is irreversibly destroyed or deteriorated, then government's essential attribute as a trustee over that substance has been eviscerated. Were government to attempt such an abdication, courts could enjoin government from doing so. In other words, courts can require legislatures to not act where it would have otherwise acted; yet, when the same result occurs through inaction, courts have been reluctant to place an affirmative duty on the legislature. The distinction is mere formalism, a principle untethered from its rationale.

Government defendants in public trust litigation tend to characterize their fundamental fiduciary obligations as "political questions" inappropriate for judicial review. This framing has dominated the government defendants' briefs in climate trust cases, for example. But whether government has a fundamental constitutional obligation to oversee the atmosphere as a sovereign trust resource does not implicate the political question doctrine. Such a determination is nothing more than the vindication of a constitutional right. A judicial determination of the existence of the trust obligation and whether rights protected by the public trust doctrine have been violated is merely the courts holding the legislature and executive branches to their respective constitutional duties.

Another obstacle that has arisen in public trust cases seeking action on climate change is the claim that statutes have displaced the trust duty. This is called the displacement doctrine. However, unlike other common law rights, the public trust doctrine is not subject to statutory displacement. The public trust doctrine is not supplanted by the mere existence of legislation which addresses public trust assets. No deference is owed to administrative or legislative bodies who interpret the public trust. Mere compliance by these bodies with their legislative authority is not enough to determine if their actions comport with the requirements of the public trust doctrine.

The public trust doctrine, enforced by the courts, is an important check on how the political branches manage trust assets: the principle requires government trustees to protect trust assets for present and future generations and does not allow them to abdicate their fiduciary duty to prevent substantial impairment to the trust property. In the words of one court, "The check and balance of judicial review provides a level of protection against improvident dissipation of an irreplaceable public asset." Professor Sax explained that public trust law "is a technique by which courts may mend perceived imperfections in the legislative and administrative process."

Judicial inaction, on the other hand, effectively forecloses policy options for future legislatures. If the trust assets are completely and irreversibly depleted or destroyed, then the future legislature is denied its authority to ask and answer the questions related to trust management. If the substance of the trust is irreparably degraded, certain legislative policies are rendered obsolete. Appropriate judicial action preserves the constitutional role of the legislative branch by ensuring that a question not properly foreclosed is preserved for future legislatures.

As public trustees, government agencies and legislatures must manage public natural wealth for the *sole benefit* of the citizens, rather than to promote their own political interests or the singular interests of their allied industries. As the Supreme Court said long ago, "[T]he power or control lodged in the State, resulting from this common ownership, is to be exercised, like all other powers of government, as a trust for the benefit of the people, and not as a prerogative for the advantage of the government, as distinct from the people, or for the benefit of private individuals as distinguished from the public good." This rule carries out the basic assumption underlying American democracy: that government must exist only to serve the people. Professor Sax recognized the alignment between the public trust and popular sovereignty and explained the trust concept as rooted in basic democratic principles.

The Corpus of the Trust: Employing the Logic of Precedent

The public trust principle identifies some natural resources as belonging to the public, subject to such protection that they may endure and continue to support the survival and welfare of future generations. In other words, it puts some resources off limits to strictly private ownership and prohibits actions that lead to the destruction of the trust resource. Yet, as explored further below, the classic American property tradition viewed the balancing of property rights as purely artifacts of private law. The government would act as referee leading government officials to fall into the pattern of thinking that they must permit destructive private use so as not to interfere with private property "rights."

Professor Sax introduced a fuller paradigm to American law by unveiling a legal tradition of *public* property rights tracing back to ancient Rome and undergirding civilizations throughout the world. He showed, through meticulous compilation and analysis of cases, that the norm recognizing public property rights was incorporated into American jurisprudence through early decisions and remains to provide ecological protection. We explore in further detail below this *public* side of property law illuminated by Professor Sax, but first we ask what resources are subject to public trust protection?

In a trust construct, the wealth subject to protection is called the "*res*" or "corpus" of the trust. In a financial trust used for a college education, for example, the "*res*" or "corpus" consists of monetary wealth or other income-producing assets such as stocks, bonds, and rental properties that the trustee will use to pay tuition for the benefit of the student who is the beneficiary. In the case of a public trust, the wealth is ecological commonwealth needed to sustain society for the benefit of present and future generations who are, collectively, the legal beneficiaries of the public trust.

As Professor Sax compiled and analyzed the early public trust cases in American law, he observed that most involved waterways and shorelines. For example, in the seminal American case, *Illinois Central Railroad v. Illinois*, decided in 1892, the U.S. Supreme Court conferred public trust protection to the shoreline of Lake Michigan. The circumstances leading to the case were rather shocking: the Illinois state legislature had conveyed the entire waterfront of Chicago to a private railroad company. Back then, the shoreline was needed by the citizens for fishing, navigation, and commerce, yet the legislature (likely under corrupt influence) basically transferred to the Illinois Central Railroad a private monopoly over this essential societal resource. The Supreme Court declared that the legislature had no power or authority to make such a conveyance, because the shoreline was held in public trust to serve the public. Describing the shoreline as property of a "special character," and "property in which the whole people are interested," the Court elaborated: "The ownership of the navigable waters of the harbor and of the lands under them *is a subject of public concern to the whole people of the State.*" The Court's approach can be captured as the "public concern" test. As Professor Charles Wilkinson explained this focus on public concern: "The public trust doctrine is rooted in the precept that some resources are so central to the well-being of the community that they must be protected by distinctive, judge-made principles."

Based on the logic of *Illinois Central's* public concern test, more resources than just surface water and shorelands would appear to fall logically within the scope of trust protection. Certainly air, wildlife, forests, groundwater, oceans, soils, grasslands, and the full plethora of natural resources remain integral to society. Are any of those resources *not* a matter of "public concern," particularly in a coming climate age that will deliver unprecedented challenges for community adaptation to new ecological realities? Drought, sea-level rise, flooding, fire, insect spread, disease, and crop loss seem to place a premium on *all natural resources*, making it hazardous to excise any from the trust's protection. The reality is that ecosystem components operate as one integral system supporting life. While courts have lagged far behind the scientific understanding of ecosystem dynamics, it is now broadly understood that we cannot simply sacrifice some key resources and expect the others to maintain their function. As Aldo Leopold famously said so long ago, "To keep every cog and wheel is the first precaution of intelligent tinkering."

With these concerns in mind, Professor Sax interpreted the public trust principle in broad fashion, characterizing it as a principle animated by the core logic of protecting ecosystem integrity. Not willing to confine the public trust and its relevance to historic conditions, he charted the principle in a way responsive to society's changing needs. While acknowledging, "The historical scope of public trust law is quite narrow," he wrote: "Certainly the principle of the public trust is broader than its traditional application indicates." Sax saw the public trust as a reservoir of principled logic that could be applied beyond the historic application to waterways. He wrote, "Of all the concepts known to American law, only the public trust doctrine seems to have the breadth and substantive content which might make it useful as a tool of general application for citizens seeking to develop a comprehensive legal approach to resource management problems." He elaborated by giving examples to which this principle could be applied, stating:

> [I]t seems that the delicate mixture of procedural and substantive protections which the courts have applied in conventional public trust cases would be equally applicable and equally appropriate in controversies involving air pollution, the dissemination of pesticides, the location of rights of way for utilities, and strip mining or wetland filling on private lands in a state where governmental permits are required.

The reach of the public trust depends on judicial interpretation. Like the great doctrines derived through our common law jurisprudence, the public trust is a principle devised by courts. Where there is no specific statute limiting their application of extant legal principles, judges have always created and interpreted legal principles using reasoned logic and relying on the authority of precedent (which means judgments and reasoning from past cases). Through careful assaying of judicial opinions, the judiciary can craft principles capable of being both faithful to tradition yet responsive to contemporary lived circumstances. This is the power of "common law" created by courts. As one court described the common law:

> The very essence of the common law is flexibility and adaptability. It does not consist of fixed rules but it is the best product of human reason applied to the premises of the ordinary and extraordinary conditions of life.... If the common law should become ... crystallized ... it would cease to be the common law of history and would be an inelastic and arbitrary code. [O]ne of the established principles of the common law [is] that precedents must yield to the reason of different or modified conditions.

Despite the resistance of government officials to apply the public trust to 21st century problems, many if not most courts describe the doctrine as flexible, geared to accommodating new societal needs rather than confining the law to serve history's requirements. Even back in 1893, the Supreme Court of Minnesota set the tone for this judicial approach by finding that the public trust should protect not just the traditional interests of fishing, navigation and commerce, but should also protect the public's interest in "sailing, rowing, fishing, fowling, bathing, skating ... and *other public uses which cannot now be enumerated or even anticipated.*"

This wisdom applied a century ago by judges who could not have possibly anticipated the potentially cataclysmic consequences of climate change holds even more force today. Modern courts describe the public trust as "not fixed or static," but a principle to "be molded and extended to meet changing conditions and needs of the public it was created to benefit." Many (though not all) courts have extended the trust to a broader array of natural resources, including dry sand beaches, fish and wildlife, air and atmosphere, and groundwater. Still, some judges are reluctant to modernize the trust. An Oregon county circuit court judge, for example, said that the public trust in that state extends only to the submerged lands along navigable waters. Taking a classic *private* property view, the judge found air and atmosphere could not be "property" subject to the public trust, because they were "not acquired or traded for economic value and hence [they are] not a commodity." To that judge, atmosphere was simply empty, uncontrolled, valueless space—not something that "can be measured or divided and used." Accordingly, he refused to extend public trust protection to air and atmosphere—not recognizing that the incapacity of the resource to be transformed into a commodity was the very essence of its public nature. Youth plaintiffs in that case appealed the decision to the Oregon Supreme Court, and the case is pending as of this writing.

Some courts, however, have moved public trust interpretation closer toward a full *ecological res* approach to bring the law more in compliance with the actual laws of Nature. Courts take a first step in that direction when they recognize the intertwined and indivisible nature of ecosystems—and the artificiality of the legal system's compartmentalization of them into neat cubbyholes of surface water, air, forests, wildlife, soils, groundwater, and the like. As an astute trial judge in Washington state noted, the public trust's required protection of navigable waterways equally requires protection of the atmosphere from greenhouse gas emissions, because atmosphere and submerged lands remain inextricably connected. Judge Hollis Hill said, "to argue that GHG emissions do not affect navigable waters is nonsensical...." A federal district court in a landmark climate public trust case, *Juliana v. United States*, referred broadly to the "natural resources trust," describing the scope of the doctrine as extending to "resources important enough to the people to warrant public trust protection."

Decisions such as these follow the path charted by Joseph Sax when he noted that the logic of the public trust decisions applied equally to other natural resources well beyond the streambeds and navigable waterways that were the focus of 18th and 19th century cases.

The Fiduciary Obligations of a Government Trustee

Professor Sax observed that citizens were increasingly seeking recourse in court to force legislatures and agencies to protect ecology. He viewed the public trust as the only principle both general enough and flexible enough to respond to the host of emerging environmental problems. He deemed that, for this principle to be an effective tool of judicial protection, "it must contain some concept of a legal right in the general public." Embedded in the structure of any trust is a legal right assertible by the beneficiaries against the trustee for mismanaging the trust. By describing natural resources as held in a public "trust," the courts of this country bring to bear a rich tradition of jurisprudence that holds trustees accountable to the beneficiaries.

A trust of any sort—whether public or private—divides ownership of the trust wealth between the trustee and the beneficiaries. The trustee is charged with managing the trust assets. The number-one rule of a trust is that the trustee must manage the trust assets for the benefit of the designated beneficiaries, rather than for the trustee's own benefit. While the beneficiaries have no authority to manage the property, they (and they alone) gain the clear benefit of the trust.

The law imposes a well-established set of requirements called fiduciary obligations on the trustee. These are basic standards of care and loyalty to ensure that the property is well managed and not used to benefit anyone other than the named beneficiaries. These fiduciary obligations are enforceable in court by the beneficiaries—which, in the public trust context, are present and future generations of citizens (while only live citizens can walk into court, they represent the interests of their posterity as well as themselves).

Many public trust cases have borrowed the fiduciary obligations enshrined in private trust law as it has developed over centuries. When Professor Sax wrote his article, he focused mainly on government's restrictions in alienating public trust property (putting it into private ownership). But by introducing and explaining the public trust as an entire framework, he gave the courts an analytical paradigm necessary to apply the full suite of fiduciary obligations that had been well-refined in private trust law. The list below gives a summary of the key duties assembled from some modern public trust cases decided since Professor Sax wrote his pioneering article (many of the cases rely extensively on his work). Together they form a coherent framework of government accountability in managing ecology.

As a preliminary matter, however, it is important to clarify the relationship of these basic fiduciary duties to statutory law. Courts have made clear that agencies are not excused from their public trust responsibility just because they met the terms of a statute. In fact, since legislatures are themselves deemed trustees, the statutes are measured according to whether they carry out the trust obligations. As one court said, "Mere compliance by [agencies] with their legislative authority is not sufficient to determine if their actions comport with the requirements of the public trust doctrine. *The public trust doctrine at all times forms the outer boundaries of permissible government action with respect to public trust resources.*" As you review these specific obligations, consider how differently the environment would be managed if courts forced government to abide by them.

Protect the Resources (the Trust Assets) from "Substantial Impairment"

The fiduciary obligation carrying the most practical importance is quite basic: the trustee has a firm duty to protect the wealth of the trust. As one federal district court made clear, "the natural resources trust operates according to basic trust principles, which impose upon the trustee a fiduciary duty to protect the trust property against damage or destruction." Because future generations are, without exception, recognized beneficiaries of the public trust, the principle aims to protect and sustain natural wealth for their inheritance. Applying this classic duty to public trustees, courts have said that agencies and legislatures must prevent "substantial impairment" of public trust resources. Courts emphasize that this duty is active, not passive: a trustee may not sit idle and allow the trust property to "fall into ruin on his watch." As one court put it, "The trust reposed in the state is not a passive trust; it is governmental, active, and administrative, requir[ing] the lawmaking body to act in all cases where action is necessary, not only to preserve the trust, but to promote it." Scores of other courts have described this duty as "affirmative," requiring the government's "continuous supervision and control" over the public's crucial resources.

Maximize the Societal Value of Natural Resources

Leading trust cases require government trustees to manage trust resources in a way that maximizes their benefits to the people. Most polluting uses of air, water, and soil would fail under a trust approach. Existing statutes allow a corporation to pollute these valuable resources to the extent that they do not force the internalization of all production costs—minimizing, rather than maximizing, the societal value of the resource.

Scrutiny of Private Use

Government trustees may not manage public natural commonwealth for the primary purpose of serving private interests. The trust's basic purpose is to reserve resources for public use, access, and benefit. The trust does not altogether prohibit private use of public trust resources, but rather aims to harness private interests to promote the public good. A trustee may privatize public trust assets only when doing so (1) clearly aids a public trust purpose; and (2) does not cause "substantial impairment" to the public's interest in the remaining lands and waters.

Keep the Trust Resources in Public Ownership

The public trust principle imposes strict limitations on when the government can privatize a resource held in public trust. It can only do so if the conveyance (1) furthers the public's interest in the trust resource; and (2) does not cause substantial impairment to the remaining resources. Many courts have applied this test to bar the state from conveying tidelands to private parties, in order to protect the public's interest in fishing, navigation, commerce, and recreation. Some courts have said that the government cannot fully convey private title to dry sand beaches, because doing so would allow private owners to exclude citizens from this area that serves important public needs, including recreation. Even where a state did convey private title to such areas in the past, courts find that private landowners do not have complete title, but rather share their title (called *jus privatum*) with the public (which holds an interest called *jus publicum*).

Restore the Trust

A trustee must restore a trust asset that has been damaged. This basic principle seeks to return the beneficiaries to their rightful position by making the trust whole again. Trustees have an affirmative obligation to recoup monetary damages against third parties that harm or destroy trust assets. In the public trust context, for example, the duty demands recovery of natural resource damages against oil companies that cause spills in the ocean.

The Duty of Loyalty

Trustees may not manage public commonwealth for their own political or private gain. The trust imposes steadfast, undivided loyalty towards the designated beneficiaries and prohibits conflicts of interest that could engender even the possibility for the trustee to self-deal. The fiduciary duty of loyalty remains exacting and rigorous, "not the duty to resist temptation, but to eliminate temptation, as the former is assumed to be impossible. . . ." This duty of loyalty is the primary tool to ensure that government works for the benefit of the people, as a true democracy requires. While Professor Sax did not analyze this duty in his scholarship, it comes directly from his premise that government must manage ecosystems for the benefit of citizens.

Professor Sax identified a serious, deep-seated problem with the growing field of environmental law. He observed that legislatures and agencies often took actions contrary to the public's best interests, due to inordinate political pressure imposed by powerful private interests. This fundamental duty of loyalty, if enforced by courts, could perhaps root out the core problem with government today: the corruptive influence of campaign contributions on the part of private interests who stand to benefit from legislative and executive branch decisions on environmental issues. Campaign financing creates exactly the kind of temptation that the trust abhors. Self-dealing, which is strictly prohibited by the trust's duty of loyalty, manifests habitually when legislators or political appointees in the executive branch make decisions to reward their industry campaign funders.

The problem is not that this corruption goes unrecognized, but that it has become institutionalized, and greatly exacerbated by the U.S. Supreme Court's *Citizens United v. Federal Election Commission* decision, which treats corporations as natural persons for purposes of direct contributions to political campaigns. The *Citizens United* opinion remains difficult to legally dislodge, because the Court categorically held that corporations have constitutionally protected First Amendment rights to make such campaign contributions. But the fiduciary duty of loyalty at the core of the trust structure that Sax identified can delegitimize this political behavior, not by contesting the right of the corporations to make the contributions, but by challenging the ability of officials to involve themselves in decisions that are tainted by campaign contributions. The fiduciary duty of loyalty would require lawmakers to recuse themselves from decisions in which a corporate-affiliated campaign donor has a significant interest. This would not require the showing of a corrupt *quid pro quo*. The trust paradigm of loyalty to citizens would seemingly steer American government back towards the democratic ideals that the Founders aimed to secure in establishing the United States government.

In sum, the public trust repositions all players in their relationship to natural resources and natural systems. The doctrine makes government officials fiduciary trustees rather than mere political actors, and it bears no tolerance toward disloyal public servants. Nature is a priceless public endowment consisting of tangible and quantifiable assets, instead of a vague "environment" with amorphous value. Citizens stand as beneficiaries holding a clear public property interest in crucial natural resources, rather than as weak political actors. The approach does not view the polluters as equal claimants to the trust assets. They may have more political power, but the role of our political institutions is to safeguard democracy rather that to give it over to the most powerful members of the political sphere. But this paradigm requires enforcement of fiduciary obligations, for without a rigorous judicial role, a "trust" is not a trust at all.

The Court's Role in Enforcing the Trust

Professor Sax determined that, for the public doctrine to provide a satisfactory tool, it must be enforceable against the government. His scholarship thus delved deeply into the role of courts, as enforcers of the trust, "shaping public policy with respect to a wide spectrum of resource interests." This was a truly a pioneering endeavor. Sax wrote at the dawn of modern environmental era at a time in which Congress was actively passing statutes such as the Clean Air Act, the Clean Water Act, the National Environmental Policy Act, and many others. The American public had fought hard to get these environmental laws passed by Congress. Twenty million Americans participated in peaceful demonstrations on the first Earth Day, April 22, 1970, to make the environment a national priority, and there was great faith that these laws would work to improve the doleful environmental conditions facing the nation. The focus of this era was on the two political branches of government—the legislature and executive branch agencies—and not yet on the courts.

Professor Sax illuminated the necessary role of the judiciary in environmental policy, showing that the courts could and did enforce the trust, and that such enforcement served as a vital check in the system of democracy. But the full impact of his judicial analysis is now just being realized. For decades, environmental litigation consisted almost exclusively of statutory claims, not public trust claims, and created a framework of judging that relegated the judicial branch to a passive position.

Over time, courts applying the statutes have developed a strong "deference doctrine" that gives tremendous latitude to agency decisions. Judges uncritically presume that agencies will faithfully carry out their statutory commands, and their deference to agencies often precludes effective and probing review. This restrained attitude has greatly diminished the judicial branch as a vital check in the three-branch system of government. In retrospect, the statutes dramatically shifted the balance of power between the three branches of government. One federal appellate judge recently announced a "Wake Up Call for Judges," objecting that an "enfeebled" judicial branch contributes to a "wholesale failure of the legal system to protect humanity from the collapse of finite natural resources by the uncontrolled pursuit of short-term profits."

Recently environmental litigants have turned to the public trust to seek redress in court when agencies allow broadscale environmental damage. The public trust puts the courts in a much different posture and summons judicial capacity in ways that statutory claims tend not to, for several reasons. First, public trust claims can be macro in scope. They seek to hold agents of the state to the fiduciary responsibility of protecting ecological assets. Second, trust claims seek to hold public officials accountable to *substantive* fiduciary obligations, not just procedural formalities. Substantive fiduciary performance looks to actual protection of the asset, regardless of whether government followed correct statutory procedures in resource management. Third, a trust claim may assert breach of the duty of loyalty to public beneficiaries. Fourth, a trust claim does not trigger judicial deference to agency technical decisions. Courts typically approach a trustee's fiduciary performance with a strict evidentiary review. Finally, a trust claim may challenge legislative action as well as agency action. Statutory claims never address legislative dysfunction, because the bounds of review are set by the statute. If a court finds a law in violation of the public trust duty to citizens, it may not rewrite the law itself, but it can send the matter back to the legislature as a "legislative remand," a tool that Professor Sax described in his landmark article.

What is the remedy in a public trust case? First, the court may order an "accounting" of the resource which informs the beneficiaries of the condition of the trust. An accounting for a river held in trust might require a full disclosure of all of the pollution in the river (and its sources), the water levels and withdrawals from the river, other threats, and uses and other ecological resources supported by the river (fish and wildlife for example). The second feature is an enforceable plan to stop the damage to the trust and restore the ecological wealth that has been lost by the public trustees. For a river, this might take the form of an enforceable cleanup plan and a plan to change the water permitting system to allow enough water in the river to maximize the public uses. The courts typically maintain continuing supervision over these processes. A final trust remedy is the "backstop injunction," which is an order from the court to keep the situation from getting worse. In the river context, for example, the court may enjoin a damaging water diversion or to prevent an agency from issuing a permit to pollute the river. While the features of a trust remedy may be complex, the tools used by courts in fashioning such relief are hardly unknown to judges. They are the common tools with which every judge has great familiarity. While environmental statutes introduced a host of narrow procedural remedies to the field of environmental law, these fundamental remedial tools remain available to courts deciding public trust claims.

Lawyers craft the cases that they bring to court. Professor Sax's article contained wisdom for lawyers seeking to apply the public trust. He cautioned against "extreme and doctrinaire positions" and wrote, "A litigation theory which begins with a sophisticated analysis of public trust principles-setting out alternatives for the achievement of a reasonable development of trust lands with minimal infringement of public use-is likely to obtain a far more sympathetic response from the bench than is one which takes a rigorous legal principle and squeezes it to death." In this vein, it is important for lawyers to map out a reasonable and feasible remedy for the court to impose if it finds a trust violation.

One of the most practical tools is a supervised remedy structure in which the parties devise a solution within the framework defined by the court. In this way, the court itself does not fashion the remedy, but rather scrutinizes a proffered solution for consistency with the legal rights and duties and supervises its enforcement. This model has widely been used in complex litigation. It positions the court in a way that does not usurp the executive branch's authority yet enables judges to ensure compliance with the law that they define through their holdings.

As the nation enters a radically different ecological age, courts are increasingly called upon to grasp their constitutionally appointed role in governance. In one groundbreaking public trust case protecting public rights to water resources, the Hawaiian Supreme Court emphasized, "The check and balance of judicial review provides a level of protection against improvident disposition of an irreplaceable *res*." At this perilous moment defined by climate crisis, youth have invoked the ancient public trust to protect ecological stability which is the condition necessary for human survival.

Applying the Public Trust to the Climate Emergency: Atmospheric Trust Litigation

It would be hard to dream up an environmental catastrophe with more dire consequences to more people than the climate crisis. Scientists are clear that runaway heating threatens human lives and the welfare of global civilization. The time remaining in which to slash carbon emissions is frighteningly narrow due to "tipping point" thresholds of nature. These are feedback processes capable of flooding the atmosphere with carbon emissions. For example, when trees die in a heating world, they burn and release the carbon they have stored, further increasing the atmosphere's load of carbon dioxide. When human-caused warming melts the permafrost situated across the northern latitudes, vast amounts of greenhouse gasses release into the atmosphere. There are many such feedback processes that threaten to send the climate situation spiraling out of control. Breach these tipping points, scientists warn, and we will trigger runaway planetary heating *regardless* of any subsequent decarbonization of the economy or society. No one suggests that civilization can survive runaway planetary heating.

In 2011, the non-profit organization, Our Children's Trust, launched a bold campaign known as Atmospheric Trust Litigation (ATL) on behalf of youth to force climate protection. This unprecedented legal strategy consists of lawsuits or administrative petitions filed against every state government as well as a lawsuit against the federal government. The youth plaintiffs and petitioners assert that the atmosphere is held in public trust and that their government has a fiduciary duty to protect and restore it.

The crux of the matter boils down to something quite simple. Government has known about this growing crisis for decades and has continued to subsidize and perpetuate a fossil fuel energy system despite the danger it poses to the future. Since the early 1970s, the Clean Air Act and other major environmental statutes provided the authority to regulate greenhouse gas emissions and phase out fossil fuel extraction. Nonetheless, the government promoted the fossil fuel energy system despite the environmental laws and the knowledge of the harms being created. The United States is now the leading oil producer in the world. The youth have invoked the public trust to slam the brakes on a heedless energy policy before the world plunges over the climate cliff. Plaintiffs seek court-supervised, science-based, enforceable plans to reduce carbon emissions at a rate necessary to restore a safe climate system.

The ATL campaign has its origins in Professor Sax's seminal work. Indeed, the ATL story shows how one scholar can set a pioneering pathway for others to follow and build upon as society encounters new threats. Professor Sax suggested applying the public trust to air and atmosphere in his famous 1969 article but did not develop the idea. For 30 years, the concept rested there, largely dormant.

In 2001, Professor Gerald Torres (one of the co-authors of this essay) gave a groundbreaking lecture that later became an article entitled "*Who Owns the Sky.*" He compiled exhaustive legal research and provided cogent reasoning to argue that the public trust logically applied to air for the same reasons it applied to the other traditional water-based resources. Indeed, air was one of the public resources expressly identified by the influential Institutes of Justinian in its ancient delineation of public rights to crucial resources. Now, nearly five decades after Sax first suggested the trust's application to air, the idea is solidifying in many courts. A California court recently stated, "From ancient Roman roots, the English common law has developed a doctrine enshrining humanity's entitlement to air and water as a public trust."

The next step was to develop a full litigation strategy through which the public trust principle could be invoked to confront climate crisis and hold governments accountable for transitioning away from dangerous fossil fuels. The other co-author of this essay, Professor Mary Christina Wood, took on that challenge and wrote a series of book chapters and articles outlining the strategy of "Atmospheric Trust Litigation." She developed a framework through which youth could invoke the public trust in every state in America and conceivably in many other nations as well. The trust concept, having such ancient legal roots, is integral to governments worldwide. In scores of opinions drawing on Professor Sax's scholarship, courts of several other countries—most notably India and the Philippines—had already characterized the trust as an attribute of sovereignty enforceable by citizens against their governments. Professor Wood suggested a model of domestic climate litigation that could be adapted worldwide.

In 2010, Julia Olson, an accomplished environmental litigator who had achieved notable success in the areas of wilderness and forest preservation, decided to bring the ATL strategy to court. She formed the non-profit organization Our Children's Trust, and in 2011, that organization launched the ATL campaign, consisting of lawsuits and administrative petitions on behalf of youth in every state in the United States. It was an unprecedented legal crusade: all of the petitions and lawsuits asserted the same duty to protect the atmosphere held in trust. Since those initial legal proceedings, the global legal campaign has accelerated and includes lawsuits filed or planned in partnership with other attorneys operating in the Netherlands, France, Canada, England, Belgium, Australia, Pakistan, Colombia, Norway, Ukraine, Uganda, India, the Philippines, and elsewhere. The suits reflect laws that are unique to each nation, but the underlying thread of governmental duty to citizens remains constant in all cases, unifying the cases in a coherent legal framework.

The youth gained early backing for the ATL campaign by leading scientist experts from around the world, including Dr. James Hansen, the famous scientist who was serving as the nation's chief climate scientist at NASA's Goddard Institute of Space Studies. In a brief supporting the youth, Dr. Hansen and other scientists said, "*failure to act with all deliberate speed in the face of the clear scientific evidence of the danger functionally becomes a decision to eliminate the option of preserving a habitable climate system.*" Dr. Hansen resigned from his top position at NASA in 2013 partly in order to support the young climate advocates, and he became a key scientific expert providing declarations against the federal government in Atmospheric Trust Litigation cases.

The youth also gained early support from many law professors nationwide. Because Professor Sax was widely regarded as the leading expert on the public trust, his backing was crucial. Amicus briefs ("friend of the court" briefs) were filed—and are still being filed—on behalf of law professors in many of the ATL cases. While he was alive (during the first three years of the ATL campaign, from 2011-2014), Joseph Sax was the lead signatory to all those briefs. In his final illness, Joe Sax's last decisive action as a legal scholar was signing his name to an amicus brief filed in support of the youth in a lawsuit challenging the federal government's failure to protect the atmosphere so crucial to their survival.

Building a new area of law is not an easy matter. The first round of ATL cases were mixed. While some judges ruled that the atmosphere was held in public trust, many dismissed these early cases based on the overriding sentiment that the courts should have no role in the climate crisis. To their thinking, climate was a problem for the other branches of government. That, of course, was the point of the litigation: to hold the other branches accountable for addressing this problem. They were instead fueling the emergency through their affirmative fossil fuel policy. In this early round of cases, climate became the hot potato tossed between the three branches, never lingering long enough for the sustained attention justice demanded.

Many judges approached these cases as if they were ordinary lawsuits. Seeking perhaps to simply rid themselves of the controversy, some characterized climate as a "political question" not suited to judicial resolution. These early decisions placed unwarranted confidence in the political branches of government to prevent the very danger that agency actions were continuing to perpetuate. The decisions succumbed—as did several notable climate tort cases before them—to what Professor Douglas Kysar and Henry Weaver identify as judicial nihilism—"[d]enying [their] own expansive power, [these courts] cowered before catastrophe." As Kysar and Weaver point out, judicial inaction is far from neutral. The failure of courts to carry out their constitutional role enables growing climate violence carried out by the other branches. Hawaii Supreme Court Associate Justice Michael Wilson writes, "As the archetypal peril of earth with collapsing ecosystems approaches, legal narratives limiting judicial review of carbon-caused global warming will become anachronisms."

The tide began to turn when a Washington court judge found a state constitutional public trust right to a protected atmosphere, saying that the children's "very survival depends upon the will of their elders to act now, decisively and unequivocally, to stem the tide of global warming...." Courts in other countries began to hand down notable victories for citizens in climate cases, some holding their governments accountable for hard-number emissions reduction. In 2015, the historic *Juliana v. United States* case was filed on behalf of 21 youth plaintiffs against the federal government. The plaintiffs were young people in states across the nation who were suffering intense climate harm, including loss of homes from sea level rise, loss of food supply, extreme flooding, wildfires, crop failures, exacerbated asthma, and a myriad of other harms. Scientist James Hansen joined as a plaintiff guardian representing future generations. The *Juliana* case challenged, quite literally, the entire fossil fuel policy of the United States and has often been called "the biggest case on the planet."

The *Juliana* case incorporates two claims against the federal government. One asserts the youth's public trust rights to a stable atmosphere, and the other asserts the due process right to be free from affirmative government action endangering the lives, liberty, and property of the 21 young people. Supported by thousands of pages of documentation, the plaintiffs showed that the government had known for decades of the growing climate emergency and yet perpetuated a fossil fuel energy policy that could only exacerbate it. The alleged, "Defendants have acted with deliberate indifference to the peril they knowingly created."

An early victory in the case happened in November 2016, when presiding Judge Ann Aiken issued a groundbreaking decision affirming that the youth's claims had a basis in law. Recognizing that this was "no ordinary lawsuit" and that it was a civil rights action rather than a standard environmental action, the court denied the government's and industry's motions to dismiss the case. Judge Aiken stated, "*I have no doubt that the right to a climate system capable of sustaining human life is fundamental to a free and ordered society.*" The ruling swept the globe and inspired a growing wave of international cases.

The case then headed to trial, scheduled for October 29, 2018. Building upon 20 depositions and thousands of pages of expert declarations and supporting documents, the much-anticipated trial promised to be the "trial of the century," because it represented the very first time the nation's fossil fuel policy would meet climate science in court. In an astonishing turn of events in June 2018, the fossil fuel industry, which had intervened in the case early on, withdrew *en masse* from the lawsuit when faced with requests for discovery and admissions. The monumental nature of the case caused the Trump government lawyers to double down their efforts to resist trial, using serial motions and other tactics designed to force an early appeal and derail the normal judicial process. Though initially such efforts repeatedly failed at all levels of the judicial system (including twice in the U.S. Supreme Court), the case finally went up on early appeal to the Ninth Circuit where it now stands.

Due to the dangerous proximity of climate tipping points, attorneys for the youth plaintiffs took the unusual step in February, 2019 of filing an Urgent Motion for Preliminary Injunction to stop 100 projects that the Trump Administration had poised for release before the youths' appeal could even be heard. These projects could use up much or all of the remaining narrow budget necessary to keep the planet from heating over 1.5 degrees C (the science-based limit for catastrophic heating). As Dr. Hanson declared in an amicus brief in one atmospheric trust case, judicial relief "may be the best, the last, and, at this late stage, the only real chance to preserve a habitable planet for young people and future generations."

Conclusion

Despite the good intentions, high aspirations, and hard work of many citizens, lawyers, and government officials, modern environmental law has turned into a system that permits wholesale destruction and pollution of crucial natural resources—exactly the opposite of its laudable purposes. This dysfunction is rooted in a fundamental breakdown of democracy that Professor Sax observed long ago. A discrete and insular minority—powerful private interests—maintain illegitimate power over government agencies and legislatures while the public, diffused and not organized, proves a weak counterweight.

Professor Sax identified, explained, and brought to modern environmental law a principle that drills to the core of government purpose. It defines an enduring government obligation to protect the ecological resources needed by the citizens, today and tomorrow. It prevents monopolization of crucial resources by private property interests. It demands government loyalty to the public in decision-making. Strict fiduciary obligations require care and caution in managing the invaluable natural wealth. The principle remains the bedrock obligation, with constitutional force as an attribute of sovereignty that government cannot alienate.

The public trust pulls environmental law out of deep statutory canyons where it has languished for decades and situates it in a fundamental rights framework, one in which citizens can hold their government officials accountable for representing their interests, as the promise of democracy has always purported to do. These reserved public trust rights held by the people are the same ones that animated the Magna Carta and Gandhi's famous Salt March to the sea.

As has always been the case, the public trust comes to life only through the work of many people. Professor Sax was the pioneering pathbreaker. In this time of historic danger, citizens all over the world are using the trust he illuminated to appeal to courts to force their governments to protect and restore the climate system necessary to support all life on Earth. If there is a habitable planet at the end of this century, it may well be because courageous judges stepped up at this pivotal moment to safeguard the crucial resources that have always been necessary for the endurance of humanity and civilization.

Chapter 7

Elinor Ostrom, Pioneer of the Commons (and Much More)

Daniel H. Cole[1]

Introduction

Elinor Ostrom was not a "pioneer" of environmental law in the conventional sense, but she pioneered a way of thinking about rule-based natural resource conservation that has strongly influenced many, if not all, environmental law scholars since the early 1990s. Her book *Governing the Commons: The Evolution of Institutions for Collective Action* (Cambridge 1990) changed the way nearly everyone today thinks about the "tragedy of the commons" and potential means of avoiding it. The Swedish Academy cited Ostrom's book when it awarded her the 2009 Nobel Memorial Prize in Economic Sciences, making her the first woman (and second political scientist) to receive that prize.

This appreciation of Ostrom's work will focus, of course, on *Governing the Commons*, which has influenced generations of environmental law scholars. In addition, I will attempt to place that work within a larger context of Elinor and Vincent Ostroms' efforts to create a multidisciplinary school of thought, using methods from throughout the social sciences—including law—for understanding social-ecological dilemmas and the diverse rule-based solutions that diverse

---

[1] Daniel H. Cole is Professor of Law and Professor of Public and Environmental Affairs at Indiana University, Bloomington. Professor Cole is author or editor of twelve books and more than 60 articles, book chapters, and essays many of which overlap the boundaries of law, economics, and political science, focusing on property rights and systems, environmental protection, and natural resources management, and comparative governance systems more broadly. He recently completed, with Michael D. McGinnis, editing a four-volume collection, *Elinor Ostrom and the Bloomington School of Political Economy* (Lexington Books 2015-18). In 2012, Cole and Ostrom co-edited *Property in Land and Other Resources* (Lincoln Institute). In the past few years, he has published law and policy articles on polycentric approaches to climate change, including a 2015 paper in the leading climate science journal, *Nature Climate Change*. Various publications of his have been translated into French, Italian, and Chinese. Professor Cole is a Life Member of Clare Hall (College for Advanced Study), University of Cambridge.

communities produce through collective action to avoid, ameliorate, or resolve them. This school of thought, alternately described as one of political economy, public choice, or institutional analysis, is known as the "Bloomington School."[2]

The reason for widening the focus to include that larger school of thought, is to suggest that Ostrom's influence among legal scholars should extend beyond the influence of *Governing the Commons*. The broader context is crucial for appreciating: (1) the value of interdisciplinary cooperation and mixed-methods approaches for understanding and resolving environmental problems; (2) how legal "action situations" arising at operational, policy, and constitutional levels might be analyzed more systematically and with greater utility for both legal scholars and scholars in cognate disciplines, using Ostrom's IAD framework;[3] and (3) the different types of rules and the various functions they perform. These wider lessons extend far beyond the legal subfields of environmental and natural resources law, of course. They mark an important, though unacknowledged contribution to analytical jurisprudence, which, if put into widespread use, could facilitate more productive interactions between legal scholars and other social scientists.

Before Governing the Commons

Ostrom's 1965 PhD on Groundwater Management in Southern California

Elinor ("Lin") Ostrom received both her BA and PhD in Political Science from UCLA, where she met her mentor, PhD supervisor, and eventual husband, Vincent Ostrom. They established a scholarly partnership the depth and breadth of which remains underappreciated. Elinor joined Vincent's team of research assistants studying groundwater allocation in Los Angeles. This was Lin's initial introduction to the collective-action problems associated with common-pool resources (CPRs). And it became the subject of her PhD dissertation, which later became one of her many examples of how resource users can sometimes avoid commons tragedies without the need for markets or government intervention.

---

[2] William C. Mitchell, *Virginia, Rochester, and Bloomington: Twenty-Five Years of Public Choice and Political Science*, 56 Pub. Choice 101, 112 (1988) (first reference to a distinctive "Bloomington school" of public choice); Abigail Bennett, Leslie Acton, Graham Epstein Rebecca Gruby and Meteja Nenadvoic, *Embracing conceptual diversity to integrate power and institutional analysis: Introducing a relational typology*, 12 Int'l J. Commons 330, 332 (referring to the "Bloomington School of institutional analysis"); Dario Castiglione and Filippo Sabetti, *Creativity, Diversity and Governance—Extending the Ostroms' Research Program, in* F. Sabetti & D. Castiglione, eds., Institutional Diversity in Self-Governing Societies: The Bloomington School and Beyond xiii (2017) (referring to the "Bloomington School of Political Economy").

[3] *See infra* Creating an Analytical Framework for the Study of Social and Combined Social-Ecological Phenomena.

As described in *Governing the Commons*, Ostrom's dissertation studied mechanisms devised by groundwater users in the Los Angeles metropolitan area to end "competitive pumping," which was rapidly depleting groundwater supplies. The chief difficulty was in the incentives created by existing legal rules governing "ownership" of groundwater. Those legal rules were unusually complicated because they combined elements of prior appropriation doctrine, correlative rights doctrine, which subordinates the rights of senior appropriators to the owners of lands immediately above groundwater aquifers, and prescriptive rights. The legal confusion created by this admixture of rules was exacerbated by uncertainty over the amount of water a given groundwater basin could sustainably supply (i.e., the "safe yield").

To clarify the situation, parties resorted to the court system, not to allocate the water by decree but as a mechanism for bargaining in the shadow of the law. The courts became clearinghouses for information that water users, including municipalities such as Pasadena, large irrigation companies, and small landowners, relied upon to successfully negotiate their own agreements, which the courts then ratified. In effect, the courts served as "action arenas" (a term later incorporated into Ostrom's IAD framework, which is described *infra*) within which successful collective action was achieved. Instead of a regulatory solution *imposed* from above or marketization of the resource system, the water basins were successfully managed under "a *polycentric set* of limited-purpose governmental enterprises, which involved active participation by private water companies and voluntary producer associations. This system is neither centrally owned nor centrally regulated," and compliance with the negotiated agreements was virtually complete.[4]

In 1965, Elinor and Vincent Ostrom moved to Indiana University. She was the "trailing spouse," was not hired onto the tenure track but as an adjunct to teach an intro-level political science course on Saturday mornings. Vincent already was well known among political scientists and public administration scholars for his work on the politics of public finance, particularly his scholarly opposition to the then-rampant consolidationist movement sweeping municipal governments around the country. During the 1950s, in response to claims that government services were overly fragmented and, therefore, inefficient, municipalities began consolidating school districts, police and fire departments, and various other public-service providers. Some of this consolidation was no doubt driven by changing demographics, as the population became increasingly urban and suburban. But it was also based on presumptions about economies of scale that were hardly ever critically examined, either theoretically or empirically.

In 1961, Vincent, along with co-authors Charles Tiebout and Robert Warren, published a provocative and influential attack on the consolidationist

[4] Elinor Ostrom, Governing the Commons: The Evolution of Institutions for Collective Action (1990) 136.

movement for its presumption of continuous economies of scale in public service production and provision.[5] Their work argued that apparently fragmented public service provision by small units with overlapping jurisdictions actually could be *more* efficient than large, consolidated providers, depending on the type of service relative to the service area. Whereas a port authority might of necessity be controlled at the largest level of municipal governance, local trash pick-up, for example, might more efficiently operate at a neighborhood level with competing service providers. In other words, a "polycentric" governance approach, based implicitly on a conception of subsidiarity,[6] could be more efficient and effective than a unitary, consolidated governance system.

This hypothesis was a twist on Charles Tiebout's earlier (1956) model of sorting by public services consumers, who could "vote with their feet," moving from one place to another to obtain better public service.[7] Ostrom, Tiebout, and Warren (1961) suggested that public service consumers might be able to vote among competing providers of public services without moving at all.

Police Studies

In 1973, the Ostroms created the Workshop in Political Theory and Policy Analysis at Indiana University as an independent research center designed to bring together researchers from diverse disciplines to work together on common problems, including but not limited to problems of natural common-pool resources (CPRs), and various mechanisms used around the world for resolving them. Today, the Workshop is most famous as the home of CPR studies. But before Elinor Ostrom began work in earnest on *Governing the Commons* (1990), she spent most of the 1970s empirically grounding Vincent's theory of polycentric governance. With teams of graduate students and colleagues, she carefully constructed intricate natural experiments in various cities, including Indianapolis, Chicago, and St. Louis, to test whether larger, smaller, or medium-sized governance units—police departments, fire departments, transportation departments (road repair)—tended to perform best according to a number of objective and subjective (as perceived by their "consumers") performance measures. The studies found that small units always performed better than large, consolidated

[5] Vincent Ostrom, Charles M. Tiebout, and Robert Warren, *The Organization of Government in Metropolitan Areas: A Theoretical Inquiry*, 55 Amer. Pol. Sci. Rev. 831 (1961).

[6] As a political doctrine, subsidiarity refers to matching the governance level to the scale of the problem to be managed. *See* Andreas Føllesdal, *Survey Article: Subsidiarity*, 6 J. Pol. Phil. 190 (1998). However, "polycentricity" goes beyond the concept of subsidiarity in calling for varying amounts of competition and cooperation among public service providers, to be determined empirically. Ostrom, Tiebout, and Warren, *supra* note 5.

[7] Charles M. Tiebout, *A Pure Theory of Local Expenditures*, 64 J. Pol. Econ. 416 (1956).

units, and medium-sized units performed best overall.[8] It is important to note that, though these were not studies involving natural resources, they were studies of CPRs. Fire and police protection, among other governmental functions, meet the Ostroms' strict definition of common-pool resource, as set out in the next section.

Defining a "Common-Pool Resource"

Long before *Governing the Commons*, in 1977 Elinor and Vincent Ostrom published a seminal paper in a little noticed book.[9] The paper, "Public Goods and Public Choices," had important implications for all of Elinor's later work on governance systems, covering both natural and artifactual resources. In it, she and Vincent completed a typology of "goods" created by the economist Paul Samuelson,[10] who first distinguished between public goods and private goods on two dimensions: rivalrousness in consumption (i.e., whether the good is subtractable, degradable, or depletable) and cost of exclusion. Most ordinary goods, traded in markets, are "private goods" because relative scarcity renders consumption rivalrous—if one person buys a scoop of ice cream and consumes it, that particular scoop of ice cream no longer is available for another consumer. Meanwhile, non-paying customers can cost-effectively be excluded from accessing ice cream by suppliers (i.e., shop, truck or cart vendors). (For more examples, see Table 1, below). Some goods, however, do not exhibit these qualities. For example, solar energy from the sun which is necessary for life to exist on earth is not rivalrous in consumption because, no matter how much of it one person uses just as much exists for everyone else in the world. At the same time, restricting access to solar energy is simply not possible at any finite cost.[11] Some public goods are not natural but must be created by humans, such as standard weights and measures.

Samuelson's model of "goods" begged for two more categories. If public goods are both non-subtractable and nonexcludable, and private goods are

---

[8] Elinor Ostrom, *Between Markets and States: Polycentric Governance of Complex Economic Systems*, 100 Amer. Econ. Rev. 641, 644 (2010) (the published version of Ostrom's 2009 Nobel Prize address); Elinor Ostrom, Roger B. Parks and Gordon Whitaker, Patterns of Metropolitan Policing (1978).

[9] Vincent Ostrom and Elinor Ostrom, *Public Goods and Public Choices*, in E.S. Savas, ed., Alternatives to Delivering Public Services: Toward Improved Performance (1977), *reprinted in* D.H. Cole & M.D. McGinnis, Elinor Ostrom and the Bloomington School of Political Economy: Vol. 2, Resource Governance 3 (2015).

[10] Paul A. Samuelson, *The Pure Theory of Public Expenditure*, 36 Rev. Econ. & Stat. 387 (1954).

[11] Note that "solar energy" is not a synonym for sunlight, which in certain cases can be rivalrous in consumption. *Cite Fountainbleu Hotel case.*

Table 1. Four Types of Goods.

		Subtractability of Use	
		High	Low
Difficulty of Excluding Potential Beneficiaries	High	*Common-pool resources*: groundwater basins; lakes; irrigation systems; fisheries; forests	*Public goods*: solar radiation; national defense; standard weights & measures
	Low	*Private goods*: food; clothing; automobiles; computers	*Toll goods*: theaters; private clubs; many churches; "tollways"

Source: Adapted from Ostrom [1997] 2011 at 7, Fig. 1.1

both subtractable and excludable, it is reasonable to suppose that some goods might be excludable but not subtractable, and still others subtractable but not excludable. In 1965, James Buchanan identified the category of "club goods" as examples of the former.[12] Such goods include country club golf courses, which can cost-effectively be fenced in to exclude non-members, but the paying members are not so numerous as to create at any time rivalrousness in consumption on the 18 holes (for other examples see Table 1). It is important to note, however, that a "club" good might become rivalrous in consumption at some congestion point, e.g., if the club lets in too many members so that its golf course becomes over-crowded. The Ostroms subsequently relabeled "club goods" as "toll goods" to emphasize that it is not only private groups that supply such goods but also public agencies (at both large and small scales of governance).[13] In addition, the Ostroms completed the typology of "goods" with CPRs, a category that combines subtractability (i.e., rivalrousness in consumption) with high costs of exclusion.[14] It would be incorrect to label such goods as "public goods" that are either "impure," "subtractable," or "congestible," because lack of rivalrousness in consumption is a defining characteristic of "public good." On Samuelson's definition, adopted by the Ostroms, if a good is subtractable it cannot be a public good but must be some other type of good—which the Ostroms labeled CPR.

Scholars sometimes mistakenly conflate the "type" of a good with a property system used to manage that good, as if the type of good determines the set of appropriate management institutions. In fact, as Ostrom demonstrated in subsequent works,[15] a wide variety of management institutions are applied to each

[12] James Buchanan, *An Economic Theory of Clubs*, 32 ECONOMICA 1 (1965).

[13] Ostrom and Ostrom, *in* COLE & MCGINNIS, EDS., *supra* note 9.

[14] *Id.*

[15] Daniel H. Cole and Elinor Ostrom, *The Variety of Property Systems and Rights in Natural Resources, in* D.H. COLE & E. OSTROM, EDS., PROPERTY IN LAND AND OTHER RESOURCES 37 (2012).

of the types of goods, as defined in Table 1. For example, what is probably the most famous painting in the world, *La Giaconda* (more commonly known as the "Mona Lisa"), is technically a private good, but it is not privately owned. Under French heritage laws, the painting is owned by the public and cannot be sold. By contrast, a public good like national defense is often co-provided by public and private suppliers. And while knowledge is a pure public good, the specific form it takes may be a private good under intellectual property laws. Because the "nature" of a good does not necessarily determine a specific management regime, it is very important not to conflate the good and the management system. For this reason, it is not appropriate to refer to a common-pool resource (CPR) as a common-property resource (also CPR) because common-pool resources are not always managed as common property, as that term is understood today to mean a group of user-owners who exclude others. In addition, to conflate common-pool resources (biophysical things) with institutional structures designed to manage them (e.g., property rights) is a Rylean "category mistake."[16]

The Ostroms adopted John Searle's conceptual distinction between "brute" facts about the world and "social" or "institutional" facts.[17] Brute facts refer to things in the world that exist regardless of what humans believe. For example, if we are walking towards a river, it does not matter whether we notice it or acknowledge its existence, nor does it doesn't matter what we think it is or what we call it. If we continue walking toward it, eventually our feet will get wet. Social or institutional facts, by contrast, depend entirely on human intentionality—a combination of collective intent on the part of the relevant community and collective acceptance by that same community.[18] Laws are institutional facts, as are social norms, scientific models of the world, religious injunctions, even language itself, preceding all other social facts. It can be said that true "laws" of physics represent brute rather than institutional facts, but the use of the word "law" in that context reflects physical/chemical cause and effect relations. Those same physical/chemical cause and effect relations are absent when the same term is used in reference to formal institutions governing individual behavior and social interactions in a society.

Finally, as noted at the end of Section I, not all CPRs are "natural" resources. Police and fire departments are as well. Although they are often portrayed as public goods, the services they provide are subtractable, at least beyond some

---

[16] Gilbert Ryle, The Concept of Mind (1949); Daniel H. Cole, *'Economic Property Rights' as 'nonsense upon stilts': a comment on Hodgson*, 11 J. Inst'l Econ. 725 (2015).

[17] John R. Searle, The Construction of Social Reality (1995); Vincent Ostrom, *Where to Begin?*, 25 J. Federalism 45 (1995); Elinor Ostrom, *The 2005 James Madison Award Lectures: Converting Threats into Opportunities,* 39 PS: Pol. Sci. & Pol. 3, 6 (2006), *reprinted in* D.H. Cole & M.C. McGinnis, eds., Elinor Ostrom and the Bloomington School of Political Economy: Volume 1, Polycentricity in Public Administration and Political Science 307. 315-16 (2015).

[18] John R. Searle, *What is an institution?*, 1 J. Inst. Econ. 1 (2005).

congestion point. Great fires in London (1666), Chicago (1871), and San Francisco (1906) are only the most obvious cases where demand for fire protection services greatly outstripped the supply—something that is, strictly speaking, not possible for a "public good.". The same is true of public libraries, though private libraries would be considered "toll" goods.

Creating an Analytical Framework for the Study of Social and Combined Social-Ecological Phenomena

Elinor Ostrom's Institutional Analysis & Development (IAD) framework, which unfortunately remains largely unknown to legal scholars, has been described as "one of most developed and sophisticated attempts to use institutional and stakeholder assessment in order to link theory and practice, analysis and policy."[19] It is very widely used, in particular, by social scientists studying CPR problems.[20] Interestingly, however, it was not Ostrom's work on natural resource systems that first motivated her efforts to create the framework but her more general interest in creating an analytical system to understand "the complexity and diversity of the field settings," referring to her studies of municipal fire, policing, and other services.[21] It was also in response to Vincent Ostrom's demand for an analytically more rigorous language for understanding public administration and policy.[22]

The first iteration of the IAD framework appeared in 1978.[23] Since then, it has been subject to almost constant revision, in accordance with the Ostroms' insistence on empirically-grounding theory, or in this case meta-theory, to the greatest extent possible. Indeed, Lin Ostrom continued to make minor changes in the framework during the last decade of her life.[24] The version presented in Figure 1 comes from her most detailed exposition of the IAD framework.[25]

According to Ostrom, "[t]he IAD framework has its roots in classic political economy (specifically the work of Hobbes, Montesquieu, Hume, Smith,

[19] Paul Aligica, *Institutional and stakeholder mapping: frameworks for policy analysis and institutional change*, 6 PUB. ADMIN. REV. 79, 89 (2006).

[20] A Google Scholar search conducted on July 11, 2019 using the phrase "IAD framework" yielded 3,550 entries.

[21] OSTROM 2010, *supra* note 8, at 645.

[22] Vincent Ostrom, *Language, Theory and Empirical Research in Policy Analysis*, 3 POL. STUD. J. 274 (1975).

[23] Larry L. Kiser and Elinor Ostrom, *Three Worlds of Action: A Metatheoretical Synthesis of Institutional Approaches," in* E. Ostrom, ed., STRATEGIES OF POLITICAL INQUIRY 179 (1978).

[24] Compare ELINOR OSTROM, UNDERSTANDING INSTITUTIONAL DIVERSITY 15, Fig. 1.2 (2005) (a book which contains her most detailed explication of the framework) with her Nobel Prize address, Ostrom 2010, *supra* note 8, at 646, Fig. 2.

[25] OSTROM 2005, *supra* note 24, at 15, Fig. 1.2.

Figure 1. The Institutional Analysis & Development framework.

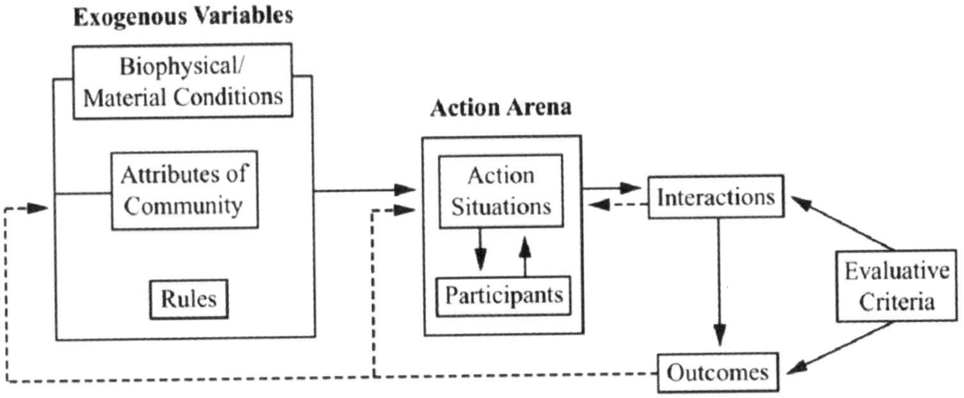

Source: Ostrom 2005.

Hamilton, Madison, and Tocqueville), neoclassical microeconomic theory, institutional economics (the work of Commons ... and Coase ...); public choice theory" (including work by Buchanan, Tullock, Riker); "transaction-cost economics (North ... [and] Williamson ...), and noncooperative game theory...."[26] Despite that, the IAD framework is not itself a substantive or normative theory or a model. Rather, it is what Elinor Ostrom once referred to as a "metatheoretical conceptual map"—an analytical device comprised of the most basic variables and relations between them involved in all collective choice problems.[27] As such, it is designed to be consistent with a wide variety of theories and models to be chosen by the analyst. The framework's only obvious normative commitment is to methodological individualism, which only limits the framework's utility for scholars who are pure social-constructivists. This is in keeping with the Ostroms' shared faith in individual agency, including the ability of ordinary people, working together, to solve shared problems (as in the successful cases recounted in *Governing the Commons*). The Ostrom's other major normative commitment, to polycentricism, has no necessary bearing on the IAD framework or its applications. It remains primarily a tool of positive diagnosis and, to a lesser extent, prediction.

The centerpiece of the IAD framework is the "action situation," located social interactions occur, whether for the purpose of making (a) "constitutional-level" decisions, which establish the meta-rules (the rules for making rules);

---

[26] Elinor Ostrom, Roy Gardner, and James Walker, Rules, Games and Common-Pool Resources 25 (1994).

[27] Amy R. Poteete, Marco A. Janssen, and Elinor Ostrom, Working Together: Collective Action, the Commons, and Multiple Methods in Practice 40 (2010).

(b) the policy level (often referred to as the "collective-choice" level[28]) where the formal "rules of the game"[29] are promulgated (in accordance with constitutional meta-rules); or (c) the "operational level" of everyday relations in markets, churches, courts, private associations, social media, book clubs, households, etc., which are governed by constitutional- and policy-level rules. Importantly, the outcomes of operational level interactions can lead to efforts to change rules at the policy or constitutional level.

What happens in any focal action situation will be largely determined by the (misleadingly named) "exogenous variables" in the left-hand column of Figure 1. Those variables are only exogenous if the focal action situation involves a single-play game or the first-round of an iterative game. In all other cases (that is, the vast majority of cases of interest), they are endogenized to the framework by virtue of feedback loops. It is more useful to think of them as "preexisting conditions" prior to any focal action situation; many of them will be outcomes of prior interactions (again highlighting the framework's recursive nature). The three boxes of "Biophysical/Material Conditions," "Attributes of Community," and "Rules" are supposed to include all of the important variables that may influence, but not necessarily determine, what will happen in the action situation. Within the "Biophysical/Material conditions" box exist all the relevant "brute facts," as defined earlier, which are mainly relevant for action situations involving combined social-ecological problems.[30] The "Attributes of the Community" include the actors, the various positions they hold, including (in the case of a courthouse) "Attorney," "Defendant," "Plaintiff," "Judge," "Bailiff," "Witness," "Juror," and so on. In many action situations, power relations will be effectively determined by those positions, each of which is associated with a separate set of attributes and governed by rules which might be similar or different. For instance, among the Actors mentioned above, only the Judge has the power to hold someone in contempt of court. US judges do not, however, have the power to interrogate witnesses. Only attorneys are allowed to question

[28] I prefer the label "policy level" to "collective-choice level" because constitutional-level choices are also "collective choices." Although it is possible to talk about constitutional "policy," that term is more conventionally associated with legislative and administrative choices made within the overarching system of constitutional rules.

[29] See DOUGLASS C. NORTH, INSTITUTIONS, INSTITUTIONAL CHANGE AND ECONOMIC PERFORMANCE 3 (1990). Ostrom defined "institutions" with slight variations throughout her works, but always consistently with North's phrase, "rules of the game." Compare OSTROM 2005, *supra* note 24, at 132 ("Broadly defined, institutions are the prescriptions that humans use to organize all forms of repetitive and structured interactions. . . ."); *Id.* at 179 (following North's distinction between institutions and organizations); OSTROM 1990, *supra* note 4, at 51 ("'Institutions' can be defined as the set of working rules. . . .").

[30] It would be unusual, indeed, for biophysical conditions to affect interactions in action arenas such as courtrooms and legislative committee rooms, unless biophysical conditions are at issue in a specific case or certain biophysical conditions, e.g., failure of an air conditioner, effects interactions in some way.

witnesses, but they must do so in accordance with the Rules of Evidence, which the Judge enforces. Those Rules of Evidence come from the third box, "Rules" (often labeled "Working Rules" or "Rules-in-use"), which include the sum-total of formal (e.g., legal) rules and informal social norms that might affect interactions and, therefore, outcomes once the fully- or boundedly-rational Actors enter the Action Situation with whatever positions, beliefs, and strategies they hold.

Rules, including formal laws, social norms and hybrids,[31] condition the interactions of all Actors when they enter an action situation. Schlager and Ostrom define "rules" as "generally agreed-upon and enforced prescriptions that require, forbid, or permit specific actions for more than a single individual."[32] This statement can usefully be decomposed into two elements that together comprise a rule: (1) deontic specification, i.e., the rule must specify actions that specified actors may, must, or must not perform; and (2) levels of compliance/enforcement, i.e., the rule must be obeyed and/or enforced to some, inevitably uncertain level below which it would no longer be considered a rule but something less, such as a guideline, recommendation, ethic, signal, expression, or simply an empty gesture.[33] For the sake of conceptual clarity, the examples of rules provided in this paper intentionally steer clear of the admittedly fuzzy boundaries of both deontic specification and obeisance/enforcement.

Instead of just listing rules, Ostrom created a classification of rules by function to enable more finely grained institutional analysis, as shown in Table 2 (below). Ostrom also developed an "institutional grammar" to understand what kinds of sentences (in ordinary language) establish rules, as described above, and norms.[34] The grammar becomes quite complex, but its basic "ADICO" syntax, set out in Table 3 (below) is easy enough to grasp.

Once again, Ostrom's goal in developing the IAD framework, including her functional classification of rules and grammar of institutions was primarily diagnostic—to better understand social and combined social-ecological dilemmas requiring collection action for resolution. Through careful use of these tools, Ostrom believed, social scientists could develop better, more complete

---

[31] On the classification of rules as formal, informal, and hybrid, *see* Daniel H. Cole, *Laws, Norms, and the Institutional Analysis and Development Framework*, 13 J. Inst. Econ. 829 (2017).

[32] Edella Schlager and Elinor Ostrom, *Property-rights regimes and natural resources: a conceptual analysis*, 68 Land Econ. 249, 252 (1992).

[33] Frank Elmes, *Government and people: III: when is a law not a law?*, 39 Police J. 47, 51 (1966) ("The laws of the land share one great weakness with all other laws; they are not laws unless they are enforced."). It might also be said that laws are not really laws if they are unenforceable. *See* Daniel H. Cole, Instituting Environmental Protection: From Red to Green in Poland Ch. 3 (1998).

[34] Sue E.S. Crawford and Elinor Ostrom, *A Grammar of Institutions*, 89 Amer. Pol. Sci. Rev. 582 (1995); Ostrom, *supra* note 22, Ch. 5.

Table 2. Ostrom's Functional Classification of Rule-Types.

Type of Rule	Function of Rule
Boundary rules	Define (1) who is eligible to hold a certain position (e.g., "president" or "defendant"), (2) the process by which positions are assigned to actors (e.g., by appointment, vote, or succession), and (3) how positions may be exited (e.g., term-limits, firing, retirement, or death).
Position rules	Create positions (e.g., member, judge, plaintiff, voter, representative) that actors may hold.
Choice rules	Prescribe actions actors in positions must, must not, or may take in various circumstances (e.g., attorneys *must* comply with rules of professional responsibility, *must not* breach their fiduciary obligations to clients, and *may* plead on behalf of their client).
Aggregation rules	Determine how many, and which, players must participate in a given collective- or operational-choice decision (e.g., majority v. super-majority v. unanimity voting requirement for members of Congress, a corporate board, or a jury to, respectively, make laws, promulgate corporate by-laws, and render verdicts).
Information rules	Authorize channels of information flows available to participants, including assignation of obligations, permissions, or prohibitions on communication (e.g., rules of evidence in court, permission to reprint published information subject to copyright, embargoes on press releases, and judicial gag orders).
Payoff rules	Assign rewards or sanctions to particular actions that have been taken or based on outcomes (e.g., criminal, civil or administrative penalties for violations of law, loss of employment for sexual harassment, ostracism for violating important social norms of a community).
Scope rules	Delimit the range of possible outcomes (e.g., a trial court can only decide the case before it, and cannot establish a general rule applicable in all future cases; a federal administrative agency cannot act outside the scope of authority designated by Congress; a university president may be allowed to make some decisions unilaterally but others only with the approval of the Board of Trustees.

Adapted from Cole, *supra* note 31, at 837, Table 1.

case studies and experiments, which could be incorporated in meta-analyses and various other types of qualitative and quantitative analyses.

CPR Studies and *Governing the Commons*

Before Ostrom (with a team of PhD students) began compiling case studies for *Governing the Commons*, she and colleagues put together a coding manual, based in the IAD framework, to record a consistent set of variables for each CPR

Table 3. The ADICO Syntax for an Institutional Grammar.

A. Attributes	Defines the actors, within a given action situation, to whom the "institutional statement" applies (e.g., applicants for the bar)
D. Deontic	Refers to the three modal verbs of "choice rules": "must" (obliged); "must not" (forbidden); and "may" (permitted)
I. "Aim"	Denotes the actions or outcomes to which the deontic operators apply (e.g., to become an attorney (the A*im*), an applicant must pass the bar exam)
C. "Conditions"	Defines when and where an action or outcome is permissible, obligatory, or forbidden (e.g., the bar passage obligation is waived in Wisconsin for graduates from accredited law schools in that state and in the District of Columbia for attorneys who have bar accreditation from at least one state)
O. "Or else"	Defines the consequences for not obeying the rule established in the "institutional statement" (e.g., practicing law without having been admitted to the bar is illegal and punishable (depending on the jurisdiction–a boundary rule) as a misdemeanor, with imprisonment for up to one year and fines up to $1000, or a felony with imprisonment for up to five years and fines of $5000 or more per offense)

Source: Derived from Ostrom, *supra* note 22, Ch. 5 and Crawford and Ostrom, *supra* note 34.

study.[35] But the coding manual proved only moderately useful because various scholars from diverse disciplines did not use the same terms or give the same meaning to the same terms, which made coding difficult and, in some cases, impossible. "To obtain sufficient information about 47 irrigation systems, the team screened over 450 documents. They screened several hundred papers to obtain sufficient information on 30 coastal fisheries located around the world."[36] The team contacted authors of earlier studies in an effort to gain greater clarity on variables, but with only limited success. In Ostrom's mind, this frustrating experience demonstrated the need for a common analytical framework, such as the IAD. The value of case studies utilizing a common analytical framework would be much greater than case studies that could not be used in a meta-analysis. From the start, the IAD framework was conceived as a *general* diagnostic tool. Ostrom's work on *Governing the Commons* underscored the importance of its generalizability.

Ostrom's research that led to *Governing the Commons* was the proximate result of a National Research Council committee convened in the mid-1980s to study jointly managed resources, i.e., CPRs. The Committee was comprised of members from various disciplines, all of whom agreed to use (and improve) the

---

[35] Ostrom 2010, *supra* note 8, at 649.

[36] Amy R. Poteete, Marco A. Janssen, and Elinor Ostrom, Working Together: Collective Action, the Commons, and Multiple Methods in Practice 93 (2010).

IAD framework as a basis for identifying common variables in cases of successful and failed management. They identified more than 1,000 case studies written by scholars throughout the world.[37]

But *Governing the Commons* had deeper roots extending back to Ostrom's PhD dissertation and two important publications that appeared within a few years of her dissertation. One was the 1965 publication of Mancur Olson's PhD dissertation, *The Logic of Collective Action.*[38] The other was the 1968 publication of "The Tragedy of the Commons" by biologist Garrett Hardin.[39] (*Governing the Commons* also may be considered a response to Harold Demsetz's 1967 article, "Toward a Theory of Property Rights,"[40] but that work was not an explicit target for Ostrom in the way the other two were.)

Olson's book is neatly summarized by a quote from David Hume, who wrote 200 years before Olson was born. In his *Treatise on Human Nature*,[41] Hume made the following observation of what Olson later described as the "free-rider" problem that hinders collective action within large groups:

> Two neighbors may agree to drain a meadow, which they possess in common; because 'tis easy for them to know each other's mind; and each must perceive, that the immediate consequence of his failing in his part is, the abandonment of the whole project. But 'tis very difficult, and indeed impossible, that a thousand persons shou'd agree any such action; it being difficult for them to concert so complicated a design, and still more difficult for them to execute it; while each seeks a pretext to free himself of the trouble and expence, and wou'd lay the whole burden on others.[42]

Based on her 1965 dissertation and other studies of CPRs, Ostrom may have agreed with Hume and Olson that collective action within large groups can

---

[37] Annual Reviews Conversations, "An Interview with Elinor Ostrom" at 9 (2010) (accessed at https://www.google.com/url?sa=t&rct=j&q=&esrc=s&source=web&cd=2&ved=2ahUKEwiR193PoszjAhWUds0KHQo1DoIQFjABegQIBhAB&url=http%3A%2F%2Fwww.annualreviews.org%2Fuserimages%2FContentEditor%2F1326999553977%2FElinorOstromTranscript.pdf&usg=AOvVaw12yH3CSLgVVQmwH3cjO'sYZ on July 23, 2019).

[38] Mancur Olson, The Logic of Collective Action: Public Goods and the Theory of Groups (1965).

[39] Garrett Hardin, *The Tragedy of the Commons*, 162 Sci. 1243 (1968). Hardin was building on empirically-grounded theories developed by fisheries economists earlier in the twentieth century. *See* Jens Warming, *Om 'grunderete' af fiskegrunde,* Nationalokonomisk Tidskrift 495 (1911), *translated in* P. Anderson, trans., *On Rent of a Fishing Grounds: A Translation of Jen's Warmings 1911 Article, with an Introduction*, 15 Hist. Pol. Econ. 391 (1983); H. Scott Gordon, *The Economic Theory of a Common Property Resource*, 62 J. Pol. Econ. 122 (1954); Anthony D. Scott, *The Fishery: The Objectives of Sole Ownership*, 63 J. Pol. Econ. 203 (1955).

[40] Harold Demsetz, *Toward a Theory of Property Rights*, 57 Amer. Econ. Rev. 347 (1967).

[41] David Hume, A Treatise on Human Nature, L.A. Selby Brigge, ed. ([1739-40] 1978).

[42] *Id.* at 538.

be difficult, but her own research, even at that early date, proved it was not "impossible."

Ostrom's disagreement with Hardin was basically the same, but it went even deeper because, unlike Olson, Hardin proposed means of averting the "Tragedy of the Commons," which in Ostrom's view were too limited. In addition, Elinor and Vincent both became horrified at Hardin's proposals for draconian remedies for commons tragedies, including restrictions on childbearing and forced sterilization, which inevitably impede individual agency.[43] Hardin's presumption that such top-down "panacea" solutions could work led Elinor to refer to him, on the record, as a "totalitarian."[44] From her perspective, Hardin was blinded by his own inability to conceive that even large groups of ordinary people—numbering more than 10,000 farmers in one of the Spanish irrigation systems she studied—could successfully manage to conserve CPRs as common property systems over very long periods of time. The notion that common property/regulatory regimes for managing CPRs only works at a very small scale remains a common misunderstanding of her work.

Despite the fact that *Governing the Commons* contains an important theoretical component, most readers have focused on the empirical case studies and meta-analyses, treating the book as a work of economic anthropology, disconnected to the rest of the Ostroms' research program. Nevertheless, the book provided scholars and policymakers with a third possible way of averting commons tragedies. Hardin had offered two: A Hobbesian solution of state regulation of access to and use of CPRs (which Hardin referred to as "socialistic") and privatization of parcels of the CPR (which he referred to as capitalistic).[45] Ostrom provided a third: co-management by the users themselves as common property (which actually describes a huge variety of institutional solutions).

In *Governing the Commons,* Ostrom discussed both successes and failures of CPRs. The goal of her meta-analysis was to see whether she could discern regularities among the successful cases that were not present, or were less present, in the cases of failure. Based on her institutional diagnoses, she was able to come up with a "speculative" set of "Design Principles," which she characterized as tentative necessary ingredients for a successful CPR management system.

More recent research has confirmed that Ostrom's "Design Principles" (see Table 4) have significant predictive value. A 2010 analysis of 91 studies by scholars who assessed the relevance of the principles for explaining the success or failure of CPR management found that two-thirds of the studies confirmed the

---

[43] Garrett Hardin, *Political Requirements for Preserving Our Common Heritage, in* H.P. Brokaw, ed., Wildlife and America 310 (1978); Ostrom 2010, *supra* note 8.

[44] "An Interview with Elinor Ostrom," *supra* note 37, at 8.

[45] Hardin, *supra* note 39. Demsetz, *supra* note 40, had already argued, a year before Hardin published "The Tragedy of the Commons," that only Hardin's second solution had any hope of working.

Table 4. Design Principles for long-enduring CPR institutions.

1. Clearly defined boundaries: Individuals or groups with rights to withdraw resource units from the CPR must be clearly defined, as must the boundaries of the CPR itself.
2. Congruence between appropriation and provision rules and local conditions: Appropriation rules restricting time, place, technology, and/or quantity of resource units are related to local conditions and to provision rules requiring labor, material, and/or money.
3. Collective-choice arrangements: Most individuals affected by the operational rules can participate in modifying the operational rules.
4. Monitoring: Monitors, who actively audit CPR conditions and appropriator behavior, are accountable to the appropriators or are the appropriators.
5. Graduated sanctions: Appropriators who violate operational rules are likely to be assessed graduate sanctions (depending on the seriousness and context of the offense) by other appropriators, by officials accountable to these appropriators, or both.
6. Conflict-resolution mechanisms: Appropriators and their officials have rapid access to low-cost local arenas to resolve conflicts among appropriators or between appropriators and officials.
7. Minimal recognition of rights to organize: The rights of appropriators to devise their own institutions are not challenged by external governmental authorities.

For CPRs that are parts of larger systems:

8. Nested enterprises: Appropriation, provision, monitoring, enforcement, conflict resolution, and governance activities are organized in multiple layers of nested enterprises.

Source: Ostrom 1990, *supra* note 4, at 90 Table 3.1.

significance of most of the "Design Principles." Among those that did not, some scholars thought the principles too rigid and/or failed to adequately distinguish between ecological and social conditions. But most of the criticisms came from abstract studies rather than empirical studies.[46] The authors of the 2010 analysis suggested some tweaks to Ostrom's list of "Design Principles,"[47] which she immediately accepted.[48]

One alleged problem with "Design Principles" resulted mainly from Ostrom's choice of label, which implied that successful CPR management systems could be "designed" simply by following the "blueprint" Ostrom allegedly offered.[49] Indeed, Ostrom regretted her use of the label "Design Principles," conceding that it generated unnecessary confusion.[50] In fact, those principles were nothing more than a list of common elements or features that were found,

---

[46] Michael Cox, Gwen Arnold, and Sergio Villamayor-Tomás, *A Review and Reassessment of Design Principles for Community-Based Natural Resource Management*, 15 Ecol. & Soc. 38 (2010).

[47] *Id.* at 53, Table 4.

[48] Ostrom 2010, *supra* note 8, at 653.

[49] Cox, Arnold, and Villamayor-Tomás, *supra* note 46, at 51.

[50] Ostrom 2010, *supra* note 8, at 654 fn. 5.

in the aggregate, to be present in successful CPR management cases. They were common features, which she posited, *could* be necessary features. But she never intended to create a "blueprint" for "designing" a successful CPR management system. That would have been wholly out of character for a scholar who so strongly believed in the importance of context, complexity, and the absence of panacea solutions for social and combined social-ecological dilemmas.[51]

After *Governing the Commons (In Brief)*

After she completed *Governing the Commons*, Elinor Ostrom conducted additional CPR studies with an eye toward developing large databases of cases for analysis and meta-analysis in order to improve both her theories—in the form of the "Design Principles" she hypothesized in *Governing the Commons*—and her analytical framework for diagnosing social and social-ecological dilemmas. She and colleagues also began developing and testing formal game theoretic models of CPR problems, consistent with the IAD framework, which could be tested in an experimental lab as well as in the field. That work quickly yielded two important, but often overlooked books, *Trust & Reciprocity*[52] and *Rules, Games, and Common-Pool Resources.*[53] As their titles indicate, these books are very much about the role mutual trust plays in motivating collective action to conserve a CPR, and how mutual trust is built over time and sometimes lost, often more quickly. The upshot is that CPR problems, contrary to the understanding of many game theorists, are not noncooperative games like the Prisoner's Dilemma; rather, they are in the nature of what Amartya Sen labeled "assurance games" (such as the "Stag Hunt"), which have alternative cooperative and noncooperative equilibrium outcomes.[54] Instead of certain payoffs, assurance games have probabilistic, expected payoffs, where the players' perceived probabilities of cooperation are largely determined by trust or its absence and, in turn, determine whether the outcome is a noncooperative or cooperative equilibrium.[55]

In 2005, Ostrom published her most complete and detailed explication of her diagnostic approach to analyzing institutions using the IAD framework.[56]

---

[51] *See* OSTROM 2005, *supra* note 24, at 242-3, 254.

[52] ELINOR OSTROM AND JAMES WALKER, EDS., TRUST & RECIPROCITY: INTERDISCIPLINARY LESSONS FROM EXPERIMENTAL RESEARCH (1993).

[53] OSTROM, GARDNER, AND WALKER, *supra* note 26.

[54] Amartya K. Sen, *Isolation, assurance, and the social rate of discount*, 81 QUART. J. ECON. 112 (1967).

[55] See Daniel H. Cole and Peter Z. Grossman, *Institutions Matter! Why the Herder Problem is not a Prisoner's Dilemma*, 69 THEORY &DECISION 219 (2010).

[56] OSTROM 2005, *supra* note 24.

But as that book was going to press, ecologist colleagues were pressing Ostrom to rework her framework in a major way to better account for ecological variables—in their view, the "biophysical conditions" box of the IAD framework was a black box. She responded by developing, along with modelers Marco Janssen and J. Marty Anderies, the "Social-Ecological Systems" (or SES) framework. Compared to the IAD framework, the SES framework incorporates a much larger menu of social and ecological variables and sub-variables.[57] However, despite the new title, the SES framework was not intended to be an alternative, substitute or replacement for the IAD framework. Rather, it was supposed to subsume the IAD framework. In other words, the IAD framework is supposed to be built into the SES framework. But scholars have not appreciated that point. Many scholars have used the SES framework,[58] but they treat it as an alternative to the IAD framework, which continues to be more widely used.. Ostrom began an effort in 2009 to more fully integrate the IAD and SES frameworks,[59] and some of her colleagues have continued that work since her death in 2012.[60]

As Ostrom continued her field research, experiments, and amendments to her analytical frameworks, she and colleagues at the Ostrom Workshop created important repositories of case studies on CPRs, including the International Forestry Resources and Institutions (IFRI) database, established in 1992 (housed at the University of Michigan since 2006), and the Social-Ecological Systems Meta-Analysis (SESMED) Database (now housed at Dartmouth), which are freely accessible. The IFRI database currently involves a network of 14 collaborating research centers around the world and contains detailed information about biodiversity, livelihoods of forest actors, institutions, and forest carbon for more than 250 sites in 15 countries. All of these cases are coded similarly using the IAD framework to facilitate both qualitative analysis (including meta-analysis) and quantitative analysis.[61] Created more recently, the SESMED database currently contains 21 meta-analyses, which scholars use to improve Ostrom's

---

[57] *See* John M. Anderies, Marco A. Janssen and Elinor Ostrom, *A Framework to Analyze the Robustness of Social-Ecological Systems from an Institutional Perspective,* 9 ECOL. & SOC. 18 (2004); Marco A. Janssen, John M. Anderies, and Elinor Ostrom, *Robustness of Social-Ecological Systems to Spatial and Temporal Variability,* 20 SOC. &NAT. RES. 307 (2007); Elinor Ostrom, *A General Framework for Analyzing Sustainability of Social-Ecological Systems,* 325 SCI. 419 (2009).

[58] A Google Scholar search, conducted on July 24, 2019, using the search terms "SES framework," returned 1,550 distinct entries.

[59] *See* DANIEL H. COLE AND MICHAEL D. MCGINNIS, EDS., ELINOR OSTROM AND THE BLOOMINGTON SCHOOL OF POLITICAL ECONOMY: VOL. 4, POLICY APPLICATIONS AND EXTENSIONS xviii (2018).

[60] See Daniel H. Cole, Graham Epstein, Michael D. McGinnis, *The Utility of Combining the IAD and SES Frameworks,* 13 INT'L J. COMMONS 244 (2019).

[61] The IFRI database and coding manual can be downloaded here: http://www.forestlivelihoods.org/ifri-dataset/ (accessed July 24, 2019).

analytical frameworks and "Design Principles."[62] Finally, the Ostrom Workshop houses the "Digital Library of the Commons," which is a freely accessible collection of published and unpublished literature on CPRs.[63]

In the first decade of the 2000s, Ostrom branched out from natural CPRs to what might be called "artefactual" CPRs, including the so-called "knowledge commons." With a Workshop colleague, Charlotte Hess, she organized a 2004 "Workshop on Scholarly Communication as a Commons," which led in 2007 to the publication of a book, *Understanding Knowledge as a Commons*.[64] It helped to animate what has grown into a large community of scholars, who hold regular meetings, working on various aspects of information-related commons dilemmas, from intellectual property bottlenecks to rare-disease research consortia.[65]

A year or so later, Ostrom was asked by the World Bank to draft a paper on polycentric approaches to climate change, a natural CPR at a scale almost inconceivably greater than any of the local CPRs problems Ostrom had dealt with previously. Although, in 1995 she had published a book with Robert Keohane, *Local Commons and Global Interdependence*, which hinted at her thinking as to how her and Vincent's works might scale up to treat social and social-ecological dilemmas at the international and global level.[66] She and Keohane observed that if countries were treated like individuals in local CPR problems, then the scale of required collective action would not be so daunting. She had studied regional CPRs involving more than 10,000 actors. At the level of global governance, fewer than 200 exist. Of course, the heterogeneity of those actors, who might not even share mental models of the world) grows almost exponentially as we move from bilateral to multilateral to global negotiations. And, of course, there are principle-agent problems between negotiators and their political bosses. These issues were not sufficiently dealt with in that 1995 book.

Nevertheless, Ostrom had a good deal to say about the potential utility of more polycentric approaches to climate change (in addition to or in place of a single global regime) in her 2009 World Bank report.[67] Her main points were that: (1) polycentric approaches create greater opportunities for experimentation

---

[62] See the SESMED database at https://sesmad.dartmouth.edu/pages/intro (accessed on July 24, 2019).

[63] See the Digital Library of the Commons at http://dlc.dlib.indiana.edu/dlc/community-list (accessed on July 24, 2019).

[64] Charlotte Hess and Elinor Ostrom, eds., Understanding Knowledge Commons: From Theory to Practice (2007).

[65] *See* Brett M. Frischmann, Michael J. Madison, and Katherine Strandburg, Governing Knowledge Commons (2014), which was the output of a 2011 conference, which Ostrom attended, at NYU Law School.

[66] Robert O. Keohane and Elinor Ostrom, eds., Local Commons and Global Interdependence (1995).

[67] Elinor Ostrom, "A Polycentric Approach for Coping with Climate Change," World Bank Policy Research Working Paper 5095 (2009).

and learning within and between different levels of governance; and (2) the greater number of bilateral and multilateral interactions among actors *could* help build mutual trust between them, potentially facilitating greater cooperation and better outcomes. As an example, consider the effect of the US-China (bilateral) Climate Working Group, which held regular and productive meetings between 2013 and 2015. In a relatively short period of time, they built up mutual trust sufficiently to agree on a series of pacts to cut greenhouse gas emissions. Although those agreements concerned relatively low-hanging fruit, they gave a big boost to global negotiations in the run-up to the 2015 Paris Agreement.[68]

Ostrom's 2009 World Bank working paper ignited an important and still ongoing discussion in the scholarly literature about polycentric approaches, especially among scholars who had grown disillusioned with the UN process as "the only game in town." Ideas for various kinds of polycentric approaches, including "building blocks," "regime complexes," and "bottom-up systems" were all published within a few short years after Ostrom's World Bank paper.[69] Neither Ostrom nor the scholars she motivated to write about polycentric approaches to climate change suggested that such an approach would provide a panacea solution to the largest collective-action problem the world has ever confronted. They merely suggested ways in which polycentric interactions could help to create the necessary conditions for successful mitigation and adaptation.

Conclusion: Elinor Ostrom's Legacy for Legal Scholars

Elinor Ostrom's legacy for legal scholars is much greater than most legal scholars are aware, especially if the only work of Ostrom's they have read is *Governing the Commons.* Of course, that work, which was cited by the Nobel Prize Committee in 2009, it remains her most influential work. Indeed, legal scholars have cited *Governing the Commons* in nearly 1,000 articles.[70] But there is far more in Ostrom's work of potential value to legal scholarship than her admittedly very important demonstration that CPR users can successfully govern their

---

[68] See Daniel H. Cole, *Advantages of a polycentric approach to climate change policy*, 5 NATURE CLIMATE CHANGE 114, 116 (2015).

[69] *See, e.g.*, Jouni Paavola, *Climate Change: The Ultimate Tragedy of the Commons?*, *in* D.H. COLE AND E. OSTROM, EDS., PROPERTY IN LAND AND OTHER RESOURCES 417 (2012); Robert O. Keohane and David G. Victor, *The Regime Complex for Climate Change,* 9 PERSP. POL. 7 (2011); Daniel H. Cole, *From Global to Polycentric Climate Change*, 2 CLIMATE L. 395 (2011); Richard B. Stewart, Michael Oppenheimer, and Bryce Rudyk, *Building Blocks for Global Climate Protection,* 32 STAN. ENVTL L.J. 341 (2013); Raphael Leal-Arcas, *Top-down versus Bottom-up Approaches for Climate Change Negotiations: An Analysis*, 6 IUP J. GOV. &PUB. POL. 7 (2011).

[70] Hein Online search in "Core U.S. Journals," using search term "Governing the Commons" (accessed July 25, 2019). The count is over-inclusive to the extent that not all of the journals listed are law journals, but under-inclusive to the extent that Hein Online does not include citations in books or book chapters.

own access to and use of resource units, via common property systems or other institutional mechanisms, for very long periods of time. In fact, all aspects of the Ostroms' research program have something of value for legal scholars, especially as legal scholars become increasingly interdisciplinary in their work.

This concluding section will suggest just two ways in which Ostrom's larger body of work, including *Governing the Commons* but extending beyond that important book, can be of great value to legal scholars. First, as part of that more analytical approach to studying law, Ostrom's functional differentiation of rule-types could be quite useful to legal scholars studying how and why societies make, implement, and enforce specific legal rules within larger systemic contexts. Legal scholars already distinguish between "substantive" and "procedural" rules, between "rules of evidence," "constitutional rules," and between "legislative rules" and "administrative rules." More finely grained legal analysis would be facilitated by Ostrom's distinctions between boundary, position, choice, aggregation, information, payoff and scope rules. As a normative matter, studying the function of rules would enable legal scholars to make better, more precisely targeted arguments for legal change. And a functional approach would force legal scholars to appreciate any socio-legal problem as comprising a *configuration* of rules, forcing them to consider how treating any single rule might affect the overall configuration. Put differently, it would force legal scholars to think of laws as part of an institutional matrix, and legal analysis as a form, but not the only form, of institutional analysis.

Second, Ostrom's rigorous analytical framework for diagnosing complex social, including legal, dilemmas could reinvigorate analytical jurisprudence.[71] Adopting the IAD framework would enable legal scholars, who already possess a comparative advantage in the methodologies of case studies and meta-analyses, to work together more productively with social scientists. Even for legal scholars who are not interested in interdisciplinary work, using the IAD framework or some variation on it would allow for more finely-grained analysis of legal "action situations," which are everywhere—in contract negotiations, legislative committee rooms, corporate board rooms, courts, and administrative agencies. Admittedly, many legal scholars are more interested in normative than positive analysis, but, as in medicine, a careful diagnosis is a prerequisite to any effective treatment. Legal scholars, to my knowledge, have never created such a comprehensive diagnostic tool of their own, but Ostrom's IAD framework would fill that role nicely.

---

[71] On modern analytical jurisprudence, *see, e.g.*, H.L.A. HART, THE CONCEPT OF LAW (1961); Hans Kelsen, *The Pure Theory of Law and Analytical Jurisprudence*, 55 HARV. L.REV. 44 (1941); Edgar Bodenheimer, *Modern Analytical Jurisprudence and the Limits of Its Usefulness*, 104 U.PENN. L.REV. 1080 (1955-56); H.L.A. Hart, *Analytical Jurisprudence in Mid-Twenteith Century: A Reply to Professor Bodenheimer*, 105 U.PENN. L.REV. 953 (1956-57); Robert S. Summers, *The New Analytical Jurists*, 41 NYU L.REV. 861 (1966).

In sum, Elinor Ostrom left a great legacy not only to environmental law scholars through *Governing the Commons* and her work on natural and artefactual CPRs. She provided an entire analytical approach to studying social and social-ecological dilemmas, which of course include legal problems. In doing so, she also improved mechanisms by which legal scholars can interact productively with scholars from other disciplines, which is crucial to solving problems in a world where no single discipline has the necessary tools to resolve complex social and combined social-ecological problems. Indeed, environmental law scholars (and legal scholars more generally) have hardly begun to appreciate the extent to which Elinor Ostrom is a "pioneer" in their field.

Chapter 8

Wes Jackson and the Advent of Agroecology

Deanell Reece Tacha[1]

A Pioneer

Pioneers are, historically, people who first come to a land or, intellectually, those offering a groundbreaking approach to an old problem. Wes Jackson, who created one of the first university Environmental Studies programs in the United States and is credited with coining the term "sustainable agriculture," is a pioneer in ecological thinking and agroecology. Though not well known in environmental law—he is not a lawyer or legal scholar—his insights offer exciting new ways to approach environmental problems through the law. Jackson's

[1] Deanell Reece Tacha is a native of Scandia, Kansas. She received her B.A. Degree from the University of Kansas and her J.D. from the University of Michigan. She served as a White House Fellow in 1971-1972 and practiced law at Hogan and Hartson in Washington D.C. briefly before returning to Kansas where she practiced privately in Concordia, Kansas. She joined the faculty of the University of Kansas School of Law in 1974. She was Vice Chancellor for Academic Affairs at the University of Kansas from 1979-1985. President Ronald Reagan appointed her to the United States Court of Appeals for the Tenth Circuit in 1985 where she served for 25 years. She was Chief Judge of that court from 2001-2008. She was a member of the United States Sentencing Commission and served as Chair of the Judicial Branch Committee and on the Executive Committee of the Judicial Conference of the United States. She was a recipient of the Edward Devitt Award for Distinguished Service to Justice in 2007 and the ABA's prestigious John Marshall Award for Distinguished Service to the Legal Profession in 2008. She is a past President of the American Inns of Court and recipient of its Sherman Christensen Award. She retired from the federal judiciary in 2011 and became Dean of the Pepperdine University School of Law where she served until 2017. She is currently affiliated with JAMS as a neutral consultant, arbitrator, and mediator. She is a frequent presenter and author on law-related topics. She is a member of Phi Beta Kappa, the American Law Institute, and the Kansas Bar Association. She is a co-founder of Freedoms Frontier National Heritage Area and involved in numerous civic and philanthropic organizations. She is a member of the United Methodist Church and serves on the Judicial Council for that worldwide church. She and her husband, John, have four children and six grandchildren and live in Lawrence Kansas.

interdisciplinary thinking has challenged the conventional wisdom for more than four decades in ways that environmental lawyers and scholars should consider.

History and ecology weave their weave through Jackson's thoughts. Take those two terms, "pioneer" and "groundbreaking," for example. This Kansas farm boy would point out that his ancestors who moved to the prairie were of course not the first to come to the land but instead displaced a native population. And the groundbreaking those ancestors engaged in when they plowed the prairie to grow grain is at the heart of our ecological crises. Both terms require critical reflection.

To set the stage for such reflection, Jackson goes back much further in time, 10,000 years, to the invention of agriculture and the beginning of humans' social and ecological challenges. He argues that instead of focusing on problems *in* agriculture, we have to address "the problem *of* agriculture" and how it left us floundering as a "species out of context."[2] We didn't evolve as farmers or living in large-scale societies. Jackson suggests that's why we are in so much trouble today.

While invoking a deeper sense of history and a more radical approach to ecology, Jackson understands that nuts-and-bolts law and policy are crucial tools in dealing with the urgent problems we face and offers proposals for moving toward not only a more sustainable way of growing food but also a sustainable human presence on the planet more generally.

Jackson's prescriptions for modern technological society recommend radical changes in the goals, methodologies, and strategies for the contemporary lawyer and policy maker. The basic underpinnings of the law relating to property rights, regulation of property, and the role of individuals, governments, and worldwide commitment to a sustainable future for human life—all require rethinking if we were to adopt Jackson's new look at very old environmental issues.

The Vision

Wes Jackson spends a lot of time thinking about how topsoil is "the capital stock of the planet."[3] While humans in different places at different times have farmed in varied ways, the grain agriculture that provides the majority of our calories requires annual tilling of the soil and leads to dramatic loss of topsoil. That story goes back to ancient times, as Greece and Rome depleted their soils,

---

[2] Wes Jackson, First Annual E. F. Schumacher Lecture: Call for a Revolution in Agriculture (Oct. 1981), https://centerforneweconomics.org/publications/call-for-a-revolution-in-agriculture/.

[3] Fred Bahnson, *Farmed Out: Wes Jackson on the Need to Reinvent Agriculture*, The Sun (Oct. 2010), https://www.thesunmagazine.org/issues/418/farmed-out.

losing that capital stock to rain and wind, flushed into rivers and to oceans, not to be replaced for millennia to come.

Many people know the story of the 1930s Dust Bowl, when the combination of a prolonged drought, high winds, and failed efforts to prevent soil erosion on the Great Plains denuded the landscape, bankrupted farmers, and, worst of all, stripped the land of the soil organic matter and nutrients that would reduce the productivity of that land for generations to come. But in the 1970s, U.S. topsoil was still eroding, leading Jackson to begin thinking about new ways to approach grain agriculture. What once was native prairie sustained only by soil, water, and sunlight had become modern industrial farms dependent on fertilizers, pesticides, irrigation, and other human developments that required fossil fuels—the mirror opposite of natural ecosystems.

Recognizing the foundational problem of soil erosion and degradation, Jackson went to work, attempting to build a system of food production that could be self-sustaining, economically feasible, ever-renewing, and promising for the future of the species. He states it this way:

> Is it possible to build an agriculture based on the prairie as standard or model? I saw a sharp contrast between the major features of the wheat field and the major features of the prairie. The wheat field features annuals in monoculture; the prairie features perennials in polyculture, or mixtures. Because all of our high-yielding crops are annuals or are treated as such, crucial questions must be answered. Can perennialism and high yield go together? If so, can a polyculture of perennials outfield a monoculture of perennials? Can an ecosystem sponsor its own fertility? Is it realistic to think we can manage such complexity adequately to avoid the problem of pests outcompeting us?[4]

Research on what Jackson named Natural Systems Agriculture—perennial grains grown in mixtures to mimic natural ecosystems—continues to make progress, albeit slowly, at The Land Institute (TLI) in Salina, Kansas. Although TLI is best known for that scientific work, the organization began as an alternative school that Jackson co-founded in 1976. That educational mission has always been at the core of his sense of mission—to nudge a modern technological industrial society to think about what it would mean to embrace an ecological worldview.

Although his personality is refreshingly modest, the force of his intellect and the range of his ideas can be breathtaking. His scientific training is in genetics, but his vision is planetary in scope and, like so many foundational thinkers, he understands that all life on the planet is interrelated and interdependent and that we must frame environmental and agricultural thinking and policy on this basic understanding. As he puts it:

[4] Wes Jackson, Becoming Native to This Place 43 (The University Press of Kentucky 1994).

> As living organisms we humans are biocentric. We say, "The earth is our life-support system." In my view that's not the best way to look at it. We need to think hard about our embeddedness within the ecosphere and move ourselves down in the hierarchy.... I'd argue that we can never do better than nature. Humans draw on an array of technologies, and we sometimes must use them out of necessity, but anything we do of a technological nature, because of the scaffolding of civilization itself, draws down the ecological capital of the planet.[5]

Jackson believes that "there has not been a single human-designed product or process, including the domestication of crops and livestock, that hasn't come at the cost of the drawdown of the capital stock of the planet[,]" which means the question of "renewability can vary from a fraction of one lifetime to cosmic time."[6]

That means challenging not only the burning of fossil fuels but thinking about "the five exhaustible and relatively nonrenewable carbon pools" that humans have tapped into—the soil through agriculture, trees felled and burned to smelt ore, and then coal, oil, and natural gas.[7] These dense energy sources that built "civilization" now threaten a long-term human presence on the planet. With eight billion people on the planet, there is no going back to a pre-agricultural gathering-hunting economy. But Jackson is convinced that taking "nature as measure" when evaluating human practices is essential to our survival.[8]

The big ecological crises we face today are obvious: climate change, species extinction, chemical contamination, along with soil degradation and erosion. Many people focus on how new technology might provide solutions, and Jackson does not deny that there's a need for improved technology in dealing with immediate problems. But if we are to create a truly ecological civilization, human solutions will have to learn from natural ecosystems rather than continue to try to dominate nature. Jackson believes the place to start is how we grow grains, that "agriculture has the sole potential to provide the lead into a different relationship with our ecosphere. From that relationship can then come a more realistic assessment of the technology we adopt."[9]

---

[5] Fred Bahnson, *Farmed Out: Wes Jackson on the Need to Reinvent Agriculture*, The Sun (Oct. 2010), https://www.thesunmagazine.org/issues/418/farmed-out.

[6] Wes Jackson, Consulting the Genius of the Place: An Ecological Approach to a New Agriculture 13 (Counterpoint 2010).

[7] Wes Jackson, Consulting the Genius of the Place: An Ecological Approach to a New Agriculture 14 (Counterpoint 2010).

[8] Wes Jackson, Nature as Measure: The Selected Essays of Wes Jackson xi (Counterpoint 2011).

[9] Wes Jackson, Consulting the Genius of the Place: An Ecological Approach to a New Agriculture 15 (Counterpoint 2010).

So, in many ways, Jackson's pioneering vision is as old as the ecosphere itself. It is thinking and working toward ways to reinsert human organisms into that ecosphere in a way that interrupts natural processes as little as possible.

The Inspiration

Jackson seems to draw inspiration from almost every personal experience, passing acquaintance, reading, and research project ever encountered—starting with his upbringing on a farm near Topeka, KS, through university training, and in his role as one of the foremost advocates for sustainable agriculture as president of The Land Institute. He has absorbed, factored in, considered, and relied upon a rich array of sources of inspiration, from farmers to philosophers. He credits one simple sentence uttered by Professor Ben W. Smith of North Carolina State University in 1965—"[w]e need wilderness as a standard against which to judge our agricultural practices."—with leading him "to a still-incomplete discovery" that became Natural Systems Agriculture.[10]

In addition to his experience on the farm growing annual row crops—Jackson likes to say he was "born on the end of a hoe handle"[11]—he was also deeply influenced by his experience as a teenage boy on a South Dakota ranch belonging to his mother's cousin. In contrast to the Kansas farm where the land was plowed every year, the ranch was then, and still is, mostly unplowed. It also bordered the Rosebud and Pine Ridge reservations, and he saw first-hand how the conquest of the prairie had not only changed the landscape but destroyed Native American ways of living, and how most white ranchers ignored that reality.

The contrast between untilled ranch and the heavily tilled farm stayed with Jackson. Later, as he read the work of Aldo Leopold,[12] he put personal experience and scientific inquiry together, developing an ecological understanding that increasingly challenged the world-view of the founders of modern science such as Descartes and Bacon. Jackson sees a direct connection between the reductionism at the heart of that scientific worldview and the eventual industrialization of agriculture. Writers such as Leopold provided an intellectual "framework toward the eventual marriage of ecology and agriculture."[13]

---

[10] WES JACKSON, CONSULTING THE GENIUS OF THE PLACE: AN ECOLOGICAL APPROACH TO A NEW AGRICULTURE 33 (Counterpoint 2010).

[11] Riane Eisler, *Sustainable Agriculture—Going to the Root of the Problem: A Conversation with Wes Jackson*, 6 INTERDISCIPLINARY JOURNAL OF PARTNERSHIP STUDIES Article 2, 1 (2019) https://pubs.lib.umn.edu/index.php/ijps/article/view/1983/1459.

[12] *See* ALDO LEOPOLD, A SAND COUNTY ALMANAC AND SKETCHES HERE AND THERE (Oxford Univ. Press 1949) (featuring the essays *The Land Ethic*, *Thinking like a Mountain*, and *The Odyssey*).

[13] WES JACKSON, CONSULTING THE GENIUS OF THE PLACE: AN ECOLOGICAL APPROACH TO A NEW AGRICULTURE 33 (Counterpoint 2010).

Another source of inspiration for Jackson was his decades-long collaborative friendship with novelist and essayist Wendell Berry, one of the country's most eloquent spokespersons for agrarianism and rural life. Jackson credits Berry with deepening his literary sensibility and broadening his vision.

Throughout Jackson's work it is clear that he has been deeply influenced by a host of sources. His humility shines through in his relentless willingness to credit his thinking and his work to the influence of others. In important ways, Jackson lives out the importance of mentors, experiences, and the work of those who preceded him in shaping his own ideas and motivating his work.

The History

From that small Kansas farm where he spent his boyhood years, Jackson went on to earn a B.A. in biology at Kansas Wesleyan University in 1958, an M.A. in botany at the University of Kansas in 1960, and a Ph.D. in genetics at North Carolina State University in 1967. He taught biology at a Kansas high school and at his undergraduate alma matter before becoming a tenured full professor at California State University in Sacramento, where he established that early Environmental Studies program.

With social movements pressing for change—including the protests against the war in Vietnam, the civil-rights campaigns, and feminism—Jackson and colleagues determined that they did not want "environmentalism to be defined in a narrow 'clean-up-the mess' sort of way" because "war, racism, poverty, the growing gap between rich and poor, destruction of our environment, and consumerism were one subject."[14] They set about designing a curriculum broader than the prevailing approaches that narrowly addressed pollution, clean-up efforts, and conservation. The courses were designed to challenge students to see the sustainability of the planet as a cosmic topic connected to all other issues and debates.

Straining against the norms and practices of the modern University and longing for home, Jackson and his then-wife, Dana, left California to return to Kansas on what he describes as "a homesteading trip."[15] They founded The Land Institute in 1976, growing from a small alternative school to a world-renowned research institution dedicated to creating "an agricultural system that mimics natural systems in order to produce ample food and reduce or eliminate the negative impacts of industrial agriculture."[16]

---

[14] Wes Jackson, Consulting the Genius of the Place: An Ecological Approach to a New Agriculture 62 (Counterpoint 2010).

[15] Wes Jackson, Consulting the Genius of the Place: An Ecological Approach to a New Agriculture 63 (Counterpoint 2010).

[16] The Land Institute, https://landinstitute.org/ (last visited Aug. 16, 2019).

While directing the research at TLI, Jackson has written scholarly articles, often collaborating with the plant breeders and ecologists, but his most important writing has been for a general audience. His books (see bibliography at the end) and articles build on his experiences from the farm to the research lab, helping readers imagine what must be done to develop agricultural methods that can realistically meet the food needs of a crowded planet while rebuilding healthy ecosystems and reducing farmers' dependence on non-renewable fossil fuels.

Jackson has received scores of prizes and awards, including a MacArthur Fellowship in 1992, the Pew Conservation Scholars Award in 1992, the Right Livelihood Award in 2000, and the Louis Broomfield Award in 2010. He holds five honorary doctorates and numerous other university distinctions. He continues a full schedule of lecturing throughout the world and working with The Land Institute and other partners globally.

The Work

The Land Institute is a 501(c)(3) nonprofit organization. TLI's team of plant breeders and ecologists there have established promising collaborations with people around the country and the world—forty-one primary research colleagues worldwide, at sixteen universities in the United States and in eighteen other countries (South Africa, Turkey, Italy, China, Germany, Mali, India, Ethiopia, Canada, Sweden, Uganda, Argentina, Australia, France, Uruguay, and Denmark). Jackson originally predicted that the work of developing perennial grains, pulses and oilseed-bearing plants to be grown in ecologically intensified, diverse crop mixtures would take at least fifty to one hundred years to bear fruit, and TLI is a bit ahead of schedule. They now have "proof of concept" with Kernza, an intermediate wheatgrass that is in limited commercial production, and perennial rice is being grown in China. Work continues on wheat, sorghum, silphium (an oilseed in the sunflower family), and legumes. The scientists have taken two paths—domesticating wild species, and cross-breeding wild perennials with domesticated annuals—to try to develop plants that will produce enough seed to make viable crops for farmers.

Natural Systems Agriculture is one of many agroecological approaches to a sustainable food production. By focusing on grains, which provide about two-thirds of the calories people consume, Jackson is tackling one of the biggest challenges. While there are people growing grain with minimum-till or no-till methods (preparing the soil without disturbing the ground), the majority of farmers are plowing, and even under the most careful farm management that means soil erosion, especially when economic pressures lead farmers to maximize yields and plow more and more marginal land. The deeper roots of perennial plants hold the soil in place, and you eliminate the need for plowing. Less soil carbon being disturbed, in tandem with fewer fossil fuels being used, reduces the contribution of agriculture to global warming.

But perennials are only half the project—just as important are polycultures instead of monocultures. Crops grown in mixtures will have less to fear from weeds, pests, and pathogens, which flourish in monocultures and lead to all those chemicals. The Land Institute and its partners seek to develop "new crops arrangements [that] will be less dependent on nitrogen-based fertilizers and better-equipped to anchor soil, virtually eliminating erosion and chemical runoff."[17] Put in their words they are animated by a belief that a solution is possible:

> At The Land Institute, we believe that a solution for the 10,000 year old problem of agriculture—soil loss and degradation, ecosystem destruction, and high energy use—is not only necessary, but possible. Our goal is to fashion an agriculture as sustainable as the native ecosystems it displaced, to find a way of growing crops that rewards the farmer and the landscape more than the manufacturers of external inputs. We envision an agriculture that not only protects irreplaceable soil, but lessens our dependence on fossil fuels and damaging synthetic chemicals.[18]

Kernza, that intermediate wheatgrass, has already enjoyed some small-scale success in the marketplace. General Mills is developing Kernza products, including a breakfast cereal, and Patagonia Provisions, an offshoot of the outdoor clothing company, has produced Long Root Ale. Jackson is buoyed by the success but cautious; there will be setbacks as well as advances in this long-term research program.

Why turn to agriculture in this age where technology is providing so many new understandings, opportunities, and ways of looking at every issue that confronts civilization? Jackson believes:

> Agriculture has the discipline of ecology and evolutionary biology to help us produce food in properly functioning ecosystems. All visions of a sustainable or resilient society must rely on renewable resources. Other spheres of human activity do not have that advantage. Agriculture, broadly defined, may be the only artifact in current civilization where that potential resides.[19]

Though Jackson thinks about the native prairies of his home state, he has a wider goal:

---

[17] The Land Institute, *Transforming Agriculture with Perennial Polycultures* (2013).

[18] The Land Institute, *Transforming Agriculture with Perennial Polycultures* (2013).

[19] Wes Jackson, Consulting the Genius of the Place: An Ecological Approach to a New Agriculture 153 (Counterpoint 2010).

> The goal of our research team is to develop diverse perennial grain production systems that are as ecologically sound as former prairies. The Land Institute's mission doesn't end at the prairie boundaries of the Appalachians, the Rio Grande, or the Rockies. As Jack Ewel's research in Costa Rica implies, food worldwide can, indeed must, come to be produced by ecosystems that have the efficiency and resiliency of those natural ecosystems that were replaced by farms, forest plantations, and fisheries.[20]

The Goal

In addition to the breeding work, The Land Institute has not forgotten its origins as an alternative school. After retiring from running the organization, Jackson launched a new program called Ecosphere Studies, which aims to bring an ecological worldview to the public. Through workshops and publications, the Ecosphere Studies staff is imagining how "perennial education" can contribute to a sustainable culture.

This emphasis on education and outreach is not surprising, given the mission statement of The Land Institute:

> When people, land, and community are as one, all three members prosper; when they relate not as members but as competing interests, all three are exploited. By consulting Nature as the source and measure of that membership, The Land Institute seeks to develop an agriculture that will save soil from being lost or poisoned, while promoting a community life at once prosperous and enduring.[21]

Jackson looks far beyond the agricultural research work being done on perennial grains, motivated by his belief that the entire community must share the common goals of sustainability and constant renewal of the land, the people, and the community. In today's economy, corporate farming and technological advances in equipment and capacity exploit the soil, distance the consumer from the grower, insert lots of interruptions in the "food chain," sever people's connection with the imperative of protecting and preserving the food supply, and ruin communities where people mutually sustain each other. People will better understand the existential threats to the food supply caused by depletion of the soil and non-renewable energy when they are connected enough in community to find ways to sustain each other and slow the human assault on ecosystems. Jackson's bedrock belief in community means both a geographic community

---

[20] Wes Jackson, Consulting the Genius of the Place: An Ecological Approach to a New Agriculture 153 (Counterpoint 2010).

[21] The Land Institute, *Vision & Mission*, https://landinstitute.org/about-us/vision-mission/ (last visited Aug. 16, 2019).

where people witness first-hand the effects of humans on the landscape and a community of interest where people share the same goals and find ways to achieve those goals together.

In a project to demonstrate that in the 1990s, Jackson, friends, and The Land Institute purchased several old and run-down buildings in Matfield Green. This small rural Kansas town was in danger of disappearing, like so many rural communities that saw their economic base erode in the past half-century. With that base went the grocery store, gas station, and other services. Matfield Green had even lost its post office. Jackson and his compatriots rehabilitated several of the old buildings, including the old elementary school, which was outfitted to become a community building for meetings and programs sponsored by the Land Institute. Matfield Green also became a place where artists could live with affordable work and gallery space.

The goal of the Matfield Green program was "to use ecology as the organizing principle for human community."[22] Jackson calls the program there "ecological community accounting," where people might learn to adapt to the environment as it exists.[23] Although the Land Institute group eventually sold the properties, an arts-related revival continues to build slowly, and the old school is being renovated as studio and community activity space. One artist in the community has said, "[i]n a small community like Matfield Green [the commitment to the arts] may be the only thing that can fuel economic development, so it's extremely important."[24]

Jackson's overarching goal is to force every person to be keenly aware of the space we occupy and the way we use it, seeing the relationship to the planet and beyond. We are but specks of dust in the history of our planet, but, if we are to preserve the earth and feed its people, humankind has a particular responsibility at this time to reverse the stunning pace at which we are "burning up options for future generations," as Jackson likes to say.

In his most recent work, Jackson suggests that the route to a more ecological society is to get "creaturely," borrowing a term used earlier by his friend Berry, by which he means that we need to see ourselves as just another creature along with the other animals, plants, and microbes which are "all products of a rich, integrated evolutionary history."[25] In addition to leaving behind the

[22] Kansas Historical Society, The Land Institute Collection: Manuscript Collection No. 77 https://www.kshs.org/p/the-land-institute-collection/13779 (last visited Aug. 16, 2019).

[23] Kansas Historical Society, The Land Institute Collection: Manuscript Collection No. 77 https://www.kshs.org/p/the-land-institute-collection/13779 (last visited Aug. 16, 2019).

[24] Paula Haas, *In Matfield Green, a Glimpse of a Viable Future*, VIII SYMPHONY IN THE FLINT HILLS FIELD JOURNAL 62, 69 (2016).

[25] Wes Jackson & Robert Jensen, *Let's Get 'Creaturely': A New Worldview Can Help Us Face Ecological Crises*, Resilience (Apr. 3, 2019), https://www.resilience.org/stories/2019-04-03/lets-get-creaturely-a-new-worldview-can-help-us-face-ecological-crises/.

industrial world and its demand for amounts of energy that are destructive (both in how they are extracted and the consequences of their use), Jackson points out that a creaturely worldview will require dramatic social changes, such as increasing the farm population and reducing the size of farms so that we return to relying on people more than on so much capital and dense energy. Many other insights flow from this creaturely approach to ourselves and our world, but all involve a massive shift in humankind's tendency to "see ourselves as set apart from the rest of the larger living world ... separable from the ecosystems on which our lives depend."[26]

Jackson knows that his goals are, to say the least, difficult to accomplish in the economic, political, and social systems of the 21st century, but this is the work of a pioneer. He places his faith in the evolutionary and constructive power of nature and calls on modern society to embrace this understanding if humankind is to respond to "today's multiple cascading ecological crises."[27]

The Law

Even the most elementary student of the law will understand that Wes Jackson is essentially challenging the entire legal framework of the law that governs property and natural resources—and in particular our claims of private ownership over land, minerals, air, water, and indeed (somewhat preposterously, on reflection) ownership of every "creature" on earth. What is widely called environmental law rests almost exclusively on notions of "who owns what" and "who has the right to regulate what." Thus, property rights in the western world derive from individual or institutional "ownership" of the ground and any other valuable asset on (or in) the ground or in the air.

In many legal systems—and particularly in the United States—these much-revered property rights over natural resources are circumscribed only by the "needs" of governments either to regulate for a clearly articulated public purpose or to take the land for a fully-documented "public use." A long constitutional history in each state and in the federal government shows that we interfere with private ownership only for very limited purposes under the Due Process clauses of the state and federal Constitutions. The agony of defining the limits of the "takings" clauses of constitutions fills libraries full of law books.[28]

---

26 Wes Jackson & Robert Jensen, *Let's Get 'Creaturely': A New Worldview Can Help Us Face Ecological Crises*, Resilience (Apr. 3, 2019), https://www.resilience.org/stories/2019-04-03/lets-get-creaturely-a-new-worldview-can-help-us-face-ecological-crises/.

27 Wes Jackson & Robert Jensen, *Let's Get 'Creaturely': A New Worldview Can Help Us Face Ecological Crises*, Resilience (Apr. 3, 2019), https://www.resilience.org/stories/2019-04-03/lets-get-creaturely-a-new-worldview-can-help-us-face-ecological-crises/.

28 *See Knick v. Twp. Of Scott*, 139 S. Ct. 2162, 2167 (2019) (for one such case, recently decided, overruling precedent that required plaintiffs to litigate takings claims in state court first,

Any judge in this country will have examples of cases where he or she has had to interpret governmental powers to limit private property rights. The Clean Air Act, Clean Water Act, Endangered Species Act, and a host of other "environmental laws" are in constant litigation.[29] Such "dancing on pinheads" questions as "when should wolves be reintroduced into national parks?" have resulted in powerful administrative agencies clashing in litigation with livestock owners, local customs, and the like. There is a certain hilarious irony to the thought that the wolves or the cattle actually know the boundaries to national parks or the cattleman's grazing rights!

How, in this highly developed body of law respecting private property rights and limited regulation, can the law according to Wes Jackson fit? Not easily! The Jackson ideal of world-wide community commitment and care for the future sustainability of the food supply rests, in no small portion, on a mutual understanding that we are all responsible for protecting the planet and the food supply for generations to come. Although, to be sure, governments have had the ability to limit, to regulate (and deregulate), and to direct markets in the fossil fuel industry, none of this has presupposed *worldwide* responsibility for significantly limiting our fossil-carbon usage. Similarly, efforts at worldwide preservation or sustainability of natural resources, endangered species, or the air itself have been the subject of numerous treaties, cooperative arrangements, and high-flying, optimistic speeches, but these rarely have any effective force of law behind them. Even the most "progressive" of ecology-minded progressives—whether in the "so-called" Green Revolution of several decades ago or in the "Green New Deal" proposed today[30]—fail, in critical ways, to address this

---

potentially opening the door to even more litigation); *see also* Robert Meltz, *Takings Decisions of the U.S. Supreme Court: A Chronology*, Congressional Research Service (Jul. 20, 2015) https://fas.org/sgp/crs/misc/97-122.pdf (charting the Supreme Court's decisions on takings cases); *see generally* James E. Holloway & Donald C. Guy, *Policy Coordination and the Takings Clause: The Coordination of Natural Resource Programs Imposing Multiple Burdens on Farmers and Landowners*, 8 Fla. State Univ. Journal of Land Use and Envtl. Law 175 (2018); James E. Holloway & D. Tevis Noelting, *Takings Clause and Integrated Sustainability Policy and Regulation: The Proportionality of the Burdens of Exercising Property Rights and Paying Just Compensation*, 29 Villanova Envtl. Law Journal 1 (2018) (for recent scholarship on the takings clause in environmental law).

[29] *See* U.S. Gov't Accountability Office, GAO-15-803T, Environmental Litigation: Information on Cases against EPA and FWS and on Deadline Suits and EPA Rulemaking (2015) https://www.gao.gov/assets/680/671846.pdf (surveying environmental litigation from 1995 through 2010); Adam Gustafson, *Environmental Litigation in the Trump Administration: The First Two Years*, 50 Trends (2019) https://www.americanbar.org/groups/environment_energy_resources/publications/trends/2018-2019/march-april-2019/environmental-litigation/ (summarizing key litigation in 2017 and 2018).

[30] *See* Stan Cox, *That Green Growth at the Heart of the Green New Deal? It's Malignant*, Green Social Thought, (Jan. 13, 2019) http://greensocialthought.org/content/green-growth-heart-green-new-deal-it%E2%80%99s-malignant (for the views of one of Wes Jackson's colleagues at The Land Institute).

existential problem: How do we dramatically reduce reliance on non-renewable fossil fuels and develop vast new renewable energy capacity? Moreover, those progressives also remain largely silent on how *agricultural reform* can facilitate that sort of shift in fossil-carbon use.

So, to use an overused phrase, what would Wes Jackson do with the law? It is safe to say he would encounter (and has encountered) daunting political challenges both in the United States and around the world. Although laws and governmental powers vary substantially from nation to nation, those laws and powers tend to reflect national histories, cultures, and preferences over time. Although the United Nations has attempted various forms of environmental initiatives, starting especially in the 1970s following the famous Stockholm Conference on the Human Environment, none has thus far yielded the kind of global improvements that Wes Jackson's vision requires.[31]

Wes Jackson has urged some rather specific legal initiatives to support that vision. He, along with Wendell Berry and Fred Kirschenmann of the Leopold Center for Sustainable Agriculture went to Washington about ten years ago to try to advance what they called a "Fifty-Year Farm Bill." They sought a gradual increase in the acreage of land planted in perennials. At the time, US agricultural policy and financing under the regular "once-every-five-years" series of farm bills gave support almost exclusively to a few *annual* grains (wheat, corn, soybeans), with only 20% of agricultural loans being used to grow perennials—and those were not perennial *grains* of the sort The Land Institute is striving to develop. Their goal of the "Fifty-Year Farm Bill" was to have that situation reversed by 2059. To this end, Wes Jackson and his colleagues sought a $50 million per year appropriation to hire Ph.D.-level plant breeders and thirty ecologists to pursue the potential for increased perennial-grains production. Although this effort by Jackson and others may have had some impact on policy, it is hard to discern in specific legislation: we still have only five-year farm bills.

One of the obvious legal responses to the issues that Wes Jackson studies is to ration the use of fossil fuels. The United States has specifically rationed energy and other goods in times of emergency caused by wars or international shortages, but those rationing programs were short-lived and emergency specific. Fossil fuels are, of course, already rationed by economic condition. Those who can afford the fuels can use them so long as they can pay. Those who do not have financial resources do without automobiles, heating, and a host of other basic American expectations. Every winter we are confronted with the tragic stories of homeless or poverty-level folks who are without heat. The Wes Jackson rationing would be quite different. The formula for rationing would be some combination of spreading energy use equitably throughout communities, rewarding reduction of reliance on non-renewable energy, and stimulating a common commitment

[31] *See Generally* John W. Head, *Grasslands, Agriculture, and International Law: A Survey of Proposed Reforms* 26 Kansas Journal of Law and Public Policy 297 (2017).

to sustainability of the planet. Such an approach challenges the very heart of a "market economy" which is, and has been for centuries, the mainstay of most modern economies. Even an interim approach of price controls, incentives, and trying to control factors outside the market fails to make an appreciable difference in the human "footprint" that concerns Wes Jackson.

Many scholars recognize the basic issues that Wes Jackson puts squarely before us, but few have proposed approaches to the law that purport to transform agriculture in the way that Jackson proposes, thereby addressing the energy and ecological problems of our current form of industrial agriculture. One international-law scholar who has made such an attempt is Professor John Head at the University of Kansas. He proposes creating "a Global Corporate Trust for Agroecological Integrity in order to facilitate and manage a new agriculture in a world of legitimate eco-states."[32] There is much to recommend such an approach. On the other hand, there is no example of such a sweeping international organization that has been effective in worldwide implementation.

Such a "corporate trust" or international system of eco-states would require modern legal systems to put aside, in large measure, their heavy reliance on private property rights in natural resources and to tolerate an unprecedented level of governmental and international intervention in land use, agricultural practices, and ecological protection.

The current state of American law suggests that it will take broad public understanding of the ecosystem crises that Wes Jackson warns about before the law can "catch up" with where the science and most scholars agree the planet is headed. Small comfort, but the rapid onset of melting glaciers, cataclysmic weather events, the extinction of many plant and animal species, and depletion of the topsoil may impact all people so dramatically in such a short period of time that the inhabitants of the planet in this century—indeed, in the next few decades—may have to face up to the need for very new legal approaches to the "old problems" that Wes Jackson recognizes and seeks to bring to national and international attention.

The Legacy

Let's return to Jackson's assertion that we are a species out of context. Humans evolved for hundreds of thousands of years as gatherers and hunters in small band-level groups. Agriculture changed not only how we eat but how we organize society, giving rise to cities, empires, nations. Our evolutionary history shaped us for living in small social organizations, which is why it's not surprising how hard we have to struggle—and how often we fail—to make our out-of-context social systems work to everyone's benefit.

---

[32] For a synopsis of his recent book on that subject, *see* Appendix 1.

Drawing on his scientific training and his early experience with prairies, both plowed and unbroken, Jackson has spent decades searching for ways that the human community can create ways for "joyful participation" in the universe in a renewable and sustainable way. If we cannot achieve that in agriculture first, Jackson doubts that sustainability is possible, which has led to his decades-long focus on Natural Systems Agriculture and Ecosphere Studies. Experts who once scoffed at ideas like Jackson's are slowly coming to terms with the crises we face and the need for radical change.

As ordinary people observe and experience directly the changes in climate and the natural world for themselves, Jackson hopes the constituency for that radical change will grow, allowing challenges to the law to reflect the changing priorities and concerns. Jackson remains buoyed by natural optimism, rooted in community, supported by scientific experimentation, and undergirded by a sense of the spirituality of the endeavor. Jackson is pragmatic when working to advance an ecological worldview, but also is a dreamer. As he is fond of saying "If your life's work can be accomplish in your lifetime, you're not thinking big enough."[33]

Wes Jackson Books

Author

Wes Jackson, *New Roots for Agriculture* (Lincoln: University of Nebraska Press, 1980).

Wes Jackson, *Altars of Unhewn Stone: Science and the Earth* (San Francisco: North Point Press, 1987). Reprint: Wooster Book Co. (2006)

Wes Jackson, *Becoming Native to This Place* (Lexington: University Press of Kentucky, 1994). Paperback: Counterpoint (1996)

Wes Jackson, *Nature as Measure: The Selected Essays of Wes Jackson* (Berkeley, CA: Counterpoint, 2011).

Wes Jackson, *Consulting the Genius of the Place: An Ecological Approach to a New Agriculture* (Berkeley, CA: Counterpoint, 2011).

Editor

Wes Jackson, ed., *Man and the Environment* (Dubuque, IA: W.C. Brown, 1971) (3rd edition in 1979)

[33] The Land Institute, *About the Land Institute*, https://landinstitute.org/about-us/ (last visited Aug. 16, 2019).

Wes Jackson, Wendell Berry, and Bruce Colman, eds., *Meeting the Expectations of the Land: Essays in Sustainable Agriculture and Stewardship* (San Francisco: North Point Press, 1984),

William Vitek and Wes Jackson, eds., *Rooted in the Land: Essays on Community and Place* (New Haven, CT: Yale University Press, 1996).

Bill Vitek and Wes Jackson, eds., *The Virtues of Ignorance: Complexity, Sustainability, and the Limits of Knowledge* (Lexington: University Press of Kentucky, 2008).

Appendix 1

A "bare-bones legal and policy brief": Creating a Global Corporate Trust for Agroecological Integrity in order to facilitate and manage a new agriculture in a world of legitimate eco-states

J. W. Head

The following few pages offer an outline of a brief—similar in style to a legal brief—summarizing the principal points made in the six chapters of the book A GLOBAL CORPORATE TRUST FOR AGROECOLOGICAL INTEGRITY: NEW AGRICULTURE IN A WORLD OF LEGITIMATE ECO-STATES (2019).

Proposition #1. *The form of "extractive" agriculture that humans have developed over about 10,000 years can and should be replaced with a new natural-systems form of agriculture—agroecological husbandry—but such a fundamental transformation involves extensive legal and institutional challenges.*

1. **Modern extractive agriculture can and should be replaced with agroecological husbandry** as a means of grain and legume production for human use.
   A. **Modern agriculture is "extractive"** in ways that reflect its most fundamental character as developed over about 10,000 years, and it has become dramatically more extractive recently by its overwhelming dependence on fossil carbon. For this and other reasons, modern extractive agriculture is **unsustainable** in several ways—particularly, as an ecological matter, as an economic matter, and as a social matter—and has thus created a crisis. Moreover, the crisis of agriculture fits within a **larger ecospheric context** that involves not only the pedosphere (soil) but also the atmosphere (especially with implications for climate change), the hydrosphere (water quality and availability), and the biosphere's diversity (now threatened by widespread extinctions).

B. **Agroecological husbandry**—a natural-systems form of grain-and-legume production featuring perennial (not annual) crops grown in polycultures (not monocultures)—now presents a viable alternative, as a scientific matter, to modern extractive agriculture, because of very recent developments in agricultural research (especially plant breeding, ecology, and evolutionary biology). Importantly, it **promises to avoid the economic, ecological, and social unsustainability of modern extractive agriculture** while yielding commercially-feasible supplies of grains—which today comprise roughly two-thirds of human caloric intake worldwide. Accordingly, agroecological husbandry, along with some other alternative forms of food production, warrant close and urgent study and development.

2. However, a transition from modern extractive agriculture to agroecological husbandry poses not only scientific challenges but also **a cluster of serious legal challenges**—and of these challenges, the institutional ones are probably the most difficult.

   A. Numerous **long-term changes should be made in substantive law at the national level**—especially in the USA as the principal "engine" of modern extractive agriculture, but also elsewhere in the world as well—in order to reorient agricultural subsidies, adopt the Precautionary Principle, stiffen agriculture-specific anti-pollution protections, enhance the size and diversity of rural populations and the diversity of crops they produce, and support education and research aimed at facilitating the transition to agroecological husbandry—not just (i) to hasten the development of perennial grains and the designs for their production in polyculture settings adapted to all regions of the world where food production is feasible, but also (ii) to generate a broadly-internalized "land ethic" within new generations of humans through intense public-education programs in "ecosphere studies".

   B. **At the international level, a Global Convention on Agroecology should be broadly adopted** to announce principles and reflect the obligations of contracting states to implement those principles—emphasizing, for instance, (i) the need for a reintegration of humans with the rest of the natural world, (ii) the responsibility that humans have to restore the Earth's ecological integrity, (iii) the urgency of making a transition away from modern extractive agriculture and toward a natural-systems form of food production, (iv) the inviolability of certain "safeguard rights" of all people that are to be protected during such a transition, (v) the special urgency of global climate change and its relationship with agriculture, and (vi) the duty of cooperation and for "special and differential treatment" among members of the international community—including non-state entities as well as states—in making fundamental reforms to agriculture.

C. However, the necessary **national and international legal reforms will turn on fundamental institutional changes at the global level**, including a reconceptualization of state sovereignty that (i) is closely analogous to the reframing of agriculture to reflect perenniality and diversity and (ii) will lead to a new form of governance for agroecological issues.

Proposition #2. *Building the necessary legal, institutional, and conceptual foundations for a transition to agroecological husbandry would involve several steps. Some would give special attention to aligning governance structures with physical realities of agriculture and ecology; some, by contrast, would involve reforming old notions of sovereignty and the "nation-state" emerging out of sixteenth-century Europe and adopting instead a concept of the eco-state and a form of "pluralistic sovereignty" that would provide an effective system of agroecological governance.*

3. As a physical matter—that is, taking into account realities of geography and ecology—the world already reveals **natural categories that would provide a basis for ecological governance** through "eco-states".
   A. The world's ecosystems, far from being chaotic, fall into a relatively small number of terrestrial **biomes**—categories of land cover, climate, soil composition, and species distribution—that (i) are relatively distinct from each other but that appear in similar form in various parts of the world and (ii) relate directly (unlike the "anthro-states" that we are familiar with) to agricultural and ecological realities, and in fact the great preponderance of grain and legume production (which accounts for roughly two-thirds of global human caloric intake) occurs in just four of these biomes worldwide.
   B. These biomes can serve as the **territorial foundation for eco-states**, so that each eco-state would encompass those territories, wherever located in the world, that fall within a particular biome, thus "integrating nature and society" in a way that gives the highest possible priority to ecological factors in determining how humans will manage and reform agricultural production therein.
4. As a legal and conceptual matter, **creating the "eco-state" system** would involve introducing a substitute for outmoded concepts of sovereignty and the so-called "nation-state" (more accurately referred to as the "anthro-state"), thereby establishing "new roots for sovereignty" better suited to addressing agroecological needs and realities and highlighting the need for devolution, local control, and the reality of political and cultural diversity in the world.

A. For starters, we need to "**escape the sixteenth century**" and the hold it has over our concepts of sovereignty, so that more contemporary views of global ecological governance can gain broad interest and acceptance.
B. In doing so, we can draw from numerous examples and **models of blended and layered sovereignty** found in various transboundary regions and political systems of the world, some of which do reflect ecological realities and priorities (such as biosphere reserves and river system management regimes, and even the deep seabed) but most of which have far too little authority or legal personality to provide adequate environmental governance.
C. Eco-states would have such authority and legal personality, and they would carry the responsibility for agroecological governance at the local level over territories based on biomes—and indeed their character and composition would make for a new form of "**pluralistic sovereignty**" featuring (i) legitimacy through perenniality and (ii) strength through diversity.

Proposition #3. *Complementing and facilitating the steps noted in Proposition #2 (adopting a new form of "pluralistic sovereignty" and establishing eco-states with international legal personality) would be the establishing of a new international organization—the Global Corporate Trust for Agroecological Integrity—which would avoid the shortcomings seen in existing international institutions (including those whose work focuses directly on agriculture) and would represent instead a "fourth generation" international organization designed to ensure that our species recognizes and discharges its responsibility as trustees for generations to come, whose well-being turns on agricultural reform and ecological restoration.*

5. The development of **the world's existing international organizations, and the efforts they have made to address global agricultural issues in particular, must be regarded as wholly inadequate** thus far and ill-suited to handle greater challenges to come, including global climate change. For historical and political and ideological reasons, this is hardly surprising.
   A. **Public international institutions**—those created by (anthro-)states and having only those entities as their members (and masters)—**are still quite novel**, emerging on the world stage only a hundred years ago in unsteady form and only seventy years ago in a form that constituted them as having personality in international law. They have evolved through three "generations."
   B. The **international organizations focusing especially on agriculture issues**, while doing creditable and worthwhile work, give most of their attention to expanding food production and improving rural economic

circumstances, and not to either (i) a radical reform of the agricultural system *per se* or (ii) an overriding concern for restoring ecosystems. Responding to a blend of competing influences and conflicting signals, these organizations take a "no-negative-effects" approach on ecological issues instead of seeking to thoroughly blend agriculture and ecology and guard the latter against the former.

C. Building on a framework of critical analysis developed in the context of global economic organizations, it appears clear that **those public international institutions focusing most on agriculture are inadequate to address agroecological issues effectively or to facilitate a change to global governance** in a way that will facilitate the adoption of natural systems agriculture and a framework of eco-states to manage it in accord with ecosystem integrity.

D. However, the disappointments encountered thus far in the performance of international organizations should not cause us to abandon the **multilateralist philosophy** that prompted their creation, because (i) like any new form of human effort at social cooperation, early attempts are naturally imperfect, (ii) the cluster of existential global crises we face today are more serious than earlier ones, and (iii) we have new legal doctrines and instruments available now—especially a well-developed global public trust doctrine—that enable us to design better institutional responses than in earlier times.

6. It is possible and necessary to start a new generation of international organizations that will avoid the problems plaguing the existing ones and thereby restore confidence in applying multilateral efforts in order to address global challenges and crises. **A Global Corporate Trust for Agroecological Integrity can be designed to facilitate the transition to a natural-systems form of agriculture** that is consistent with the fundamental goal of ecological restoration and protection. This design would draw from but depart radically from earlier institutional frameworks by instituting a novel system of participatory governance and by facilitating the work of the various eco-states referred to above.

A. Drawing on earlier experience, and putting to use those new legal doctrines and instruments, the **GCTAI, with ecological restoration and preservation at its heart**, (i) would have adequate power and authority to facilitate a transition away from modern extractive agriculture to a natural-systems agriculture, (ii) would involve not only anthro-states but also other entities (including eco-states, civil society, and representatives of other stakeholders), (iii) would have adequate funding and capacity for financial operations necessary to its mandate, and (iv) would have a governance structure that discards obsolete features of existing organizations and replaces them with features suitable for striking workable balance among many competing interests—with ecological integrity a non-negotiable value and objective.

B. In sum, although several very serious difficulties face advocates for legal and institutional reform designed to facilitate a transition to a natural-systems form of agriculture that contributes to, rather than detracts from, agroecological integrity, **it is reasonable to believe that these difficulties can be overcome**: (i) humans are inventive and resourceful; (ii) existential crises now facing us—particularly climate change and soil degradation, but also accelerating extinctions and drops in water quality and availability—will undoubtedly force *some* changes, thereby boosting the chances that *designed* changes can be made; and (iii) there are clear historical precedents for the specific legal reforms that are involved in a call to revise sovereignty, create eco-states, and to establish an institution such as the GCTAI.

Chapter 9

Judge Richard Dickson Cudahy: The Last New Deal Judge February 2, 1926–September 22, 2015

Joseph P. Tomain[1]

Judge Richard Cudahy can be claimed as the Dean of the Energy Bar. Nevertheless, his inclusion, in *Pioneers of Environmental Law* is more than warranted. Throughout his 40-year public career as an administrator, judge, teacher, and scholar, he has been aware of and sensitive to environmental law. More importantly, he has persistently emphasized the physical reality that environmental consequences flow through every stage of the energy fuel cycle—energy and the environment are to be treated together, not independently of each other. To that end, his opinions and law review articles stress the necessity of taking the environment into account as energy policy is designed and implemented.

Richard Dickson Cudahy was born on February 2, 1926 and raised in Milwaukee, Wisconsin. February 2nd is most certainly an auspicious birthday date for an Irishman because Dick shared it with another one—James Joyce. There is real Irish in his blood as his grandfather, Patrick, was an immigrant from the old sod. His grandparents on his mother's side, though, were English with long roots in the United States with a number of relatives having served in the Civil War including in the Vicksburg campaign.

---

[1] Joseph P. Tomain is Dean Emeritus and the Wilbert and Helen Ziegler Professor of Law at the University Of Cincinnati College of Law. Dean Tomain began law teaching in 1976 and has written extensively in the energy law field having published over a dozen books on the topic. His other publications include books on law and the humanities as well as on the role of government regulation in our democracy. In addition to serving as chair and member of various community organizations, Dean Tomain also has held positions as Visiting Environmental Scholar, Lewis & Clark Law School; Distinguished Visiting Energy Professor, Vermont Law School; Visiting Scholar in the Program of Liberal Studies, University of Notre Dame; Visiting Fellow, Harris Manchester College, Oxford University; Fulbright Senior Specialist in law in Cambodia; and National Endowment for the Humanities Summer Fellow, Stanford University.

The Cudahy family business was Midwest meatpacking. His paternal grandfather opened the Cudahy Brothers Company later renamed Patrick Cudahy, Inc. and one of his great uncles worked for P. D. Armour who operated a rival firm which later became Armour & Co. His father ran the family business, as he would years later.

Dick was educated in private schools—Country Day in Milwaukee and, for a time, the Canterbury School in New Milford Connecticut, a Catholic college prep school. He applied and was admitted to Yale College although he spent the beginning of his college education at Northwestern University before transferring to West Point from which he graduated in 1948 with a degree in military engineering.

After graduating from the US Military Academy, Dick entered active duty in the Air Force Administration in Spokane, Washington, home of the Strategic Air Command. It was there that he received his first taste of lawyering when he was assigned to the base legal office where he defended soldiers being tried by court-martial. In addition to defense, he also prosecuted those cases.

After his tour, Dick attended Yale Law School and graduated in 1955. Upon graduation, he clerked for Second Circuit Judge Charles Clark, the former Dean of Yale Law. After his clerkship, he worked in the Legal Advisors Office of the State Department before entering private practice in Chicago with the then firm of Isham, Lincoln and Beale. At Isham, Cudahy began his long association with economic regulation in general and with energy regulation in particular. He had the opportunity to engage public utility law through the firm's representation of Commonwealth Edison.

After a few years of law practice, the judge's father, who was running the meatpacking business, became ill and Dick was recruited to become CEO of Patrick Cudahy, Inc. for 10 years. This on the job training would prove useful for his regulatory work. Not so much because of the regulations governing meatpacking, rather because running a for-profit firm gave him an opportunity to understand how private firms price products and earn their profits. Additionally, he learned the economics of how businesses operate; the differences between for-profit firms that operate in competitive markets and those that are highly regulated; and the significance of the structural differences between regulated and nonregulated businesses. During that period, he became an adjunct law professor at Marquette Law School. He would also go on to teach at the University of Wisconsin and George Washington University law schools and he developed a close relationship with DePaul Law School as well.

In the early 60s, Dick became actively involved in Democratic politics. He started as a low level staffer on the John F. Kennedy campaign. Later he became head of the Wisconsin Democratic Party where he was a delegate to the infamous 1968 Democratic National Convention in Chicago. Shortly after that, he managed William Proxmire's successful United States Senate run in 1970. Then after an ill-fated run for Wisconsin Attorney General, Dick returned to private practice before beginning his career in public service after being appointed to the Wisconsin Public Service Commission (PSC). It is here he cut his teeth on utility regulation and on matters of energy and the environment. To him being appointed to the PSC, where he stayed for three years from 1972-1975, proved to be:

> "[A] pretty good deal because this was getting into a period when energy and utilities and communications and all this kind of thing were developing huge problems and presenting big challenges, environmental being one of them, obviously."[2]

Thus in the early 1970s, shortly after the dawn of environmental regulation and in the midst of the "energy crises" of that decade, Judge Cudahy was well aware of the direct connection between environmental law and policy and the emerging field of energy law and policy.

Rounding out the judge's professional biography, after the PSC, he returned to private practice to start the Washington office of Isham where he was in charge of a major utility case involving interconnections among power companies for transmitting wholesale electricity in interstate commerce. More about that case later. After a short stint in Washington, he was appointed to the Seventh Circuit by President Carter in 1979 and moved to Chicago to assume the bench.

The opportunity to provide a tribute to Judge Richard Cudahy at the end of the second decade of the 21st century is doubly important. First, although he is primarily known as the energy specialist, both as a judge and as a scholar, Dick was one of the first in the energy field to recognize the importance of linking energy and the environment. Because of this, it is fitting that he should be included in this volume on environmental pioneers.

Secondly, the subtitle of this essay, *The Last New Deal Judge*, marks an interesting point in our jurisprudence and in our political history. The rise of the anti-administrativists,[3] including a potential majority of Justices on the United States Supreme Court,[4] poses a direct challenge, if not an existential threat, to the modern administrative state. As Penn Law Professor Sophia Z. Lee writes "the scholars, judges, lawyers, advocacy groups questioning the constitutional foundations of the modern state have reached critical mass."[5] These scholars

---

[2] Collins Fitzpatrick, The Oral History of Richard D. Cudahy 119 (2010).

[3] Gillian E. Metzger, *Forward: 1930s Redux: The Administrative State Under Siege*, 131 Harv. L. Rev. 1 (2017).

[4] *See Kisor v. Wilkie*, 588 U.S. __ (2019) available at https://www.supremecourt.gov/opinions/18pdf/18-15_9p6b.pdf; *Gundy v. United States*, 588 U.S. __ (2019) available at https://www.supremecourt.gov/opinions/18pdf/17-6086_2b8e.pdf.

[5] Sophia Z. Lee, *Our Administered Constitution: Administrative Constitutionalism from the Founding to the Present*, 168 U. Pa. L. Rev. ___ (2020).

challenge the very constitutional existence of the regulatory state; and they have been labeled as advocating "the Constitution in exile."[6] The Exiles believe that constitutional law took a severely wrong turn during the New Deal and that the country would be better off returning to the *Lochner* era if not to the Gilded Age itself. As his career demonstrates, this is a sentiment that Dick Cudahy would not have shared.

Two Cases

Prior to 1974, Dick Cudahy had been a Second Circuit law clerk, a State Department attorney, a Chicago lawyer, a CEO, and a Democratic political operative. His reward? A seat on the Wisconsin Public Service Commission (PSC), which he chaired before returning to private practice in Washington, DC. At the commission, he wrote an important concurring opinion on the marginal cost pricing of electricity the importance of which still stands today and has contemporary significance for the clean energy transition.

In one sense, *In re Madison Gas & Electric*,[7] was a run-of-the-mill electric rate case in which the local utility sought to increase its revenue requirement by applying ordinary rate design concepts. In another sense, the case became, and remains, significant because of the arguments brought by the intervenors, most notably the Environmental Defense Fund. The PSC saw it as a "national test case" on electric rate design. The controversy surrounded the use of the utility's declining block rate structure, also known as a volumetric rate. In brief, declining block rates are designed so that a utility's fixed costs are covered in early blocks of the rate. Then, as consumers continued to use electricity the price declines. While consumers enjoy price decreases for consuming more, the rate design encourages overconsumption and when fossil fuels are being burned overconsumption contributes to over pollution.

The commission was well aware of the significance of case writing: "This order covers the first comprehensive hearing testing the appropriateness of these traditional rate designs in view of new and different conditions faced by the public utility."[8] Those new and different conditions involved the then energy shortage, rising prices, increasing inflation, growing dependence on foreign oil, and environmental harm. Indeed, the commission recognized that the case had been, "like no other in the commission's history" and that its opinion regarding the

---

[6] Douglas Ginsburg, *Delegation Running Riot*, REGULATION 83 (Vol. 1 1995) (reviewing DAVID SCHOENBROD, POWER WITHOUT RESPONSIBILITY: HOW CONGRESS ABUSES THE PEOPLE THROUGH DELEGATION (1993); Jeffery Rosen, *The Unregulated Offensive*, N.Y. TIMES MAGAZINE (April 17, 2005).

[7] *In re Madison Gas & Elec.*, 59 Wis. PSC 70 (August 8, 1974); 5 P.U.R. 4th 28 (Wisc. P.S.C. 1974).

[8] 59 Wis. PSC at 74.

socioeconomics of electric rate design was "unique."[9] *Madison Gas* did become a national test case for electric rate design which, in fact, is still ongoing.[10]

The PSC knew that the best solution for the negative externalities of pollution would be to impose a pollution tax on utilities. Of course, the commission had no such jurisdiction and it had to play with the cards it was dealt. In particular, the commission could affect consumption through rate design and instead of encouraging consumption a rate design could price electricity at its long-run marginal cost as best as it could.[11] In this way: (1) consumers would receive more accurate price signals; (2) electricity would be consumed at near its real price; and (3) with minor tuning, such as the time-of-use rates, price signals and demand would both be more accurate (i.e. more efficient).

In his concurring opinion, Judge Cudahy paid close attention to rate design particularly as it related to a changing industry and society:

> "The instant case ... primarily concerns the structure or design of prices and the relationship of such structure to demand, to the efficient allocation of resources, to wasteful use of resources, to conservation, to environmental protection, to revenue erosion and also to the more conventional (albeit vital) concerns such as revenue requirement."[12]

And further,

> "Electricity has become a very much more precious commodity than it was previously believed to be. Conservation and a strict accounting of costs both pecuniary and environmental have become the order of the day.... It seems clearly justified to explore more exacting cost determinations than we previously thought appropriate."[13]

Madison Gas provided an opportunity for the PSC to look deeply at the traditional rate structure and criticize the dominant focus on a utility's revenue requirement as the first, and often only, order of business. The PSC's scrutiny of declining block rates was significant for two reasons. First, it recognized changes

---

[9] *Id.* at 81.

[10] *See, e.g.*, Richard L. Revesz & Burcin Unel, *Managing the Future of the Electricity Grid: Modernizing Rate Design*, 44 Harv. Envt. L. Rev. 43 (2020).

[11] The Commission acknowledged the difficulty of accurately determining short run marginal cost and opted for pricing electricity at its long-run incremental cost. In the end, the commission imposed a flat rate as distinguished from either declining block rate, an inverted rate, or a peak load pricing rate. These economics concepts are fully explained in the opinion and in Richard D. Cudahy & J. Robert Malko, *Electric Peak-Load Pricing: Madison Gas and Beyond*, 1976 Wisc. L. Rev. 47 (1976).

[12] 5 P.U.R. 4th 51 (Wisc. P.S.C. 1974).

[13] *In re Madison Gas & Elec.*, 59 Wis. PSC70 *supra* note 7 at 90.

in the electric industry and, second, it recognized the necessity for a new way of thinking about traditional utility regulation more generally.

A declining block rate structure works well under two circumstances. First, a utility must continue to realize economies of scale. In other words, it works when the unit cost of electricity declines as more is produced. In that way, a utility's revenue requirement can be satisfied and consumers' electricity bills will either stay flat or decline. In an era when a regulated industry is expanding and is continuing to realize scale economies, there is an added bonus for public utility commissions, their workload is light, most often non-controversial, and it is politically under the radar. Consequently, during industry expansion with declining block rates, everyone is (seemingly) happy.

Second, a utility can enjoy the benefits of declining block rates as long as it ignores the social costs of pollution. As long as external costs are ignored, then the declining block rates appear to reflect actual costs. Again, in appearance only, the decreasing costs of declining block rates seem to favor the utility and its consumers. However, declining block rates neglect social realities including: (1) pollution; (2) the incentive for more capital investment; (3) inefficient higher production; (4) inefficient higher consumption; (5) ultimately increasing rates due to increasing fixed costs; and (6) and the failure to conserve energy.

Both of the requirements for effective declining block rates—scale economies and ignoring social costs—are problematic. They are also related.

Utilities cannot satisfy the first requirement for two reasons. The first reason is that economies of scale do not continue indefinitely. At some point, such as reaching a technological plateau, economies of scale are exhausted and per-unit costs increase. The second reason is that the traditional rate formula encouraged capital expansion, which also cannot continue indefinitely.

Under traditional rate regulation, utilities were encouraged to build more plant and at some point the electricity market would be saturated such that additional plant only imposed costs on the system, it did not realize a reduction in prices. The economic phenomenon known as the Averch-Johnson effect[14] simply meant that utilities would overbuild. And they did; and the price of electricity rose; and ratepayers were unhappy; and public utility commissions had challenges to meet.

The second requirement could not be satisfied for the obvious reason that the social cost of pollution cannot be ignored forever. A utility and its shareholders may not realize those costs, but society certainly absorbs them. The two reasons are related by the fact that generating electricity from cheap fossil fuels creates pollution and imposes those costs on society at large.

The traditional rate structure had a built-in bias. Because economies of scale were realized until the mid-1960s, utility commissions could safely focus

---

[14] Harvey Averch & Leland L. Johnson, *Behavior of the Firm Under Regulatory Constraint*, 52 AM. ECON REV. 1052 (1962).

on a utility's revenue requirement. The problem with concentrating on revenue, even when consumers were seemingly happy, is that costs were ignored and price signals to consumers were distorted. As noted, electricity was over consumed. With more accurate price signals, in particular peak-load pricing, consumers who consumed during peak would pay a premium and those that consumed off-peak would enjoy something of a discount. Although *Madison Gas* discussed marginal cost pricing, the commission imposed flat rates based upon the evidence before it. Commissioner Cudahy used his concurrence to discuss the necessity of internalizing social costs into electricity prices. Ideally, of course, a carbon tax could be used but taxation was beyond the purview of the PSC. To internalize the social cost of carbon, get thee to the legislature.

After *Madison Gas* was decided, Judge Cudahy and PSC chief economist, J. Robert Malko, published a law review article on the case that would endorse the desirability of peak-load pricing. The article began by acknowledging how wasteful promotional rate structures were and by acknowledging social and economic changes. The authors identified the then "energy dilemma" as encompassing general inflation and "strong environmental concerns" among others.[15]

The article went on to describe in some detail four basic types of rate design which included (1) declining block rates; (2) flat rates; (3) inverted rates; and (4) peak-load rates. The core idea driving the article was that marginal cost pricing was the most efficient way to price electricity because it provided consumer's with a more accurate pricing scheme. When fully implemented, consumers had more choice available to them regarding how much they wanted to pay for electricity based upon time of use.[16] We are still battling over the implementation of time-of-use rates not because of economic theory but rather because of the difficulty that comes with metering enough homes to make peak-load pricing more widely available.

The authors also noted the problem of negative externalities, more particularly, that the costs of pollution to society are not fully accounted for even with more marginal cost sensitive rate designs. If all negative externalities could be fully internalized, then it may be possible to achieve the socially optimal allocation of resources.[17] The authors recognized, as did the majority opinion in *Madison Gas*, that the best way to achieve such internalization would be through a carbon tax of some sort. The authors further acknowledged that the such decisions necessarily involves political choices about the type of society and economy in which we wish to live. They knew that the PSC was not the body to make such choices; it was the legislature.

---

[15] Cudahy & Malko, *supra* note 11 at 48.

[16] *Id.* at 59.

[17] *Id.* at 65.

Still, even recognizing the limitations of the commission, it did not mean that the PSC lacked any ability to address carbon pollution. Indeed, the theme of the article is that peak-load pricing should be more fully studied and applied if for no other reason than it would serve as a disincentive to continue capital investment in excess plant particularly plants that would generate excess pollution together with excess electricity at excess prices. The traditional focus on a utility's revenue requirement simply encouraged capital investment as a way to increase returns thus driving up the cost of electricity unnecessarily.

Madison Gas was a case decided early in Dick Cudahy's public service career. After serving on the Wisconsin Public Service Commission, he returned to private practice and again specialized in public utilities.

Madison Gas was decided in 1974 and at that time the electric industry was beginning a transition that is yet to be fully realized. The transition was brought about for technological and regulatory (or political) reasons. The technological issue has already been noted. The industry had overbuilt and new electricity providers with cheaper electricity were waiting in the wings. The regulatory (or political) reason was that the electricity industry was simply following in the footsteps of the general deregulatory mood in the country at the time particularly after having seen a significant deregulation of natural gas and oil.

The electric industry transition greatly accelerated in 1978 with the passage of the Public Utilities Regulatory Policy Act (PURPA).[18] PURPA was one part of a more ambitious energy package known as the National Energy Act of 1978. In one crucial respect, PURPA was a great surprise. The legislation was intended to accomplish two things in the electric industry. First, it was to contribute to the nation's energy independence by diversifying generation sources and, second, it was intended to promote energy conservation exactly along the lines that Commissioner Cudahy discussed in *Madison Gas* four years earlier.

One of the mechanisms that the legislation used to promote conservation was to tap into the cheaper electricity that was available in the market. Much energy was lost through waste heat in manufacturing and that waste heat could be captured and converted into electricity. In order to capture that excess energy, PURPA created a class of energy producers known as qualifying facilities (QFs) that had an economic incentive to produce electricity. QFs were defined as small power producers or co-generators. Manufacturers, for example, could use electricity in various processes that generated heat, then they could capture the excess heat and use it to generate more electricity. Thus, the facility could reduce energy waste as well as reduce its overall energy costs.

PURPA's surprise was that there were so many producers willing to qualify as a QF. Indeed, PURPA contained a significant incentive to qualify as such. First, QFs were not subject to Federal Power Act regulations. Next, once qualified as a

[18] The Public Utilities Regulatory Policies Act of 1978, 16 U.S.C. §2601 et seq.

QF, PURPA required that local utilities purchased all of the QFs' excess electricity at the utility's "avoided cost" of producing it. The QF could generate cheaper electricity and sell it to the utility at the utility's higher price.[19] Consequently, there was more and cheaper electricity on the market and it needed to reach customers. The complication, however, was that traditional utilities controlled the transmission and distribution wires and were reluctant to allow competitors to use them. In a word, the new electricity market confronted one big challenge—access by new entrants.

Thirty-five years after *Madison Gas*, and almost as many years after PURPA, energy regulators (agencies and judges) were confronted with the challenge of opening the electricity market by providing access. One such challenge involved improving the electricity grid or, as is sometimes said, building the smart grid. This was exactly the issue that Judge Cudahy confronted in a case involving Illinois Commerce Commission and the Federal Energy Regulatory Commission (FERC) that ended in 2014.[20]

One solution to the access problem was to treat electricity transmission as a common carrier. Under this arrangement, transmission companies would be required to allow their lines to be used by other electricity providers at nondiscriminatory rates. Privately owned transmission companies, in other words, could not game the system to their own financial benefit.

As part of that solution, regional transmission organizations (RTOs) and independent system operators (ISOs) were established to create regional electricity markets throughout the United States.[21] Although the transmission lines remained privately owned by the electric utilities, the RTO was given the responsibility of maintaining markets for energy to be used now and in the future. The RTO also has responsibility for setting interstate transmission rates that were just, reasonable, and nondiscriminatory. Today, roughly two-thirds of the electricity consumed in the United States passes through an RTO.

The RTO that serves the Midwest wanted to upgrade the grid by building high voltage transmission lines (HVTL) that have the capacity of transporting higher amounts of electricity with lower rates of line loss. HVTLs were more efficient than the lines already constructed and operating on the system. The tricky question was how to pay for those upgrades. As required by law, the RTO needed FERC approval to set rates for the new transmission facilities that

---

[19] PURPA's mandatory purchase and avoided costs requirements are alive and well. *See Winding Creek Solar LLC v. California Public Utilities Comm'n.*, D.C. No. 3:13-cv-04934 (U.S.D.C. N. Cal. July 29, 2019) available at https://statepowerproject.files.wordpress.com/2019/07/ca-9th-winding-creek-decision.pdf.

[20] *Illinois Commerce Commission v. FERC*, 576 F.3d 470 (7th Cir. 2009) (ICC I); 72 F.3d 764 (7th Cir. 2013) (ICC II); 756 F.3d 556 (7th Cir. 2014) (ICC III).

[21] Although each regional organization operates according to somewhat different rules, the major difference between an RTO and an ISO is the date that they were formed. Most regional organizations are RTOs and I will use RTOs to include ISOs.

sold wholesale power in interstate commerce. The RTO proposed, and FERC accepted, that all the utilities in that region would contribute their pro rata share of the costs. That is the charges for the grid improvement would be based on the amount of electricity sold into the RTO by each utility. The problem with the pro rata argument is that each utility would benefit differently from the new facilities and those benefits would not correspond to their pro rata share of their electricity contribution. By way of example, Commonwealth Edison estimated that it would cost them $480 million as their contribution to the upgrade but that they would only realize about $1 million in benefits.

FERC's reasons for the pro rata arrangement were fairly simple and, as the court ruled, too simplistic. First, years before the RTO was formed, utilities had such a pro rata agreement that could serve as precedent for costing out the new facilities. Second, and more notably, FERC acknowledged that benefits were difficult, if not impossible, to track. And, concomitantly, FERC reasoned that system upgrades would benefit all system users because the grid would now be more reliable and more secure. There would be less congestion and the risk of blackouts would decrease. Some utilities in the RTO objected to this arrangement arguing that it violated the fundamental principle of cost causation. They argued that only utilities that benefit from the upgrades should be responsible for paying for them.

The court, per Judge Posner, rejected all of FERC's reasoning noting that the HTVL was to be located in the eastern part of the RTO and would primarily benefit that region and not the utilities in the western part.[22] Therefore, the alignment of costs and benefits was out of whack with the pro rata payment scheme. Further, the prior pro rata agreement that was forged in 1967 among a different group of utilities carried no precedential value. Next, the fact that FERC found benefits difficult to measure was an insufficient justification for not attempting some sort of more reasonable cost allocation. Finally, Judge Posner also rejected the system benefit argument.

In his opinion, Posner acknowledged that an improved grid could reduce blackouts and, therefore, benefit the whole system. He rejected the pro rata rate arrangement because, in his view, FERC did not provide "even the roughest of ballpark estimates of those benefits."[23] Consequently, the benefits were too speculative. And, accordingly, "FERC is not authorized to approve a pricing scheme that requires a group of utilities to pay for facilities from which its members derive no benefits, or benefits that are trivial in relation to the costs sought to be shifted to its members."[24] Judge Posner simply adopted a familiar cost

[22] *Illinois Commerce Commission v. FERC*, 756 F.3d 556, 566 (7th Cir. 2014).

[23] 576 F.3d at 477.

[24] *Id.*

causation principle that links costs and benefits and rejected FERC's allocation because it was not based upon substantial evidence.

Judge Cudahy's dissent begins by describing an electricity industry in transition:

> The United States is now engaged in an urgent project to upgrade its electric transmission grid, which for years has been generally regarded as inadequate, and may become more deficient with the addition of major new anticipated loads. The existing transmission system originally served vertically integrated utilities that built their own generation relatively close to their customers. The system was not designed for long-distance power transfers between different parts of the country. The inadequacy of the present network and the urgency of the need for its improvement has only been exacerbated by the additional burdens imposed by deregulation (or restructuring), which "unbundled" generation and transmission and created a need to bring power from distant generators. Additional challenges have been posed by the demand for power from renewable generation sources (such as wind farms) that are often located in places remote from centers of electric consumption.[25]

This description more than adequately explains the reasons for his dissent. First, as a technical matter, HVTL can improve system reliability and it can carry more electricity longer distances. Consequently, according to Judge Cudahy "extra-high voltage transmission is especially fitted to be financed equally by all utilities that benefit from its role as the 'backbone' of the system"[26] as many participants in the case admitted. Moreover, pro rata rates can eliminate "fruitless controversy over the allocation of costs."[27] As far as cost causation was concerned, Judge Cudahy stated that FERC was not required to monetize benefits of reliability improvements in order to share costs because all participating units are parts of the power grid and, therefore all participating units benefit from greater grid reliability.

Judge Cudahy concludes:

> The big picture here is that FERC's proposal to spread the cost of [HVTL] on a uniform basis seems to me in the interest of efficient, high-capacity transfer capability and of the closely linked improvement of reliability, which affects the system generally. Deregulation created a demand for competitive sources of power, often at a distance. Because 500 kV and above lines satisfy these new systemic needs, their separate treatment for rate-making purposes is both sensible and innovative. While an effort to identify specific benefits to specific utilities is a traditional rate design approach and may be appropriate

[25] *Id.* at 479.

[26] *Id.* at 480.

[27] *Id.*

> for most electric plant facilities, it may miss the forest and focus on the trees when applied to very high voltage "backbone" facilities having a generalized role in supporting reliability and high capacity power transfer. Perhaps as important in this picture is the urgency of the need to build transmission and the need for incentives to that end. Pro rata assignment of costs eliminates not only lawsuits but nitpicking controversies of every sort and delays standing in the path of action. From that point of view, I think FERC may be in a better position to implement a policy leading to prompt improvement in a deficient transmission grid than this court, focused as it is on the inevitable complaints of utilities demanding more for their money.[28]

I have included this lengthy quotation for three reasons. First, for a topic as arcane and complex as the evolving electric industry, Judge Cudahy's writing is clear and direct. Second, he recognizes that the evolution of the electric industry is part of a larger deregulatory moment in the United States. Third, as discussed below, his reasoning is consistent with his New Deal approach to the relationship between courts and administrative agencies. As the judge writes in the third iteration of the case, there is a danger in a court substituting its findings on technical matters rather than relying on the FERC's analysis.[29] By way of example, Posner assumed that in the RTO electricity flows from west to east when, in fact, the development of offshore wind power would, in part, reverse that flow. With improved transmission, renewable resources could be more smoothly integrated into the grid to the benefit of the whole system.

Madison Gas and *Illinois Commerce Commission* can be read as the beginning and end of Dick Cudahy's analysis of energy law matters as a judge. In between those two cases, the energy sector, most notably the electricity industry, has undergone sweeping changes. In large part, those changes were the result of the deregulation of economic regulation that began during the Carter years and continues in various forms today.

Somewhat contrary to popular belief that Ronald Reagan was the deregulation president, it must be emphasized that deregulation started with great force during the Carter administration. Carter's deregulation began in the transportation industry with airlines and trucking, then extended to the financial sector and then, significantly for our discussion, to energy industries. Carter's 1978 National Energy Act addressed the energy crisis of the 1970s by bringing market discipline to that sector. Natural gas regulations had caused a natural gas shortage and, through price deregulation, that market was corrected. Similarly, oil price regulations imposed by the Nixon administration ended. And, also in the spirit of increased competition, that act, as the discussion of PURPA above noted, addressed competition in electricity segment of our energy portfolio. If

[28] *Id.* at 482-83.

[29] *Illinois Commerce Commission v. FERC*, 756 F.3d 556, 569 (7th Cir. 2014).

deregulation could affect the natural gas and oil industries, could the electricity industry be far behind?

The particular problem with the electric industry is that deregulation on a broad scale has not taken place. Instead, we see deregulation in the wholesale segment of the industry but much less so in the retail segment. Nevertheless, industry restructuring efforts have been substantial and Judge Cudahy's scholarly writings shed a great amount of light on that restructuring.

Deregulation

Deregulation proponents during both the Carter and Reagan administrations, and since then, have made the central claim that government regulation hampered efficiency and, therefore, reducing regulation would increase economic growth. The mantra of deregulation, however, should be spoken lightly when dealing with infrastructure industries that have been regulated for over a century.

Judge Cudahy was wary of swallowing deregulation wholesale. In an article entitled *The Folklore of Deregulation*,[30] he warned about drinking too much "free market" Kool-Aid. To him, the folklore of deregulation is the "creed that honors the way of markets as the single source of progress and prosperity—not to mention virtue, wisdom, motherhood, and apple pie."[31] And regarding deregulation advocates, he wrote: "The idea of these people was that economic regulation had to be exterminated and its grave sewn with salt least it come creeping back to strangle free competition in its crib.... Regulation was like a weed with deep roots; unless thoroughly uprooted, it would grow back more noxious than ever."[32]

The *Folklore* article analyzes deregulation in telecommunications, airlines, and electric power. Cudahy acknowledged that competition in telecommunications and airlines justified breaking the stranglehold of existing monopolies in each industry. Deregulation could be further justified when it promotes consumer welfare and encourages innovation.[33] He was concerned, though, that the airline industry may, in fact, have been too competitive. Price competition has entered the airline market from time to time, from airline to airline, and from hub to hub. In exchange for price competition, though, there is also service competition. If you have been happy with your airplane legroom and the quality of the peanuts and pretzels that are served instead of a meal, then airline

---

[30] Richard D. Cudahy, *The Folklore of Deregulation (with Apologies to Thurman Arnold)*, 15 Yale J. on Reg. 427 (1998).

[31] *Id.* at 427

[32] *Id.* at 431.

[33] *Id.* at 428-33.

deregulation is just fine. If, on the other hand, the level of service is questionable, then more remains to be done in that industry.[34] Cudahy's point was that deregulation of certain industries, particularly network or infrastructure industries, comes with costs.

The electric industry has attributes that make an easy application of deregulatory strategies more challenging. Specifically, even if competition was available for wholesale power in certain markets, the distribution and transmission (i.e. the transportation) segment of electricity still exhibited market power. The exercise of market power, was particularly evident at the retail level because local utilities continue to own and operate the lines directly to consumers' homes and businesses. There is no incentive for these privately owned transmission and distribution lines to open themselves up to their competitors at the prevailing market price. Instead, the owners of transmission and distribution lines naturally favor their own or affiliated generators and they promote practices adverse to competing electricity providers.

Cudahy saw another problem with the deregulation movement in electricity. More specifically, to the extent that new competition promoted lower prices, those prices could have a rebound effect and increase consumption specifically of fossil-fuel generated electricity. In this deregulatory scenario, environmentalists lose. The economic way of preventing increased consumption is to internalize the cost of pollution which, of course, could raise prices significantly. Cudahy saw the contradiction in deregulation. Deregulation may lower prices but increase social costs and, capturing the social cost may increase the prices. Writing in 1998, he noted that one dimension of those contradictions was illustrated by nuclear power plants that, due to their high overall costs, could be doomed by competition. He, however, confidently predicted that nuclear power would be "touted as the answer to the greenhouse problem."[35] Needless to say, 20 years later, Cudahy's confident prediction has proven true as states now move to subsidize nuclear power plants because of their zero carbon emissions attributes.[36] In that same article, he also predicted the rise of natural gas as the choice of electricity generators, which is, in fact, the case today.

What was more difficult to predict, for Judge Cudahy or anyone else for that matter, was that electricity deregulation efforts, particularly at the retail level, could become a source of massive fraud. Although the story of the California electricity crisis has been told often,[37] it is worth recounting that deregulation

---

[34] Richard D. Cudahy, *The Airlines: Destined to Fail?*, J. AIR L. & COM. 3 (2006).

[35] *Id.* 435.

[36] *See e.g.* NUCLEAR ENERGY INSTITUTE, ZERO-EMISSION CREDITS (April 2018); Peter S. Ross, *Zero-Emission Credits and the Threat to Optimal State Incentives*, 39 ENERGY L. J. 427 (2018).

[37] *See e.g.* Jacqueline Lang Weaver, *Can Energy Markets be Trusted? The Effect of the Rise and Fall of Enron on Energy Markets*, 2 HOUSTON BUS. & TAX L. J. 1 (2004); Darren Bush &

schemes can result in market manipulation much to the harm to consumers and can drive utilities to file for bankruptcy.[38]

Judge Cudahy was also concerned about the consequences of the regulation in terms of market structure and he cast a cautious eye on the central claim for increased efficiency though greater deregulation:

> "Just as it looked as if a whole new world of ruthless rivalry was about to emerge, a cloud no bigger than a man's hand appeared on the horizon. At the edge of the cloud one could barely make out the letters of a word—"Merger." For when the electric power people awoke from their long night of natural monopoly, they had to rush into each other's arms to attend unprecedented number of corporate couplings."[39]

He thus believed that it was an iron rule of deregulation that "[w]hen a capital-intensive industry is deregulated, market concentration inevitably arises."[40] He catalogs how such industries as airlines, trucking, railroads, natural gas, and telecommunications consolidated through merger after deregulation. His concern was that while the competitive forces of deregulation may be the next shiny new thing and promise competitive rewards, structural stability for the industry was not one of them.

Cudahy was not afraid of markets, he was just warning about wholesale deregulation particularly in industries unsuited to it such as vertically-integrated, investor-owned utilities. Regarding the trade-offs between markets and regulation in this industry he notes:

> "The question may be close to the larger issue of what has been gained or lost by replacing the ethos of public service with an ethos of entrepreneurship. With the latter is associated creativity and a stronger drive toward innovation, a modicum of the former remains essential to the provision of infrastructure services."[41]

For infrastructure industries, particularly electricity, full-scale deregulation was not a panacea. Instead, the industry was susceptible to partial deregulation or what became known as industry restructuring. At bottom, Judge Cudahy's concern was reliability. Could a deregulated retail market provide universal service?

Carrie Mayne, *In (Reluctant) Defense of Enron: Why Antitrust Law Fails to Protect Against Market Power When the Market Rules Encourage Its Use*, 83 Or. L. Rev. 1 (2004).

[38] Richard D. Cudahy, *Electric Deregulation After California: Down But Not Out*, 54 Admin. L. Rev. 333 (2002); *see also* Richard D. Cudahy, *Full Circle in the Formerly Regulated Industries*, 33 Loy. U. Chi. L. Rev. 767 (2002).

[39] Richard D. Cudahy, *The FERC's Policy on Electric Mergers: A Bit of Perspective*, 18 Energy L.J. 113, 119-20 (1997).

[40] *Id.*

[41] *Id.* at 360.

It did not in California where retail deregulation initiatives resulted in rolling brownouts and price spikes.

Assuming, for the moment that deregulation in telecommunications (and maybe airlines) and deregulation in some segments of certain energy industries promoted competition, such was not the case in the financial sector. Judge Cudahy is not the only one to recognize the financial havoc caused by the repeal of Glass-Steagall.[42] Eliminating the barrier between commercial banks and investment banks was the prime cause of the Great Recession of 2008. What passed as "innovative financial instruments" such as mortgage securitization, collateralized debt obligations, credit default swaps, and the like allowed commercial bankers to pretend they were investment bankers and allowed investment bankers to hedge against (and arbitrage) their own bad investments. Deregulation was the direct culprit, not an incidental bystander, of the economic recession that narrowly avoided a worldwide economic collapse.[43] For Judge Cudahy, deregulation must be seen as one tool in the regulatory toolbox; it is not the whole toolbox itself.

Electricity deregulation has proceeded in fits and starts from at least 1978 with the passage of PURPA and later with the passage of EPAct of 1992. A somewhat unintended consequence of PURPA was the recognition that the electricity market could accommodate a slew of nonutility producers and EPAct of 1992 expanded the number of such entities. The market for electricity indicated that more and cheaper electricity was available particularly for non-utility power providers. The problem was that because transmission and distribution lines were privately owned, it was difficult to get that electricity to the consumers that wanted it. The solution to the problem can be summed up in one word "wheeling." Quite simply, wheeling is one producer using another producer's line to deliver its electricity. Per Judge Cudahy, "[r]etail wheeling contemplates that every electric power customer be given an opportunity to seek out the lowest cost source of power wherever it can be found."[44] To be sure, residential consumers lack the market clout of large industrial firms that could bear the transaction costs of seeking out and trying to obtain cheaper electricity. And, therefore, larger customers led the charge for more access to cheaper power.

Just before assuming the bench, Judge Cudahy had been actively involved in litigation involving a retail wheeling case which advanced his understanding

---

[42] *See e.g.* RICHARD A. POSNER, THE CRISIS OF CAPITALIST DEMOCRACY (2010); RICHARD A. POSNER, A FAILURE OF CAPITALISM: THE CRISIS OF '08 AND THE DESCENT INTO DEPRESSION (209); JOSEPH E. STIGLITZ, FREEFALL: AMERICA, MARKETS, AND THE SINKING OF THE WORLD ECONOMY (2010); BEN S. BERNANKE, TIMOTHY F. GEITHNER & HENRY M. PAULSON, FIREFIGHTING: THE FINANCIAL CRISIS AND ITS LESSONS (2019).

[43] Richard D. Cudahy, *The Coming Demise of Deregulation*, 61 ADMIN. L. REV. 543 (2009).

[44] Richard D. Cudahy, *Retail Wheeling: Is This Revolution Necessary?*, 15 ENERGY L. J. (1994).

of this part of the industry as well as this area of law.[45] The economic interests involved with retail wheeling present a more complex problem that initially means the eye. The economic battle lines are neatly drawn between large consumers that want access to cheaper electricity and the private utilities that do not want their lines to be used without extracting economic rents from it. So far, so good. Cudahy recognized, however, that environmentalists also have a stake in retail wheeling because to the extent that electricity prices decline, then environmentalists would be concerned that there would be "no 'excess' revenues available to subsidize conservation, demand-site management programs, and other worthy causes."[46]

The conundrum that Judge Cudahy saw with retail wheeling is captured in the idea that while large industrial consumers want the "most efficient" (i.e. the cheapest) price, there may be other interests that deserve attention. In other words, the banner of competition may fly high in some markets and in some circumstances but can neglect other recognized public interests such as conservation or environmentalism. As Judge Cudahy saw it, retail wheeling presented a classic tension between competition and regulation. His chief concern was that the "foundational nature of the electric power industry ... spawns 'externalities'—social benefits and social costs which do not figure in conventional economic analyses...."[47] Cudahy knew that not only were the negative externalities of environmental pollution involved with the regulation of the industry, there were external benefits as well. Most specifically, the largest external benefit was the ready availability and affordability of a product necessary in our daily lives, or as Judge Cudahy put it "a service which is fundamental almost to the culture itself...."[48]

The very history of the electricity industry underscores its intractability in our lives. More to the point, the vitality of the industry was created not only by industrialists like Edison, Westinghouse, and Insull alone; the industry was actively promoted and supported by government regulation of electricity specifically as a network industry. Through a universal service obligation and through government power projects, citizens in rural America could enjoy the same luxurious product as citizens in our largest cities. For Judge Cudahy, the goal of universal service required government subsidization to some extent and, therefore, short-term costs might generate long-term benefits of the sort not generally acknowledged in short-term markets focused on short-term efficiencies.

Judge Cudahy was neither naïve nor ignorant of the fact that government could overregulate. From this perspective, we have overbuilt hydroelectric power

---

[45] *Central Power & Light Co. v. FERC*, 575 F.2d 937 (D.C. Cir.), *cert denied*, 439 U.S. 981 (1978); Fitzpatrick, *supra* note 2 at 132-36.

[46] Cudahy, *Retail Wheeling supra* note 44 at 352.

[47] *Id.* at 354.

[48] *Id.* at 355.

stations sometimes to the cost of the salmon industry. Moreover, he was acutely aware that fossil fuel generators imposed social costs in the form of greenhouse gas emissions, acid rain, and waste heat. Consequently, there are "benefits and costs that are generally not recognized in the books of account or in the marketplace, which as a systemic matter, seems to focus on the short-term at the expense of the long-term. The existence and fundamental importance of all these externalities suggests that everything will not be left to the invisible hand."[49] Again long-term v. short-term and market v. society trade-offs are inherent in utility regulation and must be balanced by regulators because private markets will not do so.

At bottom, the clash between the "entrepreneurial ethic" of competition and the "public utility ethic" of regulation turns on whether or not reliable and affordable universal service is readily available.[50] If the market cannot guarantee this level of service, then the fundamental point of public utility regulation has been frustrated. Cudahy worried that talk of deregulation without sufficient attendance to externalities and to the fundamental principle of universal service could mean that the anti-regulatory crowd may well affect a reversion to *Lochner* ideology[51] with the consequent undermining of the sort of New Deal regulation enacted "in the public interest." For Cudahy, the return of neo-classical economics may have limited the scope of regulators to looking at the electric industry only in terms of natural monopoly. To his way of thinking, such a narrow focus was myopic and the electric power industry was regulated not only because it was a natural monopoly "but essentially because it is a foundational industry, furnishing the nerves and sinew of the body politic."[52] Further, not only was electricity vital in our day-to-day lives; its regulation directly affected our human and natural environments.

Energy and the Environment

There are two notable anomalies involving the relationship between energy and the environment—one historical, the other physical. Historically, the discipline of environmental law gained traction with passage of the National Environment Policy Act that was signed into law by President Richard Nixon on January 1, 1970 followed shortly by the Clean Air Act of 1970 and in 1972 by the Clean Water Act. The age of environmental law had dawned. Energy law, by way of contrast, became known as a discipline only after the passage of the National Energy Act of 1978 during the Carter administration. The NEA

---

[49] *Id.* at 356.

[50] *Id.* at 357-58.

[51] *Lochner v. New York*, 198 U.S. 45 (1905).

[52] *Id.* at 361.

was comprised of five statutes passed specifically in response to the Arab Oil Embargo of 1973. The embargo precipitated what we referred to as an "energy crisis" which quadrupled the price of oil and contributed significantly to double-digit inflation and energy shortages throughout the country. The discipline of energy law did, of course, build on prior legal areas such as public utility law, natural resources law, and oil and gas law. Nevertheless, at the tail end of the 1970s decade the discipline of energy law developed as such.[53]

The physical anomaly is that from exploration and extraction through processing and distribution to consumption and disposal, the natural resources that are used to produce energy have environmental consequences. The connection between energy and the environment is a physical reality. However, because both disciplines had different antecedents, they developed independently of each other and those differences were formalized and institutionalized.[54] In other words, energy law and policy developed a distinct set of assumptions and a distinct vocabulary from that of environmental law and policy. By way of brief example, energy law involved the exploration, extraction, and production of natural resources in order to promote economic growth by providing cheap and reliable energy. As Judge Cudahy noted, though, cheap energy, is "generally not good for the environment."[55] As distinguished from energy law, environmental law involves the conservation and protection of ecosystems that can significantly affect the human environment. Additionally, each discipline was regulated independently of the other. Again, by way of brief example, the Environmental Protection Agency is the primary regulator for matters environmental as is the Department of Energy for energy matters.

Dick Cudahy understood these anomalies and as a judge and as a scholar addressed them thoughtfully. Although energy law and policy and environmental law and policy are generally treated independently of each other; they are necessarily related as PURPA revealed. PURPA had two specific aims. Given the energy crises of the 1970s, resource conservation, particularly of oil, together with energy efficiency constituted one dimension of PURPA. The other dimension was to promote competition in the electricity industry.

PURPA had both energy and environmental goals. The regulatory trick was how to treat both of them fairly and responsibly. Judge Cudahy recognized that even though efficiency is most often perceived as a market value, leaving

---

[53] *See e.g.* Fred Bosselman, *A Brief History of Energy Law in the United States Law Schools: An Introduction to the Symposium*, 86 CHI-KENT L. REV. 3 (2011).

[54] LINCOLN L. DAVIES & JOSEPH P. TOMAIN, ENERGY LAW IN THE UNITED STATES OF AMERICA 215-32 (2015).

[55] Richard D. Cudahy, *Keynote Address: Elephants at Play*, 1 ENVTL. & ENERGY L & POL. J. 77, 83 (2006). Indeed, "[t]he combustion of hydrocarbons produces unacceptable climate change and, hence, combustion of these fuels to produce energy must be eliminated or severely reduce . . ." Richard D. Cudahy, *The Bell Tolls for Hydrocarbons*, 29 ENERGY L. J. 381, 383 (2008).

electricity regulation to the market might have undesirable consequences. More specifically, if electricity regulation is left to the market then "both fuel diversity and energy conservation might be completely ignored."[56] Thus, a narrow focus on efficiency would frustrate both of PURPA's goals. Markets have many desirable consequences including achieving efficiency as well as economic growth, however, markets do not always work to achieve desirable public policy ends including reducing harms from the "greenhouse effect."[57]

Regarding conservation, Judge Cudahy wrote that "quite apart from the economic impact of conservation efforts, the need to husband resources is a fundamental prudential or ethical value." He goes on to note that conservation is "especially significant when America retains its high standing in wastefulness among advanced industrialized countries."[58] Judge Cudahy understood that conservation is part of the American tradition going back into the 19th century. While the environmental consciousness of the 1960s ushered in a recommitment to that tradition, the energy crises of the 1970s "interacted in multiple ways with various environmental issues, and these interactions manifested iron links between energy and the environment."[59] In addition to conservation, the diversification of energy resources, including the development of non-fossil fuels, was directly connected to such conservation efforts.

Regarding competition in the electric industry, even though the disciplines of energy and the environment have been regulated independently of each other and often employ different vocabularies, they are not always at odds. One of the strengths of PURPA was that it did promote competition in the electricity sector by encouraging diversity of generating sources. Some resources would be Lovins' type "soft path" renewables and others, like natural gas, would be more or less traditional. In both instances, reliance on the harder fossil fuels of oil and coal, would decline. In addition to fuel diversity, PURPA also promoted decentralization which, as Judge Cudahy noted, can improve energy security, help stabilize rates, and reduce the risks of shortage.[60] From his perspective renewable energy and conservation "should now stand on their own competitive feet"[61] and be a full part of the United States' energy portfolio. Cudahy made this assessment about renewable resources and conservation 25 years ago well before discussions of a transition from a fossil fuel economy to a clean energy future began in earnest.

---

[56] *Id.* at 421.

[57] *Id.*

[58] Richard D. Cudahy, *PURPA: The Intersection of Competition and Regulatory Policy*, 16 ENERGY L. J. 419, 420 (1995).

[59] Richard D. Cudahy, *Coming of Age in the Environment*, 30 ENVT'L. L. 15, 17 (2000).

[60] Cudahy, *PURPA supra* note 58 at 427-29.

[61] *Id.* At 428.

As society became more aware of the contribution of fossil fuel burning to climate change and global warming, it became more important to discuss energy and the environment as interrelated systems rather than as distinct from the other. Judge Cudahy accepted this linkage and looking into the 21st century noted the need to assess the global scale and dimension of the environmental problem as well as the necessity of finding creative, broad scale solutions including re-envisioning the transportation sector rather than concentrating on what he called environmental details.[62] Indeed, he understood that global warming was the "most inescapable problem confronting energy policy makers."[63] Given the multiple scientific, technological, and economic complexities of such "super-wicked" or polycentric problems, as a judge, Dick Cudahy was required to develop a sense of the relationship between the judicial and executive branches. In defining that relationship, Dick Cudahy was the quintessential New Deal judge.

New Deal Regulation

Judge Cudahy's approach to judicial decision-making fits comfortably within the classic New Deal paradigm in which the judiciary defers to administrative agencies and in which regulatory experimentation in agencies and in states themselves is seen as valuable. Even today, though, there is much weeping and gnashing of teeth about New Deal regulation. George Will, for example, throughout his recent book, *The Conservative Sensibility*,[64] blames the regulatory state and the rent-seeking that it generates on the proscriptions of 19th-century Progressives made manifest in New Deal legislation. He is not alone. New Deal antipathy is alive and well on the current Supreme Court with Justices Alito, Thomas, Kavanaugh, Gorsuch and sometimes Roberts.[65] Dick Cudahy, by way of contrast, has held fast to the principles of the administrative state developed during the New Deal.[66] Somewhat ironically, his commitment to FDR's agenda

---

[62] Cudahy, *Coming of Age*, supra note 59 at 21-22.

[63] Richard D. Cudahy, *Energy Law Journal 25th Anniversary Celebration*, 25, Energy L. J. 267, 271-72 (2004).

[64] George F. Will, The Conservative Sensibility xxii, 99-100; 120-22, 292-96 passim (2019).

[65] *See e.g.* Jeannie Suk Green, *The Supreme Court is One Vote Away From Changing How the U.S. is Governed*, The New Yorker (July 3, 2019) available at https://www.newyorker.com/news/our-columnists/the-supreme-court-is-one-vote-away-from-changing-how-the-us-is-governed; Joseph P. Tomain, *Justices Have and Eye on Control of Federal Agencies*, Columbus Dispatch (July 223, 2019) available at https://www.dispatch.com/opinion/20190723/column-justices-have-eye-on-control-of-federal-agencies.

[66] *See e.g.* James M. Landis, The Administrative Process (1938); Daniel R. Ernst, Tocqueville's Nightmare: The Administrative State Emerges in America, 1900-1940 (2014); William Forbath, *The New Deal Constitution in Exile*, 51 Duke L. J. 165 (2001).

cuts against his upbringing in which "[n]obody in my family that I know of was a Roosevelt supporter."[67]

Sitting as Chair of the Wisconsin Public Service Commission, he had the occasion to look at utility regulation up close. The principles of public utility regulation had been established during the New Deal. Those principles held fast until the mid-1970s when ideas about energy industries and their regulation came under close scrutiny. This was exactly the time of Dick's appointment to the PSC. Given the closer examination of public utility regulation, those basic principles began to evolve during his service on the PSC.

Those basic principles provide a reliable starting place to analyze changes in the electric industry and its regulation as demonstrated by his legal opinions and scholarly writings. As the discussion of *Madison Gas* demonstrated, Commissioner Cudahy was critical of the economic waste attributed to the "construction of allegedly unneeded (and *environmentally burdensome*) power plants and the potential thicket of transmission lines."[68] As noted above, he was well aware of the environmental effects of traditional practices and of the need to reform promotional rate structures that encouraged consumption. More specifically, in the 1970s due to the "energy dilemma, general inflation, increases system peak demand, capital shortages, strong environmental concerns, and other problems"[69] traditional rate designs had to be revised.

Traditional cost-of-service ratemaking contains two notable inefficiencies. First, it encouraged capital investments and utilities overbuilt plant. The key problem with overbuilding was that fixed costs became high and with higher fixed cost came higher rates. Nevertheless, under cost-of-service ratemaking, the returns on those capital investments went to shareholders. Those returns came out of the pocketbooks of ratepayers. Second, traditional ratemaking completely ignored the social cost of pollution. Consequently, the reverse Robin Hood effect of charging high rates to consumers while not counting the costs imposed on society, both for the benefit of shareholders, required a political correction.[70]

One such political correction could be a policy judgment that "the electric production process should bear *all* its social costs, even without a parallel analysis of its social benefits."[71] Cudahy knew his economics; he also knew his politics. As a matter of basic economics, marginal cost pricing could lead to more efficient

---

[67] Anita Hecht, An Oral History Interview with Dick Cudahy 12 (December 30, 2008).

[68] Richard D. Cudahy & J. Robert Malko, Electric Peak-Load Pricing: Madison Gas and Beyond, 1976 Wisc. L. Rev. 47 (1976) (emphasis added).

[69] *Id.* 49.

[70] Richard D. Cudahy, *From Socialism to Capitalism: A Winding Road*, 11 Chi. J. Int'l L. 39 (Summer 2010).

[71] Cudahy & Malko, *supra* note 11 at 67.

results. Even so, Cudahy, as a matter of pragmatist politics, envisioned a modest role for regulators.

> "The sorting out of social costs and benefits resulting from industrial processes is an inherently difficult procedure which includes many obscure value judgments. It must necessarily involve a primarily political evaluation of a fundamental sort about the type of society and economy we seek to encourage. It is certainly doubtful that a public service commission is a proper administrative agency to make this sort of evaluation. Public service commissions do make political evaluations, but their suitability for making this one is distinctly questionable."[72]

As noted above, instead of the PSC, he acknowledges that the legislature together with existing environmental agencies are chiefly responsible for forcing the internalization of external costs. Nevertheless, the PSC had some say in the matter. Peak load pricing, he reasons, is consistent with the commission's mandate to balance consumer and producer interests through ratemaking even if differential pricing may cause workers and homeowners to change some of their consumption patterns. He also notes that time differential pricing may actually stimulate the creation and marketing of new appliance technologies.[73] The PSC may be the inappropriate agency to force the internalization of all pollution costs, however, it is responsible for fair ratemaking practices.

Embedded in Judge Cudahy's understanding and support of the administrative state is a deep commitment to fundamental democratic principles. More particularly, in a complex modern world, the checks and balances of our Constitution are intentionally designed to cabin public and private power.[74] Public power is constrained by an orderly process in which the democratically elected Legislature adopts the policy preferences it deems best. It then remains with the Executive to implement those preferences in an orderly way leaving the Judiciary the responsibility of ensuring that the acts of the Legislature are constitutional and that the exercises of power by the Executive are both constitutional and conform to legislative directives.

It is important to recognize these checks and balances are not only procedural. In fact, the substantive target of the administrative state is democratic to the core—expansive democratic participation. At first glance, the concept of democratic participation may appear just to be another procedural mechanism operating in our constitutional order. However, democratic participation contains within it the very norms of liberty and equality. People must be free to

---

[72] *Id.* at 67.

[73] *Id.* at 70-72.

[74] K. Sabeel Rahman, *Reconstructing the Administrative Sate in an Era of Economic and Democratic Crisis*, 131 Harv. L. Rev. 1671, 1675-76 (2018).

engage their government and people must have equal voices in doing so. As a judge, Dick Cudahy was particularly sensitive to the litigants that appeared before him and sensitive to the civic role they played in our governmental process.

The Judge and Judging

In many ways, Richard Cudahy was the quintessential judge. He was well-educated and articulate. In addition, he possessed more than a modicum of judicial humility to go along with a solid theory of judging. The word "judging" is intentionally used as opposed to any sort of more finely honed fashionable jurisprudence such as originalism. If there is any label to put on his approach to judging it would be pragmatism, an American philosophical tradition that eschews tightly wrapped views of the world.[75] Indeed, he has been called a "judge's judge" precisely because of this approach.[76] And he was recognized as "passionate about the law and intensely concerned about the real-life consequences of court decisions."[77]

Two former law clerks summarize his "quite jurisprudence"[78] as consisting of: (1) "respect for the appellate process as a pragmatic and collective search for understanding, in which judges had to balance applying rules and taking account of the reality within which those rules had effect;" (2) he was always aware of "the consequences of any decision in the real world and how it would affect the parties;" and (3) he saw "law, regulation, and government as potential sources of public good."[79]

According to scholars, Dick Cudahy's judicial humility extended even into the realm of economic regulation. They argue that his opinions "consistently illustrate ... judicial humility on matters of economic regulation and a deferential brand of federalism that encourages states to act as laboratories for regulatory innovation."[80] Moreover, he was able to apply his economic intelligence to changing developments in various regulated industries as demonstrated, perhaps most acutely, in an antitrust decision involving the telecommunications industry

---

[75] Elizabeth Mertz & Cynthia G. Bowman, *Balanced Judicial Realism in the Service of Justice: Judge Richard D. Cudahy*, 67 DePaul L. Rev. 655 (2018).

[76] *Id.*

[77] John C. Roberts, *Judge Richard D. Cudahy: An Appreciation*, 67 DePaul L. Rev. 607, 609 (2018).

[78] *Id.* at 675-83.

[79] *Id.* at 675.

[80] Jim Rossi & Thomas J Hutton, *Judge Cudahy and the Deference Tension in United States Energy Law*, 29 Yale J. on Reg. 371, 373 (2012).

when MCI sued AT&T[81] for alleged predatory pricing.[82] Judge Cudahy rejected the upstart MCI's argument after balancing economic efficiency and consumer benefits against the political and social consequences of concentrated economic power.[83]

There is, of course, a direct connection between judicial humility and a New Deal approach to judging. More specifically, Judge Cudahy recognized not that administrative "agencies are invariably correct n their decisions and policy choices, but simply that they are in a better position than judges to balance policy values and legal obligations to make the required judgment calls on matters requiring expertise."[84] Today, this deferential approach comes under significant assault as noted earlier. It is also noteworthy that Judge Cudahy expressed skepticism about judicial economic expertise particularly in the realm of energy law and regulation given its complexity and the significance of such capital-intensive industries in our economy and in our society.[85] Quite simply, generalist judges should not be quick on the trigger to substitute their policy preferences for those of expert administrative agencies who work in the field on a daily basis.

His colleagues, as well as his clerks, recognized how prolific he was throughout his judicial career.[86] More importantly, his commitment to the judicial process was notably demonstrated by his respect for litigants and by his desire to protect individual and civil rights and liberties, and his interest in preserving access to courts.[87] A former clerk writes that "[i]n his own quiet way, he embodied a judicial philosophy characterized by wisdom, common sense, and humanity."[88] Judge Cudahy's humanity was manifest in cases ranging from criminal law to immigration and to employment law.[89] Judge Cudahy's humanity, in fact, can be captured in a tribute he wrote for Justice William Brennan:

> "[I]n the long run the judges who invoke a measure of intuition and passion are somehow more likely to benefit the powerless than the powerful.... I expect there will always be groups too small, diffuse, or reviled to obtain redress for their real grievances through majoritarian processes. These groups

---

[81] *MCI Communications Corp. v. Am. Tel & Tel Co.*, 708 F2d 1081 (7th Cir. 1983).

[82] Diane P. Wood, *Theory and Practice in Antitrust Law: Judge Cudahy's Example*, 29 Yale J. on Reg. 403 (2012).

[83] Mertz & Bowman, *supra* note 75 at 681.

[84] *Supra* note 80 at 373.

[85] *Id.* at 373-77.

[86] Richard A. Posner, *A Heartfelt, Albeit Largely Statistical, Salute to Judge Richard D. Cudahy*, 29 Yale J. on Reg. 355 (2012).

[87] Judge Alok Ahuja, *My Year with Judge Cudahy*, 67 DePaul L. Rev. 637, 638 (2018).

[88] Jack Beermen, *Barack Obama's Emancipation Proclamation: An Essay in memory of Judge Richard D. Cudahy*, 67 DePaul L. Rev. 613 (2018).

[89] *Id.*

will continue to prefer judges whose logic is informed by their sensitivity to the plight of the dispossessed and underrepresented.... This is all speculation, of course; nevertheless, it is a surmise deserving of consideration."[90]

Conclusion

Dick Cudahy was a man much admired by all who knew and worked with him. He was a man of keen intelligence and quick wit. He was also a man of the highest integrity and professionalism as well as a man of many accomplishments. A superb writer, teacher, lawyer and leader, Judge Richard Dickson Cudahy is, quite simply, the model legal professional and is someone we can all do well to emulate.

[90] Richard D. Cudahy, *Justice Brennan: The Hear has Its Own Reasons*, 10 Cardozo L. Rev. 93, 102 (1988).

Chapter 10

Distributive Water Justice: Colorado's Doctrine of Prior Appropriation Incorporates Instream Flow Rights on Behalf of the People

Gregory J. Hobbs, Jr.[1]

John Wesley Powell made his audacious pioneering run of the Colorado River one hundred and fifty years ago. He "plunged into the wildest blank spot on the map of North America outside the far north and rode a whitewater roller coaster from one side of the blank to the other side, never deviating from his

[1] Greg Hobbs: My wife, Bobbie, likes to say I'm the footloose carpetbagger who found a way into her side of the family. Born in December of 1944, I grew up in an Air Force family of five kids, me the oldest—traveling-traveling-traveling from Florida to the Panama Canal Zone to Virginia to Alaska (when it was yet a Territory) to northern California, southern California and Texas. It's truly fortuitous (destined?) that we met on Baldy Mountain in 1966 atop the Sangre de Cristos of northern New Mexico. We were serving on the staff of the Philmont Scout Ranch—through which a branch of the Santa Fe Trail curves around the Tooth of Time on its route to Fort Union. Four days after we married in Denver, her fourth-generation home, we went into the Peace Corps serving in Colombia 1967-68. Law school at Berkeley included the birth of our son Dan and daughter Emily. Federal 10th Circuit Judge William E. Doyle brought us back to Denver as his law clerk 1971-72. Thereafter I practiced law with the new Region VIII office of the EPA; with the Colorado Attorney General's office; and with Davis Graham and Stubbs and Hobbs, Trout & Raley (primarily as counsel to the Northern Colorado Water Conservancy District and its Municipal Subdistrict) until Governor Roy Romer appointed me to the Colorado Supreme Court on May 1, 1996, retiring August 31, 2015. I've been Vice-President of Water Education Colorado and its Publications Chair since the Colorado General Assembly founded it during the horrendous 2002-03 drought. Currently I serve as a Senior Water Judge mediating water cases and Co-Director of the Environmental and Natural Resources Program at the University of Denver Sturm College of Law. Along the backbone of the continent, Colorado Mother of Rivers, its peoples and its creatures, upstream and downstream, continue to call upon our shared state and interstate problem-solving abilities.

original intent."[2] Yet, of the flows bearing him up, Powell wrote in his 1879 Arid Lands Report, "[a]ll the waters of all the arid lands will be eventually taken from their natural channels, and they can be utilized only to the extent to which they are thus removed, and water rights must of necessity be severed from the natural channels."[3] His endorsement of prior appropriation water law and abolition of the riparian common law stemmed from the immense faith he placed upon irrigated agriculture to promote agrarian democracy. The "question for legislators to solve is to devise some practical means by which the water rights may be distributed among individual farmers and water monopolies prevented."[4] The "pioneers in the 'new countries' in the United States have invariably been characterized by enterprise and industry and an intense desire for the speedy development of their new homes."[5] What they most needed, along with the water, was protection against the "evils" of water company monopolies and speculative ventures controlling the means of water distribution. Powell did not foresee that prior appropriation water law would eventually produce a new breed of pioneers, intent upon keeping water in the streams while simultaneously protecting more-senior water rights.

The Colorado Doctrine of Prior Appropriation embodied in the state's 1876 constitution is a property-based system of beneficial use rights vested in water the public owns. Scholar David Schorr characterizes its adoption and implementation as an exercise in distributive justice.

> The recognition of public ownership, lobbied for by the territorial Grange, was important for providing the theoretical and legal underpinnings for the limitations on appropriation that would be applied by the state to prevent the replacement of monopoly by riparian owners with monopoly by speculating appropriators.[6]

Use rights are exercised in order of their decreed priority, based on need and water availability, integrating tributary groundwater and surface water.[7] Because Colorado has assumed McCarran Amendment jurisdiction to adjudicate federal water right claims, including Indian water rights, all water rights can be

---

[2] William deBuys (Ed.), Seeing Things Whole, The Essential John Wesley Powell 54 (Island Press 2001).

[3] John Wesley Powell, Lands of the Arid Region of the United States 42 (facsimile edition 1983 The Harvard Common Press) (1879).

[4] *Id.* at 41.

[5] *Id.*

[6] David Schorr, The Colorado Doctrine, Water Rights, Corporations, And Distributive Justice On The American Frontier 41 (Yale University Press 2012).

[7] Water Right Determination and Administration Act of 1969, Colo. Rev. Stat. §§ 37-92-101, et seq. (2018); Empire Lodge Homeowners Ass'n v. Moyer, 39 P.3d 1139, 1146-47 (Colo. 2001).

decreed to secure their administration within this larger priority-enforcement framework.[8]

Soon following adoption of the 1969 Water Right Determination and Administration Act, the Colorado General Assembly enacted the 1973 instream flow statute authorizing the Colorado Water Conservation Board (CWCB) to obtain decrees for instream flow water rights.[9] Many persons and organizations have helped to nurture this program, so much so that the Board holds close to 1,669 adjudicated stream segments covering 9,599 stream miles, as well as levels for 482 natural lakes. Through voluntary donations and acquisitions, it has added rights to 500 cubic feet per second of flow (cfs) and 9,344 acre-feet of water (AF).[10] The existence of these rights does not in any way depend upon assertion of a public trust doctrine. Rather, the CWCB has a fiduciary duty to exercise and protect these decreed rights on behalf of the people.[11]

Because instream flow rights require no diversion from the stream, the statute's constitutionality became a threshold question to its viability. Three persons deserve special recognition for the 1979 Colorado Supreme Court decision upholding these unique water rights: Senator Fred Anderson, prime sponsor of Senate Bill 97,[12] David Robbins, Deputy Attorney General for the State of Colorado who so carefully prepared the CWCB's case, and Justice James Groves, who authored the court's opinion upholding the instream flow law.[13] Subsequently, Lori Potter of the Sierra Club Legal Defense Fund, by litigating the CWCB's administrative reduction of an instream flow water right on Snowmass Creek, helped to shape formulation of the Board's fiduciary duty to the people of the state enunciated in the supreme court's 1995 *Aspen Wilderness Workshop* decision.

Run Up to the Instream Flow Program

Senator Fred Anderson of Loveland, a northern Colorado town, co-sponsored the 1969 Act, which established seven water divisions, each with a water judge, a water referee, and a division engineer responsible for water matters. He

---

[8] Navajo Dev. Co. v. Sanderson, 655 P.2d 1374 (Colo. 1982); United States v. City and County of Denver, 656 P.2d. 1 (Colo. 1982).

[9] Codified at Colo. Rev. Stat. § 37-92-102(3) (2018).

[10] Linda Bassi power point presentation, "Evolution of the Law Governing Colorado's Instream Flow & Natural Lake Level Program, Celebrating 50th Anniversary of the 1969 Act, April 5, 2019, Sturm College of Law, Denver, Colorado."

[11] Aspen Wilderness Workshop v. Colorado Water Conservation Board, 901 P.2d 1251 (Colo. 1995).

[12] S.B. 97, Act of April 23, 1973, Ch. 442, 1521-1522, 1973 Colo. Sess. Laws.

[13] Colorado River Water Conservation District v. Colorado Water Conservation Board, 594 P.2d 570 (Colo. 1979).

grew up on an irrigated farm in Larimer County and was elected to the state senate in 1966 at the age of 38. Serving for 16 years, he presided as Senate President the last eight years, retiring in 1982. The Northern Colorado Water Conservancy District promptly retained him as an advisor. His wife Anne described him well as "a mediator, a person who could take people from different sides and bring them to compromise."[14]

Established in 1937, assigned responsibility for shepherding development of the state's interstate water compact allocations through federal Bureau of Reclamation projects, the Colorado Water Conservation Board carried out its statutory roles under the leadership of Director Felix Sparks as the environmental era was dawning. A Brigadier General and former Colorado Supreme Court Justice, Sparks committed to Senator Anderson, "[y]ou want an instream flow program, you'll have an instream flow program."[15] In addition to Anderson, S.B. 97 enjoyed the sponsorship of future Colorado Governor Richard Lamm and future U.S. Congressman and Senator Hank Brown. They chose well in assigning this breakthrough in prior appropriation law to an agency supported by a full-time staff and attorney general representation, whose board is made up primarily of part-time citizen members appointed by the Governor and confirmed by the Senate from geographical locations across the state. Together, based on scientific assessment of natural stream and lake level needs, they would determine what amounts of water "for beneficial use ... are required to preserve the natural environment to a reasonable degree ... on behalf of the people of the state of Colorado ... in a manner consistent with sections 5 and 6 of article XVI of the state constitution." For the first time in Colorado water law, this legislation recognized "the need to correlate the activities of mankind with some reasonable preservation of the natural environment."[16]

Robbins faced a daunting obstacle. In a 1965 decision, the Colorado Supreme Court had struck down an instream flow water right claim filed by the Colorado River Water Conservation District. The River District's enabling statute contained a provision allowing it to obtain water rights for fishing and recreational purposes. The court held, nonetheless, that a diversion of water from the stream, such as into a pond or reservoir, would be required. The court characterized the district's instream flow claim as a "riparian right ... completely inconsistent with the doctrine of prior appropriation."[17]

---

[14] Pamela Dickman, Renowned retired senator, Loveland native Fred Anderson dies Thursday, Reporter-Herald Staff Writer, Friday, Dec. 23, 2011.

[15] Thomas v. Cech and J. William McDonald, Defend and Develop, A Brief History of the Colorado Water Conservation Board's First 75 Years 124 (Wellstone Press 2012).

[16] S.B. 97, Sections 1 and 2.

[17] Colorado River Water Conservation District v. Rocky Mountain Power Company, 406 P.2d 798, 800 (Colo.1965).

Indeed, as David Schorr observes, Colorado's constitutional framers "meant to ensure that the abolition of riparian and upstream privileges and concomitant opening to all of the opportunity to acquire water rights would not result in a tragic dilution of the resource to the point where no individual irrigator would be able to appropriate a right sufficient to irrigate his crops."[18] But, precedents of the new environmental era pointed the way for the Colorado Supreme Court to uphold the new instream flow law without a diversion from the stream. Clean and healthy air and water for humans and the environment became a state and federal priority in the early 1970s. The 1970 Clean Air Act and the 1972 Federal Water Pollution Control Act Amendments called for counter-part federal and state law programs. If a state adopted and maintained an adequate program, federal law provided for EPA to defer to it. Colorado became proactive in asserting the lead role under these statutes. In the early 1970s, the General Assembly created the Colorado Air Quality Control Commission[19] and the Water Quality Control Commission,[20] composed of part-time citizen members from across the state, to fashion control regulations. These acts contained broadly stated legislative goals guiding the work of these commissions.

In 1972, the Colorado Supreme Court upheld the constitutionality of Colorado's air act, which the General Assembly had adopted in 1970. The court's *Fry Roofing* decision set forth legal principles for judicial review of state environmental statutes.[21] First, a legislative enactment is presumptively valid; one who challenges its constitutionality bears an extremely heavy burden to establish its unconstitutionality beyond a reasonable doubt.[22] Second, the court must read a statute to ascertain whether adequate standards exist.[23] Third, the legislature may allow an agency to fill in the details of an enactment.[24] Fourth, the scope and guidelines for the Air Commission to follow "in discharging its duties and responsibilities are those which are necessary or appropriate to foster the health, peace, safety, general welfare, convenience and comfort of the people of the state, and which facilitate the enjoyment of nature, scenery, and other resources of the state."[25] These broad principles, in turn, guided the General Assembly when it formulated both the water quality control and instream flow laws in its 1973 session.

---

[18] SCHORR, THE COLORADO DOCTRINE 52.

[19] Colorado Air Act of April 10, 1970, Ch. 64 at 220-238, 1970 Colo. Sess. Laws.

[20] Colorado Water Quality Act of July 6, 1973 at 709-731, 1973 Colo. Sess. Laws.

[21] Lloyd A. Fry Roofing Company v. State Department of Health Air Pollution Variance Board, 499 P.2d 1176 (Colo. 1972).

[22] *Id.* at 1178-79.

[23] *Id.*

[24] *Id.*

[25] *Id.*

Enter David Robbins, an EPA Region 8 water quality attorney, into the Colorado Attorney General's Office in January of 1975. Newly elected Attorney General, J.D. MacFarlane of Pueblo had served in the Colorado House of Representatives from 1965 to 1969 and in the Colorado Senate from 1969 to 1973 when the 1969 Act and the early Colorado environmental laws were being formulated. He and his Deputy Attorney General, Jean Dubofsky, who later became the first female justice of the Colorado Supreme Court, created the natural resources and environmental section of the Attorney General's office. They hired Robbins to become its first leader. Robbins, a rugby player for the Denver Barbarians in the little spare time he could squeeze out, took on representation of the State Engineer's Office and the Colorado Water Conservation Board. Sporting a bushy mustache, which danced when he grinned, he went about getting to know key water legislators, attorneys and water organizations. On behalf of the state, he strategized presentations to the water courts, the Colorado Supreme Court and the United States Supreme Court leading to many important water decisions.[26]

Early on, appearing in Division 1 water court before Judge Donald Carpenter in a 1975 South Platte well case, Robbins sought to represent the State Engineer in protest of the referee's ruling. Attorneys argued that allowing such an appearance would subject water users "to the interminable will of the State Engineer." Judge Carpenter ruled that the State Engineer could not become a party to water court adjudications. Robbins appealed to the Colorado Supreme Court. Invoking the public interest, the court reversed Carpenter. In his 1977 *Wadsworth v. Kuiper* opinion, Groves wrote that, "the public has a vital interest in preserving the water resources of this state and adhering to correct rules for the allotment and administration of water."[27] So that "the people may have their day in court in the assertion of the public interest," the State and Division Engineers had standing "to protect our system of prior appropriation."[28]

Justice Groves was a Grand Junction water attorney before he took his seat on the Colorado Supreme Court on May 13, 1968. One of the founders of the Rocky Mountain Mineral Law Institute, he had served as President of the Mesa County Bar Association, then as President of the Colorado Bar Association at the age of 39. His humor was legendary. He had "a joke, an anecdote, and often a limerick which could fit any and every occasion." He composed poetry, often satirizing himself. He was a great public speaker.[29] He served as Justice until April 6, 1980. Following his 1968 *Fellhauer* opinion calling for the integration

[26] The author, assigned to Clean Air Act matters, shared an office with David Robbins at EPA Region VIII from October 1973 to January 1975, when they both moved to the Attorney General's Office.

[27] Wadsworth v. Kuiper, 562 P.2d 1114, 1115-1116, 1118 (Colo. 1977).

[28] *Id.*

[29] Edward L. Volpe, Memorial to Justice Groves, 52 Colorado Law Review (1980).

of tributary ground water and surface water,[30] the Colorado General Assembly enacted the 1969 Act providing the means to accomplish this. Justice Groves then authored the *Eagle County* decision, which the United States Supreme Court upheld in recognizing Colorado's exercise of McCarran Act waiver of sovereign immunity jurisdiction over federal agency and tribal, water claims.[31]

Robbins couldn't have had a better listener than Justice Groves when he argued for the instream flow statute's constitutionality. Leading to the court's 1979 decision approving the program, Robbins had worked with Duane Helton of the CWCB staff and Eddie Kochman of the Colorado Division of Wildlife, to select three instream flow segments for the test case. Located on the Crystal River and its tributary, Avalanche Creek on Colorado's western slope, these flow rights ranged from 10 to 100 cfs. Fish habitat and its biological needs became the initial leading example of the beneficial use environmental water needs the legislature had intended to address. Writing for the court, relying on the *Fry Roofing* decision, Justice Groves ruled that the CWCB had abided by "the terms of its delegated authority in establishing the purposes of Senate Bill 97."[32]

First, the "legislative intent is quite clear that these appropriations are to protect and preserve the natural habitat and that the decrees confirming them award priorities which are superior to the rights of those who may later appropriate."[33] Second, the legislature authorized the agency to employ "scientific expertise regarding the preservation of flora, fauna and other aspects of the natural environment." A broad statement of legislative policy is sufficient. "The legislative objective is to preserve reasonable portions of the natural environment in Colorado." Factual determinations are for the board to determine, availing itself of expert scientific opinion.[34] Third, the General Assembly had lawfully deleted the 1969 Act's statutory diversion requirement to allow these appropriations, and no provision of the Colorado constitution forbade the legislature from doing so. The language of Article XVI, Section 6, providing that the "right to divert the unappropriated waters of any natural stream to beneficial uses shall never be denied" intended "to negate any thought that Colorado would follow the riparian doctrine in the acquisition and use of water."[35] But, the CWCB was not a riparian land owner and the General Assembly had carefully slotted the CWCB appropriations into the prior appropriation's system of adjudicated priorities so as not to injure any other water rights. Deferring to the legislature, the

[30] Fellhauer v. People, 447 P.2d 986 (Colo. 1968).

[31] United States v. District Court in and for the County of Eagle, 458 P.2d 760 (Colo. 1969); 401 U.S. 520 (1971).

[32] Colorado River Water Conservation District v. Colorado Water Conservation Board, 594 P.2d 570, 578 (Colo. 1979).

[33] *Id.* at 575.

[34] *Id.* at 576.

[35] *Id.* at 573.

Supreme Court rejected its prior dicta that an instream flow right is necessarily a forbidden riparian right.

Justice Groves and the court greatly benefited from an amicus brief prepared by newly-minted Colorado attorney Ruth Wright on behalf of the League of Women Voters. She contrasted the intricacies of calculating beneficial consumptive use for irrigated cropland to the relative ease of measuring in-channel flow. "To quantify a water right which is diverted for pasture irrigation, for example, one must base the depletion on flow (cubic feet per second), on time, on acres irrigated, and on unit crop consumption."[36] Compare this complexity to an instream flow water right that can be "readily quantified as cubic feet per second of flow in the stream channel." She pointed to other examples of measuring flow in the rivers employed in water administration. Storage releases are routinely conveyed downstream to their places of use. Twin Lakes water, for example, is released into the Arkansas River and carries for "more than 100 miles to specific users on the plains." Augmentation water placed into streams to offset injurious out-of-priority depletions also maintains its full identity in water administration. In both instances, storage and augmentation releases, there is "no problem in maintaining accurate measurements of flow and deliveries."

Wright's brief also invoked the 1970s state and federal water quality laws. Instream flows can help meet water quality goals in a prior appropriation state. Co-sponsored by Senator Gary Hart of Colorado and Senator Malcolm Wallop of Wyoming, the 1977 Clean Water Act Amendments contained section 101(g), "a non-interference policy" Congress enacted to preserve water rights created under state law. This provision states that "it is the policy of Congress that the authority of each State to allocate quantities of water within its jurisdiction shall not be superseded, abrogated or otherwise impaired by this Act." Nor shall the act be construed to supersede or abrogate rights to "quantities of water which have been established by any state." [37] As Wright emphasized to the court, "In a semi-arid state such as Colorado the interrelationship between water quality, water quantity, and aquatic life is abundantly clear." Providing for instream flows within the state's appropriation system "accommodates and balances all of the uses which are beneficial to its citizens."[38]

In her distinguished career, Wright went on to become a member of the Water Quality Commission, the Colorado House of Representatives, the Great

---

[36] Ruth M. Wright, Brief of Amicus Curiae League of Women Voters of Colorado, February 8, 1979 at 7-8.

[37] P.L. 92-500, §101(g); 33 U.S.C. 1251(g).

[38] *Id.* at 12. After the court announced its decision upholding the instream flow law, Justice Groves invited Wright to lunch, as she says, "to meet the new water attorney in town." Wright also learned that the Justices had been concerned about the administrability of these new water rights within Colorado's system. Her brief had supplied useful information addressing their concerns. Ruth Wright email message to the author, May 2, 2019.

Outdoors Colorado Board, and a Director of the Northern Colorado Water Conservancy District and its Municipal Subdistrict. Her early supportive advocacy for the constitutionality of instream flows within Colorado's prior appropriation system signaled how important the CWCB's instream flow water rights would become as "an essential link" within the state's water resources system.[39]

While the General Assembly has restricted instream flow water solely to CWCB's appropriation on behalf of the people,[40] it has also enhanced the Board's authority repeatedly. A 1986 amendment, Senator Martha Ezzard sponsored with broad water user and environmental organization support, provided for the board's voluntary transactional acquisition of interests in senior water rights to improve instream flows.[41] This amendment also invited federal agencies to make recommendations to the board for instream flow rights in National Forest, National Park and Bureau of Land Management areas.[42] These and other innovations inspired creation of the non-profit Colorado Water Trust. It works to facilitate transactions between water rights owners and CWCB. From 2001 through 2018, this organization has helped to restore approximately 32,472 acre-feet of water to 323 miles of Colorado rivers and streams.[43]

---

[39] Wright Amicus Brief at 12.

[40] "The Colorado Water Conservation Board is hereby vested with the exclusive authority, on behalf of the people of the state of Colorado" to appropriate waters of the natural streams and lakes. S.B. 212, Act of June 20, 1987, Ch. 269, 1305-06, 1987 Colo. Sess. Laws. *See* Colo. Rev. Stat. §37-92-102(3) (2018). Senate Bill 10, sponsored by Senator Anderson in 1981, prohibited the Water Quality Control Commission from requiring minimum stream flows or minimum water levels in any lakes or impoundments. *See* Colo. Rev. Stat. §25-8-104 (2018).

[41] Fred Anderson, then a consultant to the Northern District, testified in support of Ezzard's bill. See Transcript of February 13, 1986 Hearing Before the House Committee on Agriculture, Natural Resources and Energy. Referring to his sponsorship of the original instream flow legislation in 1973, Anderson testified that "there's a real advantage by clarifying the acquisition and it can be of benefit to a farmer who wants to sell a portion of his right and let it be dedicated for this purpose." During the February 17, 1986 Senate floor debate on the bill, Senator Ezzard pointed out that the Colorado Wildlife Federation, Audubon Society, Nature Conservancy, and Trout Unlimited, along with the Colorado Water Congress, all supported the legislation.

[42] S.B. 91, Act of May 3, 1986, Ch. 235, 1095-96, 1986 Colo. Sess. Laws. *See* Colo. Rev. Stat §37-92-102 (3) (2018), *See also* Gregory J. Hobbs, Jr., Colorado's Instream Flow Law and Senate Bill 91: State Water Rights for Preservation of the Environment, Can They End the Federal Reserved Water Rights Instream Flow Controversy? For "How the Rivers Run, An Analysis of Current Issues in Colorado Water Law" Continuing Legal Education in Colorado, Inc. University of Denver Law School 1986.

[43] *See* https://coloradowatertrust.org/. Consulted April 19, 2019. Amy Beatie, now Colorado Deputy Attorney General for Natural Resources and the Environment, served as Executive Director of the Colorado Water Trust from 2007-2017.

Colorado's Instream Flow Program Does Not Rely on the Public Trust Doctrine

Colorado's instream flow program has grown up in contra-distinction to California's public trust doctrine, which authorizes the involuntary reallocation of existing water rights. In its 1983 Mono Lake decision, the California Supreme Court held that "parties acquiring rights in trust property generally hold those rights subject to the trust, and can assert no vested right to use those rights in a manner harmful to the trust."[44] The court went on to state that "this principle, fundamental to the concept of the public trust, applies to rights in flowing waters as well as to rights in tidelands and lakeshores; it prevents any party from acquiring a vested right to appropriate water in a manner harmful to the interests protected by the public trust."[45] Accordingly, "the state has the power to reconsider allocation decisions even though those decisions were made after due consideration of their effect on the public trust."[46]

In contrast, neither the Colorado courts, nor the water administration officials, nor the legislature has authority under the Colorado constitution to allocate, reallocate or reallocate water rights yet again. Colorado's constitution and its implementing statutes have established a system of vested rights for beneficial use of the public's water resource in order of their decreed priority. "Waters of the natural stream, including surface water and tributary groundwater thereto, are a public resource subject to the establishment of public agency or private use rights in unappropriated water for beneficial use."[47] When there is insufficient available water, junior rights are curtailed to meet the actual needs of senior adjudicated rights. Decreed CWCB instream flow and lake level appropriations enjoy the protections of, and are subject to, the constraints of the Colorado's comprehensive adjudication system that includes decreed federal and tribal water rights.

In addition, because they are appropriated on behalf of the people, the CWCB has a fiduciary duty to assert and protect them. Enter Lori Potter of the Sierra Club Legal Defense Fund who helped to shape articulation of this duty by suing against CWCB's unilateral reduction of an instream flow right the board had adjudicated. The Colorado Supreme Court's 1995 *Aspen Wilderness Workshop* opinion, as modified on rehearing, holds that the instream flow statute "makes the conservation board a unique entity charged with preserving the environment to a reasonable degree." There exists a "unique statutory fiduciary

---

[44] Nat. Audubon Soc. v. Supre. Ct. of Alpine Cty., 658 P.2d 709, 721 (Cal. 1983).

[45] *Id.* at 727.

[46] *Id.* at 728.

[47] Empire Lodge v. Moyer, 39 P.3d at 1147.

duty between the Board and the people of this state."[48] How the court got to this result is well worth recounting.

When the court first issued its opinion, it had included references to a public trust. "The Conservation Board, unlike other water users, acts on behalf of the people of the state of Colorado and is thereby burdened with a public trust. The Board initiates water appropriations in fulfillment of that trust to secure and appropriate the minimum stream flow necessary to preserve the environment."[49] Justice Mary Mullarkey's dissent red-flagged the public trust rationale, "[t]his court has never recognized the public trust doctrine with respect to water." She pointed to the court's 1979 *Emmert* decision "rejecting the public trust as a basis for assuring public recreational use of water overlying privately owned stream beds of non-navigable waterways."[50]

In the district court and supreme court, Potter represented the non-profit Aspen Wilderness Workshop, a group of citizens opposed to the CWCB's decision to reduce its wintertime instream flow appropriation by forty percent on Snowmass Creek. To accommodate its snowmaking operation, Aspen Skiing Company convinced the Board it had appropriated more water than was necessary to preserve the environment to a reasonable degree. Potter contended that the Board had no authority to reduce its decreed appropriation without returning to the water court for a change of water right. In her opening brief to the Colorado Supreme Court, she asserted that the instream flow statute imposed a "trust responsibility" on the board to exercise its full appropriation.[51] In their Amicus Brief, Northern Colorado Water Conservancy District and Southwestern Water Conservation District countered that the court should "reject the present effort to establish a public trust res in Colorado water or the public trust doctrine as a basis for water court decisions."[52] Potter's reply brief responded that her client was not "contending that the public trust substantively bars any relinquishment of instream flows by the board." Rather, "the instream flow

---

[48] Aspen Wilderness Workshop v. Colorado Water Conservation Board, 901 P.2d 1251 (Colo. 1995).

[49] Slip opinion at page 20, June 19, 1995 (on file with Colorado Supreme Court Law Library). Page 24 of the slip opinion stated that "In sum, the General Assembly vested the Conservation Board with 'exclusive authority' to appropriate water as may be required for minimum stream flows to preserve the natural environment and burdened the Board's authority with a public trust that is coterminous with its right to appropriate water."

[50] People v. Emmert, 597 P.2d 1025,1027 (1979).

[51] Appellant's Opening Brief at 10, filed with the Supreme Court in Case No. 93SC740 on April 25, 1994.

[52] Amicus Curiae Brief of Northern Colorado Water Conservancy District, Its Municipal Subdistrict, and Southwestern Water Conservation District at 14, filed on June 21, 1994. The author and his partner Bennett Raley represented the Northern District and Municipal Subdistrict.

statute imposes a special duty upon the Board to afford procedural protection to instream flow rights."[53]

CWCB, Aspen Skiing Company, and the Northern and Southwestern districts filed rehearing petitions. CWCB did not request rehearing of the court's holding that the Board must seek water court approval of modifications to decree instream flow rights. It suggested changes to delete broader language such as "the board must enforce those rights to their full extent." [54] The skiing company objected to the problematic sweep of the "fiduciary duty" the court articulated.[55] The Southwestern and Northern districts requested deletion of the "public trust" references and substitution of the words "unique statutory responsibility."[56] The court's modified final opinion of September 11, 1995, authored by Justice Gregg Scott deleted the "full enforcement" and "public trust" wording, and held that the act created "a unique statutory fiduciary duty." The court ruled that CWCB "cannot unilaterally modify" the decree and "must return to the water court to modify the original decree before reducing its appropriation on Snowmass Creek."[57]

The legislature did not disturb the court's articulation of the CWCB's fiduciary duty to the people of the state. Instead, in the very next legislative session, it formulated standards implementing this duty. In its 1996 session, Senate President Tom Norton of Weld County sponsored a statute which sets forth a detailed administrative and water court procedure applicable for considering any effort that might decrease an instream flow water right. This legislation also authorized CWCB to make instream flow appropriations to preserve the natural environment of the Colorado River endangered fishes within the state as part of the Upper Colorado River Basin Recovery Implementation Plan for the fishes.[58]

---

[53] Appellant's Reply Brief at 9, fn. 7, filed June 24, 1994.

[54] CWCB Petition for Rehearing at 4, fn. 6, filed July 7, 1995.

[55] Aspen Skiing Company Petition for Rehearing at 1, filed July 3, 1995.

[56] Southwestern District and Northern District Petition for Rehearing at 1-2, filed July 3, 1995, joined by Southeastern Colorado Water Conservancy District, Upper Arkansas Water Conservancy District and City of Colorado Springs.

[57] Aspen Wilderness Workshop, 901 P.2d at 1261.

[58] S.B. 96-064, Act of May 23, 1996, Ch. 187, 952-955, 1996 Colo. Sess. Laws. Lori Potter and the author worked with Senator Norton to write the bill's provisions. Potter's Denver Water Law Review article on the 30th Anniversary of 1969 Act addresses the Aspen Wilderness Workshop case and the General Assembly's follow-up to the court's decision. Lori Potter, The 1969 Act and Environmental Protection, 3 Univ. Den. Water L. Rev. 70-79 (1999).

Colorado Supreme Court Decisions Implement the Legislative Purposes of the Instream Flow Law

Over the five decades of its existence, the instream flow program has continued to grow in vitality and effectiveness. The link between an expert CWCB staff and representation by the Attorney General's office has led to significant court decisions. Among these are the *Central City* South Platte River change of water right/augmentation case and the *San Miguel* River CWCB instream flow water right application case. Both articulate primary purposes of the 1973 statute. First, the legislature intended these CWCB water rights to preserve stream reaches against further depletion.

> The legislature nonetheless clearly envisioned the instream flow program would obtain, in reasonable measure, its goal of preserving the environment by ensuring that certain stream reaches would not be further depleted without conditions to protect against injury. We conclude the legislature instead envisioned the primary value of an instream flow right to derive from a basic tenet of water law: its ability to preserve the stream conditions existing at the time of its appropriation.[59]

Second, the CWCB's determination that a particular instream flow will preserve the environment to a reasonable degree is a prospective policy determination, quasi-legislative in character entitled to a deferential standard of review in the water court based on the administrative record. An instream flow right when decreed "is administered within the priority system and is subject to present uses or exchanges in existence on the date of the appropriation."[60] Through a statement of opposition or protest in the water court, the Board can resist changes of water rights, augmentation plans and exchanges which "in any way materially injure instream flow rights."[61]

Central City explains that the origins of the instream flow statute trace back to the 1950's Bureau of Reclamation Frying-Pan Arkansas Project, which threatened to dry up numerous western slope headwaters streams. Specific levels of flows were permitted to bypass diversion points, but nothing prohibited other appropriators from taking the releases once they moved through the project's diversion points. The General Assembly settled on the 1973 act to provide the needed mechanism to protect flow reaches within the priority system.[62] "A val-

---

[59] Colorado Water Conservation Board v. City of Central, 125 P.3d 424, 439 (Colo. 2005).

[60] Farmers Water Development Company v. Colorado Water Conservation Board, 346 P.3d 52, 56-57, 59-60 (Colo. 2015).

[61] City of Central, 125 P. 3d at 440.

[62] *Id.* at 438.

idly adjudicated instream flow or lake level right recognizes a property right vested in the Board on behalf of the people of Colorado."[63]

The *San Miguel* case reiterates that the CWCB "acts on behalf of the people of the state of Colorado and is thereby burdened with a fiduciary duty arising out of its unique statutory responsibilities."[64] In determining to apply to the water court for a decreed instream flow right, the Board must make three determinations, that the appropriation will preserve the environment to a reasonable degree, that there is such an environment to be preserved, and the appropriation, if decreed will preserve an environment without material injury to other decreed water rights.[65] The Board cannot modify an instream flow decree on its own and must return to the water court to seek a modification of the decree.[66] On the other hand, when other rights seek modifications to their decrees to allow changes of water rights or to facilitate an augmentation plan or an exchange, protective conditions against injury to CWCB's flow rights must be included.[67]

Conclusion

Colorado's instream flow law demonstrates that a prior appropriation state can integrate instream flows into its water rights system in a manner that does not injure beneficial use rights other appropriators have previously obtained and decreed. Through voluntary transactions, the Board may also acquire water, above minimum stream flow requirements, "to improve the natural environment to a reasonable degree."[68]

Appropriators need not fear their rights will not be enforced or can be involuntarily diminished. Such a policy promotes security, reliability and flexibility in use of the public's water resource and fosters buying, selling or leasing water rights, subject to the water court process for changing rights to other uses, including instream flow uses. Many persons have nurtured this program along for its first fifty years. No doubt many will continue to do so. Most certainly there are innovations yet to come.[69]

---

[63] *Id.* at 439.

[64] Farmer's Development, 346 P. 3d at 58. The Bureau of Land Management supported CWCB's instream flow water right appropriation.

[65] *Id.* at 59.

[66] *Id.* at 60.

[67] City of Central, 125 P.3d at 440.

[68] Colo. Rev. Stat. § 37-92-102(3) (2018).

[69] This article was first published in 22 Univ. Den. Water L. Rev. 377-388 (2019).